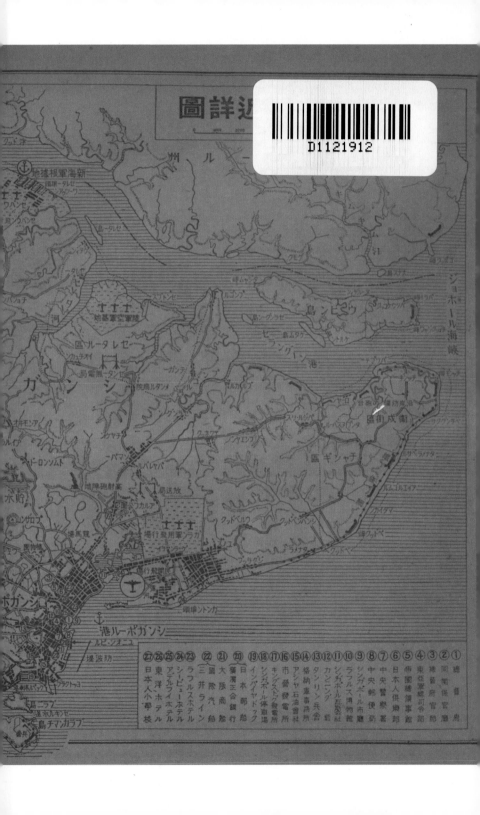

圖詳近

SINGAPORE, SINGAPURA

'*Singapore, Singapura* sparkles with life. It is a rare jewel of a book—enchanting, illuminating and at times bloody funny. Much more than a travelogue or history, this is the story of a grand adventure, told in the tradition of Conrad with the eye of Theroux and the wit of Bryson. Brilliant.'

— James Brabazon, journalist, documentary filmmaker and author of *The Break Line*

'What better way to discover Singapore than to walk across it? In this splendid book, Walton serves up the island's riches—its history, geography, economics, and, most of all, serendipity.'

— Tyler Cowen, author of *The Complacent Class and Average Is Over*

'Walton vividly traces the roots of Singapore's miraculous emergence as a global economic hub, warning that its past successes may blind it to the need to evolve in tune with a rapidly changing world. This fascinating book is an evocative guide to the past and future of a remarkable country, with universal relevance to our uncertain era of globalisation and urbanisation.'

— Alex Beard, author of *Natural Born Learners*

'Join Nicholas Walton on his intriguing voyage of discovery across the length and breadth of Singapore, exploring the island's history from the fourteenth century to the present day.'

— Mark Leonard, Director of the European Council on Foreign Relations

NICHOLAS WALTON

Singapore, Singapura

From Miracle to Complacency

HURST & COMPANY, LONDON

First published in the United Kingdom in 2018 by
C. Hurst & Co. (Publishers) Ltd.,
41 Great Russell Street, London, WC1B 3PL
© Nicholas Walton, 2018
All rights reserved.

Distributed in the United States, Canada and Latin America by
Oxford University Press, 198 Madison Avenue, New York, NY 10016,
United States of America.

The right of Nicholas Walton to be identified as the author
of this publication is asserted by him in accordance with the
Copyright, Designs and Patents Act, 1988.

A Cataloguing-in-Publication data record for this book
is available from the British Library.

ISBN: 9781787380103

This book is printed using paper from registered sustainable
and managed sources.

www.hurstpublishers.com

Printed in Great Britain by Bell & Bain Ltd, Glasgow

Endpapers: *Syonan-to*: a Japanese map of Singapore, published in *Shashin shūhō* (Photo Weekly) magazine, issue 206, 4 February 1942— a few days before the Japanese invasion and occupation of the island.

The Straits: a close-up from a 1944 RAF silk escape map of the region, showing the demarcation between British and Dutch imperial possessions.

To Luca, Jennifer and Stuart.
All three introduced me to equatorial living
and taught me to ask questions.
It worked out well.

CONTENTS

CONTENTS

ACKNOWLEDGEMENTS

I would like to thank the many people who helped me research and write this book. Some gave their time, their insights, or their encouragement; others simply provided unwitting illumination over several glasses of overpriced wine or a post-football can of beer. I apologise if I have missed anybody out. Others do not wish to be named, but I remain grateful.

Thank you to Aleks and Nick Barnes, Megat Castelcage, James Crabtree, Fernando Gandioli, Raymond Goh and AJ, Erica and John Hadfield, Margie Hall, Gordon Hewitt, Lorraine and Jay Sangani, Kenji Kwok, Collin Koh, Koh Seng Choon, Robert Kooij, John Lawson, Kishore Mahbubani, David and Nancy Marazzi, Nick Measures, Steffen Pedersen, Raghavan Raveendran, Kuik Shiao, David Skilling, Alan Soon, Yolanda Taravilla Marin, Pingtjin Thum, Tong Yee, Sudhir Vadaketh, Chris and Carol Van Beek, Keith Wallis, Tony Wagner, William Wan, Charlotte Wilkinson, Taufiq Yussef, Gremelyn Dar Zamora, and all those with whom I've played Wednesday night football.

Immense thanks are also due to the folk at Hurst, who encouraged me to write this book, and helped it along with advice and expertise. Michael Dwyer was supportive from the off, and lenient when the project took longer than he anticipated. Farhaana Arefin was an excellent editor, and helped turn thou-

ACKNOWLEDGEMENTS

sands of words into a viable book. I already knew Jon de Peyer, Daisy Leitch, and Alison Alexanian from my Genoa book, and was delighted to work with them again. Any mistakes are my responsibility entirely, and I apologise in advance to those who spot something I've missed.

Finally, I need to thank my family. My amazing wife, Ilaria, was responsible for getting us to Singapore in the first place, and was supportive and constructive throughout. Much of my time on the island was spent with our fantastic son, Luca. We explored the place together, negotiating the heat and ramshackle pavements with a pram and then a scooter, seeing things and asking questions. This book is dedicated to him, and to my parents, Jennifer and Stuart, who took me and my brother down from Durham to Nairobi back in 1974, in search of equatorial adventures and a baby sister. Thank you.

PREFACE

On 28 January 1819 a ship called the *Indiana*, commanded by Captain James Pearl, dropped anchor at St John's Island, alongside the *Enterprise*. The men on board were mostly British. Their first job was to ascertain if the Dutch had a presence on the larger island a bare handful of kilometres to the north. The answer was no. The next day a party landed on that larger island, at a point where a river met the warm seas of the narrow straits linking the Indian Ocean with the South China Sea. One of the men was the lieutenant-governor of Bencoolen, on the far side of Sumatra. His name was Stamford Raffles, and he appreciated the potential of the muddy island where he now stood. Raffles' landing on that muddy island is recognised as the founding of modern Singapore.

My own arrival in Singapore, almost two centuries later, was more prosaic. I was on the Singapore Airlines red-eye from Milan, descending over a vast flotilla of ships at anchor, dawn still an hour or so away. The prospect of setting up home in the modern world's model city state pleased me; I was busy tidying up the last pre-publications details of a book on one of its medieval precursors, the Italian city state of Genoa. I had tracked the birth, explosive growth and long decline of Venice's great rival, and written about the transsexual prostitutes and basil farmers, Sri Lankan cricketers and chocolate-makers who lived in its labyrinthine streets and *vicoli*. Singapore was a very different place. It had no medieval streets, and piecing together its history before Raffles landed on its shores two hundred years earlier was tricky. While Genoa smelled to the visiting Charles Dickens like old cheese wrapped in warm blankets, Singapore was the type of place that banned chewing gum.

Nevertheless, I saw parallels between the two. Genoa had come out fighting after finding itself in an unpromising and vulnerable situation. It harnessed hard work, tactical nous, ruthlessness, and the growing trading networks of a rapidly globalising medieval world, and flourished. Against a backdrop of tumbling rocks and arid, salty seas, Genoa had become a vital cog in the birth of the medieval economy, a crucial trading link between East and West, and a keystone in a new world order. Likewise, modern Singapore had been thrust into an unwelcoming world after being spat out by the Malay Federation in 1965. It too harnessed hard work, tactical nous, ruthlessness, and the growing trading networks of a rapidly globalising world, and it too had flourished.

The case of Genoa also carried a warning. It had remained small, agile and vital, working hard and shifting business models to stay relevant in a rapidly evolving world. But eventually, after a couple of centuries of glory, it started to lose ground and was inevitably enveloped by the fog of slow, centuries-long decline. Singapore, too, is small, agile and vital, and its admirable government has worked hard to shift business models and find relevance in a rapidly evolving world. The extraordinary successes of its first half-century of independence belied the poor inheritance of a tiny, muddy island in a hostile equatorial neighbourhood. But as it neared the fiftieth anniversary of independence (and the 200th anniversary of its founding by Raffles), valid questions were being raised about how it was going to plot its course in the future. Was the Singapore miracle a mere fifty-year affair, or would it be something more enduring?

PREFACE

These are the questions that I had in mind when I set out to write this book, the backbone of which is a 53-kilometre single-day hike across the entire country. This walk served two purposes. Firstly, it gave me a way of understanding how the place functioned, and how its history and geography intertwined with its present and future. Secondly, it illustrated just how compact the country really was. Around 900 ago, Genoa's small size was hardly unusual. In the modern world of the early twenty-first century, even if we can now frame the world as a succession of interlinked urban conglomerates rather than nation states, Singapore's size certainly is remarkable. A country that you can walk across in a single day—however ill-advised and exhausting that exercise turned out to be—is indeed tiny. Singapore's size has afforded it great advantages, such as governability and agility. But it also affords it very little room for manoeuvre or failure. All the questions that are being asked about Singapore's future have to be seen through the lens of that smallness.

There are a few notes to add. The first is to place on record that despite my misgivings about Singapore's future, I wish it well. It proved a fascinating and engaging home for my family for three and a half years. We met many lovely people and took away very many warm memories—although I will never come to terms with the island's awful climate.

Secondly, I offer a few words of explanation about the title of the book: *Singapore, Singapura*. The first word points to the modern miracle of the last fifty years since independence, and indeed the last 200 years since Raffles founded the place. The second refers to its deeper nature, embedded geographically in Southeast Asia, in the middle of an equatorial, Malay world. My use of the word "miracle" in the subtitle reflects my own admiration for what Lee Kuan Yew and the Singaporean people achieved in the half-century since independence. "Complacency" reflects what I see as the greatest threat to the miracle; Lee Kuan

PREFACE

Yew most certainly was not complacent, but I now see a different attitude creeping into facets of Singaporean life, like a multicoloured tropical mould slowly digesting the whitewashed concrete wall of a tower block. The populations and governments of other countries evidently suffer from complacency too, but Singapore's tiny size makes it uniquely vulnerable to the condition.

Thirdly, throughout the book I refer to figures in Singapore dollars (S$). As an extremely rough guide, in 2015, on the fiftieth anniversary of independence, US dollar was worth S$1.37, a euro S$1.51, and a British pound S$2.15.

Finally, although the 53-kilometre west-to-east walk was an exhausting—and ultimately rather bloody—experience, it was also exhilarating, and gave me an extraordinary physical and conceptual window into the way the entire country hangs together. Likewise, the shorter north-to-south walk that I had completed a couple of years beforehand was very well worth it. I urge others to get out of their Grab taxis and swimming pools and to set out across one of the world's most remarkable countries on foot, with a good supply of sports drinks, bandages, and dry T-shirts. However far you get, you hopefully will not regret it. Good luck.

TIMELINE

Fourteenth century: Singapore flourishes as Singapura. Civilisation ebbs and flows on the island for several centuries.

Early sixteenth century: Portuguese sailors arrive on the island, but refer to the "great ruins" there.

1819: Sir Stamford Raffles steps ashore on 29 January, beginning the history of modern Singapore. The British are allowed to establish a trading post after a treaty is signed on 6 February.

1822: Raffles returns, and is critical of how Singapore is being run. He dies in 1826, back in England.

1824: Singapore is ceded in perpetuity to the East India Company by the sultan of Johor, and the Anglo-Dutch Treaty places it firmly within the British sphere of influence.

1826: The British East India Company forms the Straits Settlements out of Singapore, Penang and Malacca.

1827: The Chinese become Singapore's largest ethnic group.

1845: The first edition of *The Straits Times* is published.

1867: The Straits Settlements become a Crown Colony.

1869: The Suez Canal opens.

1877: A Chinese Protectorate is established, to address problems within the Chinese community, including abuses of the coolie trade.

TIMELINE

1889: Chinese secret societies are banned.

1939: The great British naval base at Singapore is completed.

1942: The Japanese army invades, forcing Britain's surrender on 15 February. Among the atrocities committed by the occupiers is the *Sook Ching* massacre.

1943: Opium is outlawed by the Japanese.

1945: The Japanese occupation forces formally surrender in September, and Singapore suffers a period of rioting, looting and disorder. A British military administration takes over until March 1946.

1948: The first Singaporean elections are held, although only British subjects have the vote. Meanwhile, the Malayan Emergency begins, with British soldiers fighting communist insurgents.

1955: The Legislative Assembly elections see the mandate broadened to include non-British subjects. David Marshall of the Labour Front becomes Singapore's first chief minister. The People's Action Party (PAP) wins three seats.

1956: Riots continue to rock the island, making the British nervous about relinquishing control of internal security. Marshall resigns after failing to convince them to give Singapore complete self-rule.

1959: The PAP, led by Lee Kuan Yew (LKY), wins a landslide in Legislative Assembly elections, as Singapore moves towards self-rule.

1960: The Housing Development Board is established, with the aim of housing Singapore's people in organised communities.

1963: The Federation of Malaysia is established, including Malaya, Singapore, Sarawak and North Borneo. Albert Winsemius publishes his report on how to rebuild Singapore's economy.

TIMELINE

1965: Singapore has independence thrust upon it on 9 August, after it is expelled from the Federation.

1981: Changi airport is opened, as Singapore starts switching to higher technology industries.

1987: Singapore's Mass Rapid Transit (MRT) system is opened.

1990: LKY hands leadership over to Goh Chok Tong, but retains a great deal of authority as senior minister. Meanwhile, the number of cars on Singapore's roads is controlled by the introduction of the Certificate of Entitlement scheme.

1992: Chewing gum is banned.

2002–2003: The SARS outbreak sweeps across Asia.

2004: Lee Hsien Loong, LKY's son, becomes independent Singapore's third prime minister. Pinnacle@Duxton opens its first show flat.

2010: Marina Bay Sands opens.

2011: The opposition Workers' Party does unexpectedly well in elections, prompting a determined and considered response from the PAP.

2015: LKY dies on 23 March, ahead of the fiftieth anniversary of Singapore's independence in August. Singapore comes top in the PISA education rankings in all three categories: science, reading, and maths.

2017: Halimah Yacob is selected to be Singapore's president. The government introduces rules banning foreigners from the annual LGBT Pink Dot event. Amos Yee's asylum application is accepted by the US. I walk 53 kilometres across the island.

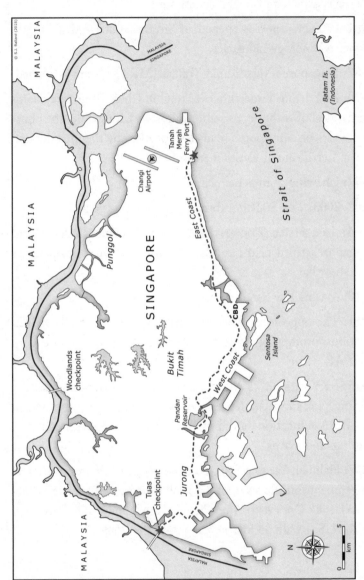

Singapore Island

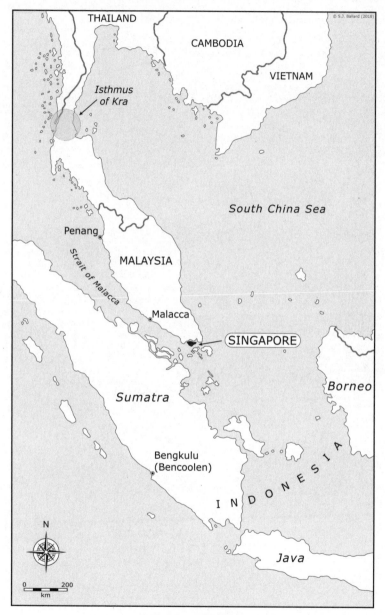

Singapore Region

THE SOUTHERN ISLANDS

SWISS ARMY KNIFE COUNTRY

The jetty at West Coast Pier was just coming off a night shift. It was an indistinct world of low-wattage lights and stray cats, off-duty firemen, and the tang of greased, oxidising metal. Somewhere above our heads a storm was fusing together, half hidden in the low equatorial clouds of a Singapore dawn. I recalled my Uber driver talking of lashing rain near Bukit Timah Plaza, and wondered if we would escape a soaking.

An office chair, set on recline to snatch a fleeting moment of rest, had been pulled under cover in expectation of rain. Cigarette smokers glanced upwards before flicking their lighters and inhaling deeply. A crew of South Asian migrant workers in dayglo orange boilersuits clambered off a flatbed, fingers securing the handles of well-filled water bottles: rain or not, it would be hot. The equator was just over there, beyond a damp horizon obscured by the flames and billowing eruptions caused by the heaviest of industry.

The swell allowed us to scramble on board the launch in twos or threes, without Captain Basir having to worry about hooking the painter to hold her steady. Then he clicked the engine up a notch and we phut-phutted away, across to a floating petrol station that was moored in the shadow of a row of half-built oil rigs. A refill and two fifty-dollar notes later, and Basir swung us south, into the channel between a crooked arm of Singapore's container port and the northeast edge of Jurong Island. The Island bristled with chimneys from a thousand petrochemical installations, while the port's skyline was a jumble of giant cranes, backs arched as they busied themselves with the endless whirring toil of containerised globalisation.

One of the smaller container ships, the *Ever Union* of the Evergreen line, pushed past us with a belch of its horn. Basir lazily adjusted to account for the wash. We rocked past a couple of car transporters, looking for all the world like floating multi-storey car parks, beaten out of iron. Then the *Mette Maersk* with its hammerhead bridge high up in the sky, leading a line of behemoths being loaded with 40-foot standardised containers. As the water opened up ahead I could see heavy rain over Kent Ridge, and a play of sunlight from a gap in the clouds over the container port. Maybe the storm would not choose us after all.

That panorama that was beginning to appear was the main reason that I had come on board Captain Basir's boat. Singapore was a tiny island, but one that hid its guts away, down here on the edge of the Straits. I wanted to bob among the container ships, plot a course between the Southern Islands, and see how the place knitted together from a suitable viewing distance. It was a way of reaching back into Singapore's past, into the old world of "Singapura," with its Malay fishing villages and equatorial lack of urgency. It would also help me see how this old world had been re-purposed in the service of the Singapore miracle.

At the edge of dystopian Jurong Island the water became choppy, Captain Basir clicked up again, and tiny droplets of spray dotted my spectacles through the open door. I wiped them, and watched flares of gas and rapidly dissipating clouds of steam being extruded by the steel-pipe chimneys of Bukom Island. The *Vega Alpha*, registered in Monrovia, cut across our bows with the resolve that came with relative size; Captain Basir measured relative courses and speeds, nudged his wheel, and put a cigarette to his lips.

According to its roof line, the Captain's launch was simply called *SC3139H*. Its windscreen wipers looked jerry-rigged, and a peculiar double-ziggurat keyring in white plastic, embossed with Arabic script, hung down from above his head. Two packets of Pall Mall cigarettes sat on his dashboard: one red, and the favoured one green. Another piece of Arabic script was scribbled onto the wall above in blue pencil. A clear plastic drawstring-bag full of milky coffee hung from a hook, a straw sticking out of its top.

Captain Basir was a local. He grew up here, among the Southern Islands, when they were part of a different world. To be precise, he grew up where a long, low stone bund stretched out ahead of us, lassoing several square kilometres of open sea in what was now known as Pulau Semakau. Back then the original Semakau Island and the neighbouring Seking Island were home to fishermen. There was a Malay village and a Chinese village, with houses propped up on stilts and shores protected by mangrove forests. Every year, the local fishermen from Singapore's swamp and sand Southern Islands used to take part in intra-island games, competing in *sampan* racing and tugs-of-war. "I was born a fisherman, ah," Basir told me. "I always fisherman, ah."

Thirty-odd years on from the young Captain Basir's eviction to a high-rise complex deep in Singapore's concrete heart, this seemed a strange place to fish. Pulau Semakau is now a state-of-the-art marine landfill in a country so short of space it has had to create viable islands out of its trash. To our west was Pawai Island, a live-fire location for Singapore's redoubtable military, rent by an explosion every fifteen minutes: a flash, a chanterelle of smoke that billowed up hundreds of metres into the sticky sky, and then a sound shockwave that found us fifteen seconds later. Raffles Lighthouse down to our southwest marked the Singaporean frontier and the western edge of a narrow channel that funnelled a quarter of the world's traded goods. Ship alarms go off incessantly in these waters, overloaded by 200 or more ships within a two-mile radius.[1]

Off in the thunderstruck east I saw the cable cars strung out across to Sentosa, the fantasy island that Singapore brands the "State of Fun," notwithstanding a past involving the British military base and post-independence political prisoners. There were the high-rise condos of Keppel Bay, looking like a witch's fingers scratching the sky, their countless evidently empty apartments hinting at copious Mainland Chinese investment. Beyond that, I could make out the profile of the peculiar high-rise banana split of the Marina Bay Sands hotel complex. Just off our starboard was the shipping superhighway of the Singapore Strait, with its relentless nose-to-tail traffic of all that the world makes and consumes. And ahead, rounded jungly pimples that were just hanging out next to the equator without sharing that existential Singaporean need to be particularly useful. They belonged to a place where there was never a shortage of land, or at least islands, and that took five hours to cross from west to east in a 747: Indonesia.

This was what had put me on board *SC3139H*. Without an understanding of Singapore's geography, how it created function out of mangrove swamps and sand, I could not understand Singapore.

My friends on board the launch had other interests. There was a pair of Singaporean couples who could have been throwing their car keys into a salad bowl after a drunken cheese fondue. Instead, they breezily chose to head out for a day of wine, *bee hoon*, and maybe even some fishing. A young Japanese man had a scary amount of professional equipment. There were a couple of older chaps, and two younger ones who were doomed to catch nothing. Then there was our guide, the man with the most Dickensian name in Southeast Asia: Megat Castelcage.

The night before he had introduced himself with a beep on our smartphones, complete with an injunction not to bring pork or bananas on board. Bananas, he sagely explained as we bobbed around the Southern Islands, scared the fish several fathoms below. He was not a full-time guide: he held down a weekday job in Singapore's Central Business District, but was spending so much time on the weekends paying for fishing trips that he decided to guide them instead. For his holidays, he went fishing.

The technique in these waters, according to Megat Castelcage, was to skewer a living prawn on your hook, through its back and out of its head, then use a weight to play the line out the 30 or 40 metres down to the coral. Captain Basir would cut the engine and the current would sweep us along to the east, until a shout of "Lines up!", frantic reeling-in, and the selection of a new spot from where to drift. Somewhere along the way we were to expect fish, while Basir eyed any ships that headed our way with occasional farts of black diesel smoke coming out of their funnels.

The two Singaporean couples opened a bottle of wine and chatted as their skewered prawns attracted little attention from the fish below. Each sentence was a merry mix of Chinese and English. One lady had a daughter at university in England, and they indulged in the Singaporean pastime of discussing different airlines before concluding that Singapore Airlines was best. Locals never referred to it as "Singapore Airlines": it is always "SIA" or (even better) "SQ," its call sign. "Fishing is not important," one of the group told me. "We are here to eat." It was a fine day to be surrounded by fibreglass and bad toilet facilities, while gazing at the geography of the planet's most remarkable country.[2]

* * *

"When I grew up as a child in Singapore its per capita income was the same as Ghana's," said Kishore Mahbubani. Singapore's foremost scholar of its place in the world had both a blistering mind and near-boundless pride in his country.[3] "Now it is higher than the UK. It's not just an economic success story. It's about infant mortality going down. It's about life expectancy going up. It's about people owning their own homes. It's about quality of education. No other country comes close."

It did not take much for Professor Mahbubani to start singing the praises of Singapore. He was justified: in half a century of independence it had shot to the top end of nearly every index of progress, from education and wealth, to crime and health. Not bad for a country small enough to walk across in one day, that did not particularly want independence in the first place. It was extraordinary, tiny, and a model for a raft of other countries who wanted to create a modern and affluent state without the encumbrances of Western-style liberal democracy.

Professor Mahbubani, like many other Singaporeans, traced his roots far beyond the island. His parents were Hindus from what became Pakistan, and left when it split from the rest of India in 1947. His entire clan dispersed to every corner of the globe. He reeled off their destinations: Suriname, Kuala Lumpur, Nigeria, Hong Kong, Japan, Texas, Guyana, Jakarta, Ghana, Mumbai, Calcutta. "I can see how lucky I was that I was born in Singapore. If my father had gone to Nigeria I'd be much richer. But I've been to Nigeria, I've been to Suriname, I've seen people's lives there. Singapore's transformation has been so spectacular."

My own personal arrival in Singapore was less dramatic than that of the professor's family. My son Luca had just turned one, and my wife was about to join the country's pampered legion of highly skilled expat workers. We had not expected to stay long, but Singapore reeled us in. In some ways that was how the place had been designed over its first five decades of independence: as a leafy low-tax magnet for international human capital.

Not long after we arrived, this tiny country celebrated the enormous progress it had made since parting ways with the Malay Federation in 1965. Although it was hardly a desert island back then, what it had achieved since that momentous split was truly nothing less than a miracle. In 1965 the country was home to sprawling and disease-ridden slums, sometimes perched on stilts above fetid water. Others lived in *kampongs* (villages) that were squirreled away in dank corners of the jungly interior. The port was there, but the British military—accounting for one fifth of Gross National Product and 10 per cent of jobs—would withdraw in 1971. Other than geography, the place had very little in the way of resources. To the north was Malaysia; to the south, Indonesia. Singapore sat between them like a nut waiting to be cracked.

It did not crack. Singapore, with the help of some far-sighted leadership, hard work, and a sense of vulnerability, pulled itself up by the bootstraps. "Since the time history began, no country has improved the living standards of its people as quickly and as comprehensively as Singapore," said Professor Mahbubani. "That's an outrageous claim: that Singapore is the most successful country since human history began. Because it's off the charts."

That outrageous claim may have been true for the country's first half-century, but would it be true for the second? When we touched down on that February morning in 2014, on the daily SIA 777 from Milan, Singapore was in a more reflective mood than usual. Preparations were well underway for its fiftieth birthday. Bulldozers and jackhammers and tremendous clanking drilling devices worked furiously. Buildings shot up and enormous infrastructure projects were laid out in concrete and steel. But in celebrating just how far the country had come in half a century, there was an unavoidable question being asked about the future: after half a century of success, was life about to get much harder for Singapore?

The challenges have certainly changed. Singapore now faced the world as a very rich country, with a cutting-edge economy. Easy wins were in the past. Beyond its borders, the benign external environment that had cushioned its rise, as a link between rising Asia and the world, was unlikely to remain quite so benign. To continue to flourish, even to survive, Singapore had to continue evolving.

This may be true for any country, but it was a hundred times truer for Singapore, because of one fundamental and startlingly obvious fact: it is tiny.

There were advantages in this. David Skilling, the director of the Landfall Strategy Group consultancy, compared Singapore to a small vessel on a turbulent sea: it was forced to confront the waves, building experience and understanding of how to survive. Vulnerability bred vitality. The *Titanic*, he noted, was big and did not have to pay quite so much attention, and look what happened there. On the other hand, we had heard about the *Titanic* because it was so, well, titanic. Just out of sight, hundreds and thousands of small vessels had been smashed to pieces and lost beneath the waves that they confronted. Singapore may have had vitality, but it would never escape vulnerability.

But what if it had lost that sense of vulnerability? What if it had become complacent? After all, vigilance is easier when incomes are low and the monsoons threaten to sweep away your attap-roofed hut. It does not come as easily when you have achieved the Singapore miracle. Even that apostle of the positive, Professor Mahbubani, recognised that this was the country's next real test.

This was something that had haunted the founding father of independent Singapore, Lee Kuan Yew. He had built his pocket-sized miracle through a combination of serendipity and the exploitation of the country's two resources: geography and people. Fifty years later this recipe no longer seemed so robust.

Singapore's geography was no longer quite the advantage that it had been. Serendipity was as unpredictable as a monsoon-season sea. And what of the Singaporean people? Did they work as hard as the feted Pioneer Generation? Were they too fond of shopping, while griping and grousing on social media? And if they were complacent, what was the impact on the country's government? Would it lose its reputation for bravery as it struggled to manage expectations and complaints?

A few comparisons illustrate just how small Singapore is. The main island is less than 50 kilometres (around 30 miles) across from one tip to the other. The entire country is 719 square kilometres in area. For perspective: London is 1,572 sq km; New York, 789 sq km; Tokyo, 2,188 sq km; Lagos is a suspiciously exact 1,000 sq km; Mexico City is 1,485 sq km; Moscow, 2,511 sq km. All of these are cities with a hinterland, full of people, industry, water, farms, sewage treatment plants, power stations, military installations. Meanwhile, you could walk across Singapore in a single day—a good working definition for a really small country.

I had already tried this out, walking from north to south. I started at Sembawang Park, near the British Royal Navy's old base on the Johor Straits, and tracked 36 kilometres or so to Labrador Park, where a British artillery battery had watched over the approaches to Keppel Harbour. The walk was an education in how Singapore organised its resources, from its carefully marshalled reservoirs, military camps and light industrial estates, to its Edwardian bungalows, high-rise public housing and fancy private condos. But, despite a few diversions along the way, it also felt like I had taken a shortcut.

Walking across Singapore, by contrast, on its longest axis, was more of a challenge. I could set off from the Malaysian border at Tuas in the west, to the effective Indonesian border at Tanah Merah ferry port in the far east. It would be 53 kilometres through the past, present, and future of a remarkable and very small country. I would get to see the guts of Singapore, and what made it tick. The walk would also help me outline the misgivings that I—and others—had about its miracle continuing. It was also a very long way for a sweaty forty-five-year-old with knackered feet. My wife thought I was a fool. But how often do you get the chance to walk across an entire country in a day?

* * *

Back out on our stretch of open sea between Singapore's southern islands and the shipping lanes, I watched the flotsam and jetsam, Asia's lost flip flops and discarded yoghurt pots, all bobbing about in the fierce current, and wished I were heading for home. But then I felt a pull on the line, as though my skewered prawn had caught on a jagged bit of coral. The pulling continued, and the realisation dawned that something, all those metres below, was fighting me. I fought back, and reeled and reeled. When it broke the surface, the fish was big enough to excite Megat Castelcage. It was a "sweet lips": not the biggest catch of the day, but big enough to impress my son.

Eventually, even Megat Castelcage decided it was time to turn for home. It was late enough to mean we were racing against the equatorial night, which snapped down on the day like a mouse trap. Basir took us around the eastern edge of Pulau Semakau, and an industrial rubbish-sorting unit that was painted Miami Vice green. Then, Pulau Bukom: hedgehogged with industrial chimneys, with the container port opposite and Jurong Island in front. We nipped around the bows of one of the *Maersk* leviathans, and back into port.

2

TUAS CHECKPOINT

A FEW HUNDRED METRES FROM MALAYSIA

Tuas was an unwelcoming place at seven in the morning for somebody on foot. In truth, it was unwelcoming for pedestrians at any hour. At best Singapore was sceptical about people wanting to wander around outdoors in 30-plus centigrade heat and near 100 per cent humidity, but the Tuas area was positively hostile. There was a bus stop, but a few yards either way the pavement simply disappeared. Everybody else was motorised, on container lorries and mopeds and buses. One posse of Bangladeshi workers, fresh off a nightshift, displayed solidarity by running from one bus to another, but even they were just trying to get to their cheap bunks, across the causeway in Malaysia.

This unforeseen hiccup meant that the grand start of my day-long hike across an entire country ended up being a witless pacing back and forth in twilit confusion, followed by an unnerving walk along the hard shoulder of a highway. After a few hundred metres I found a safer path underneath a thundering overpass, encrusted with the prints from dozens of South Asian work boots. The footprints edged to the left, I had a few more yards of hard shoulder to bear, and then I was on a proper footpath. I felt the soles of my feet stride firmly forward on concrete: something I would have plenty of time to get used to. I lengthened my stride; my walk had begun.

This 53-kilometre walk began at a border with one of Singapore's neighbours. The Tuas checkpoint was a bridge across to the western end of Johor, in Malaysia, to nearby delights such as Nusajaya, Gelang Patah, and Legoland Malaysia. Tuas was the newer of the two causeways physically linking Singapore to its erstwhile national partner: 18 kilometres to the northeast was Woodlands, where the Japanese invaded in 1942.

Tuas was a fitting place to start the walk for two reasons: firstly, modern independent Singapore began with an uneasy divorce from Malaysia in 1965; secondly, long before that, and long before a chap called Raffles realised just how strategic this island was, this land was nestled deep within a watery Malay world of trading, fishing, and petty piracy.

For centuries Singapore was just another island within a scattered maritime world of commercial linkages and nodes that stretched back a couple of millennia. Its proper name was "Pulau Ujong," which literally meant "the island at the end of the peninsula." It was just one glimmering star in the sweeping constellation of the Orang Laut, nomadic sea people who made a living around the creeks, channels and mangrove forests, in the twilight zone between the warm seas and the dank, often impenetrable interiors. Sprinkled over the islands were more established Malay villages, some locals living lives not dramatically different from Captain Basir's forebears on Pulau Semakau.

The pre-Raffles history of the island was cloudy, but intriguing. During the fourteenth century it was known as "Singapura." The name came from Sanskrit, and translated as "Lion City."[1] One story was that the founder of the kingdom, Sri Tri Buana, spotted a beast that resembled a lion when first scoping out the island. Another suggested that one of his descendants, Iskander Shah (also known as Parameswara), called it Singapura as he was seeking legitimacy for his rule by harking back to a polity called the Lion Throne. Either way, Singapura's flowering was brief. Iskander Shah fled the island after being besieged by a Javanese war-fleet, and went on to found the sultanate of Malacca.

The Malacca Straits were then—as now—an important link for trade networks, a choke point between the Pacific Asian monsoon and the Indian Ocean monsoon. Ships often had to linger for the winds associated with one of these to continue their voyage, after they had made their way using the winds associated with the other. The region was also a source of treasures, including turtle shells and sandalwood, sea cucumbers and birds' nests. The Chinese knew it as Nanyang, or the Southern Ocean, and many left the coasts of mainland China to find their fortunes in its waters. The great eunuch admiral Zheng He passed by the Dragon's Teeth on the southern edge of Singapore, but the Middle Kingdom famously, and perhaps short-sightedly, declined to pursue its maritime ambitions. There was to be no Greater Chinese Empire stretching down to these parts.

There were, however, other regional empires, based in the fertile lands of agricultural surpluses: places like Siam and Java, and the local Malay sultanates. Then Europeans arrived on their creaking wave-tossed ships from a world away, searching for spices, trading routes, and personal fortunes. The Portuguese model was to set up strategic maritime bases, which included the fortress at what they called Melaka, towards the northwest end of the eponymous Straits. The Dutch were next, taking Melaka in 1641 in their more systematic approach to commercial empire and the exploitation of Southeast Asia. They were interested in access to the vast archipelago that sprawled before them, from the fertile volcanic soils of Java to the riches of the spice islands. As such, they were more interested in the Sunda Strait, which allowed them to skirt the far edge of Sumatra before turning north, through the gap into the Java Sea. Their centuries-long presence would have a larger cartographic footprint than the Portuguese, and resulted in what became known as the Dutch East Indies, or modern Indonesia.

British involvement in the region came as a result of their interest in the trade route linking the vast markets of India and China, and to keep strategic locations such as Melaka out of the hands of their great Napoleonic rivals, the French. This came as active Dutch influence in Southeast Asia began to wane. In 1790 the British first got their hands on the island of Penang, after Francis Light of the Royal Navy persuaded the sultan of Kedah to cede the island to the East India Company for $6,000 a year. Penang itself was too far north to dominate the Malacca Straits, which led an ambitious young man, born on a ship in the Caribbean in 1783, to look for a more suitable spot for British interests. That man was Stamford Raffles, of whom we will see more later.

As European sails and ambitions shrunk the world, the sheer geographical potential of the Malacca Straits region was always going to attract attention. It was a crossroads between the monsoon winds, the Indian Ocean and the Pacific, and the vast markets of China and South Asia. It was a borderland between agrarian empires, and a narrow western gateway to the exotic treasures of the spice islands, so intoxicating to the globe-trotting Europeans. The region was not just a magnet to outside powers, but also to individuals looking to tap into these networks, and escape from lives in less promising places. The DNA that was to shape modern, successful, multi-ethnic Singapore can be traced back to the geoeconomic and geopolitical promise of this small island, deep in the heart of the Malayosphere, troubled only by fishermen, farmers and crabs, and the odd, hopeful trader.

* * *

Modern Singapore wears its age-old Malayan heritage lightly. This is in part because ethnic Malays are so heavily outnumbered in a multicultural population featuring a Chinese majority. Further back, the country's foundations were laid under the guidance of the British (despite the studied ambivalence of modern Singapore towards their former colonial rulers), lifting it out of the Malayosphere and leaving behind few traces of its earlier identity. Family links remain: "I have my parents and a brother in Malaysia," noted the leading Singaporean politician S. Rajaratnam in a 1965 speech. "I cannot force myself to regard them as foreigners."[2] Even Singapore's formal incorporation as one of its northern neighbour's states in the 1960s now feels like a doomed project, like an unlikely high school fling that is followed by very different career trajectories.

The Malaysian issue, in Singaporean minds, continues to be laced with the taboo questions of ethnicity and culture. The Malaysian population is a near-mirror image of the Singaporean one. It has small Chinese and Indian communities, but is predominantly Malay, while the same mix in its island neighbour is skewed three-quarters Chinese. Whereas Singapore is devoutly multi-ethnic in its outlook, handling the mixture like gelignite within the compressed confines of its borders, Malaysia sees itself as essentially Malay, and prepared to take measures to ensure Malay ascendancy. Back in 1933, the local Malay community pressured the British to end Chinese and Indian immigration. When the resource-rich peninsula became independent from Britain in 1957, it was as a federation of nine Malay Kingdoms. In 1963, when it expanded to include Singapore, the Federation of Malaya was careful to also take in the colonial states of Sabah and Sarawak: they would preserve its ethnic Malay preponderance, despite the addition of Singapore's hefty Chinese contingent.

Singapore's determination to be race-blind, mindful of the potential for dangerous divisions within its concentrated, linguistically and ethnically fragmented population, has been well-advised. Race riots were considered a very real security threat: they broke out in 1964, partly as a response to Malay *kampongs* being cleared and populations being relocated, as Singapore began to build modern social housing. But this critical difference in fundamental ethos had placed Singapore on a collision course with the rest of the Federation.

The collision duly happened. In August 1965, a visibly upset Prime Minister Lee Kuan Yew appeared on Singaporean television sets to announce that the little island was going its own way. It became that rarest of geopolitical entities: a reluctantly independent nation. "For me it is a moment of anguish because all my life ... I have believed in merger and the unity of these two territories," he told a press conference, before asking for a pause so that he could regain his composure.[3]

It is easy to see why even Prime Minister Lee was unnerved by independence. Singapore did not look like a viable country. It had no hinterland, no ready market for whatever it wanted to sell, no place from which to draw labour, food and water. Malaysia, on the other hand, was doing well, thanks to the postwar rubber and tin boom, and favourable geoeconomic winds from the Korean War. In 1948 it accounted for over half of all British Empire exports to the US.[4]

At any cursory glance of the map, Singapore was an integral part of the Malay world, with an artificial Chinese tinge. It was also highly vulnerable, nestling into the embrace of the southeastern tip of the Eurasian landmass, like the ball in a ball-and-socket joint. At one point (just north of Tuas), Singapore is a mere 500 metres or so away from Malaysia.

Looking southwards, the only thing that divided the new country from the Riau Islands of Indonesia was a narrow shipping lane. They sat on the other side of the 1824 dividing line that delineated the British and Dutch spheres of influence. The

Dutch East Indies had become Indonesia, and it too was no obvious friend. It was engaged in a low intensity war of regional destabilisation, known as the *Konfrontasi*. In those Cold War times, with Indochina already catching fire, its government's leftish tinge was a source of genuine concern to Singapore's governing centre-right People's Action Party (PAP).

Prime Minister Lee, then, had multiple reasons to fear for the future of his reluctantly independent state. However, having independence rudely thrust upon it turned out to be the making of Singapore, as it was forced to reinvent an age-old political unit, the city state. Many city states have prospered throughout history, from the great city states of the Mayan world to Venice and Genoa, Athens and Sparta. Singapore repurposed this model for the modern age.

Singapore's small size gave it focus, and it gave the PAP real control over the levers of the state. As it was already solving the issue of housing by moving everybody into large, urban HDB estates, it did not have to worry about diverging political interests between workers and peasants.* The population was motivated by their justified sense of vulnerability, making them more tolerant when the PAP tightened the terms of the country's democracy. They had to trust the government, and the government mostly delivered. Size and the attendant weakness and exposure also made some decisions easier: when you only had a small island, and lived in a difficult neighbourhood, what other choice did you have but to throw yourself at globalisation? Paradoxically, Singapore did not achieve its miracle despite its unpromising starting point, but did so because of it.

Meanwhile, the relationship with its erstwhile partner to the north has remained an emotional challenge. Part of it goes back

---

* The Housing Development Board, or HDB, provides accommodation for the majority of the country's residents.

to that sense of vulnerability: Singapore may have a disproportionately capable military, but Malaysia remains much bigger. And, as many taxi drivers have been keen to remind me, a large chunk of the population is ethnically Malay. "Are they loyal?" the taxi driver might ask, his gaze lingering in the mirror as he speeds up, slows down, speeds up, slows down.[5] "They're Muslim," he might add. "If there's a crisis. ..." Some people are more explicit, and it is not just the taxi drivers.

This taxi uncle talk has taken on an extra security dimension in recent years. An unnamed security source cited by *The Straits Times* in 2017 suggested that Malaysia's visa-free deal for citizens of many Islamic countries had led it to become a storage depot for deported ISIS fighters. Thirty or so had apparently been detained in airports such as Istanbul's Atatürk, before diplomatic wrangling saw them passed on to Malaysia. The source told *The Straits Times* that "instead of being deported to their last port of disembarkation, they were given the 'option' to be deported to Malaysia... We have become a dumping ground."[6] Such things are noted in Singapore, and—rightly or wrongly—confirm popular stereotypes of Malaysia going off the rails. It is, remember, just 500 metres away.

Meanwhile, Singaporeans have responded to the uncertain trajectory of modern Malaysia with two parts schadenfreude to one part anxiety. Malaysia's recent regression has been worrying because it cuts defiantly across that more familiar regional narrative of "Asia rising." For many years, Malaysia was one of the "Asian Tigers" that threatened to duplicate Japan's success in warmer waters. But recently there have been real causes for disquiet. The government of Prime Minister Najib Razak seemed to exemplify a most un-Singaporean approach to politics, tinged with patronage, corruption, inefficiency, and—perhaps most alarmingly of all—religion.[7]

The most visible evidence of this approach has been the 1MDB scandal, in which the Malaysian prime minister himself was directly accused of helping to channel many hundreds of millions of US dollars from a strategic development company into his personal bank accounts (he has denied all wrongdoing). The scandal's tentacles have even threatened to besmirch aspects of the Singaporean financial system, which its citizens view as a beacon of probity. The whole sorry business merely confirmed to Singaporeans their suspicions about the lubricating role that money and corruption play in Malaysian politics. This speaks to a cultural gulf between the two countries, rather than a narrow strait.

Meanwhile, Najib Razak seemed to lean ever more upon Islam as a source of political legitimacy, so combating any source of discontent. This, of course, harks back to the pro-Malay positive discrimination policies that have been a plank of government policy since the British left in the 1950s. The trend has become more pronounced as Singapore's economy has stalled (and the 1MDB scandal has been unearthed), with Najib's party leaning ever more heavily on conservative rural voters for support. This too has led many Singaporeans to shift uncomfortably in their seats, mindful that religion within their country's own borders could have the same explosive potential as ethnicity.

There is an awkward extra dimension to any discussion of Singapore's relationship with Malaysia. Within Singapore's government there is continuing concern over the relatively poor socioeconomic position and educational outcomes of the country's Malay community. Malays perform worse in exams, fewer go on to higher and further education, and the community is overrepresented in lower socioeconomic groups.[8] The academic John Curtis Perry has argued that there is a historical component to this: from Singapore and Malaya's earliest days of colonial development, ethnic Malays tended towards labouring jobs, farming and fishing, rather than those associated with commerce or industry.[9] Whatever the arguments explaining the differences in attainment levels, the broad trends contribute to a widely held narrative that Singapore is different because it is Chinese-dominated, rather than Malay.

Around the time that Singapore was celebrating—in effect—Malaysia spitting it out and getting on with life without the miniscule island, I asked a particularly astute and wise friend what might happen to his country if its miracle started to falter. He drew a breath and looked like he would rather I had not asked him the question. Only after some prodding did he venture an answer. "Re-join Malaysia," he muttered, under his breath. His tone said it all: for Singapore this would be less a reunification than an admission of defeat.[10]

3

THE AYE TOLL ROAD

BRAND RAFFLES

Tuas is not simply an area of container trucks, reclaimed land and burgeoning industry. Directly south of the checkpoint on my route was Raffles Marina, which promises "a full service boating haven with trappings of a country club," and berthing able to take a "megayacht." You can dine under the stars, catch a film at the Marina's "theatrette," and plan your jaunt up to Langkawi over a beer at the Discovery Pub.

Heading southeast along the Ayer Rajah Expressway (the AYE), as I did that dawn, the industry was all kept neatly to my right. To my left was the Raffles Country Club, "nestling amidst 146 hectares of luscious land" that includes two championship golf courses, an air-conditioned badminton court, and a Jackpot Room featuring sixteen whizzing, hypnotic fruit machines. Despite those fruit machines, Raffles Country Club was seriously posh. (It was also doomed: early in 2017 it was announced that the entire complex was to be bulldozed for a possible high-speed rail project, linking Singapore to Kuala Lumpur.[1] Such is the price of progress, and the price of living in a country where land is ultimately controlled by the authorities.)

The Marina and Country Club were as good an introduction as any to the man and brand Sir Stamford Raffles. A couple of centuries after he stepped fatefully onto its shores, his name graced Singapore's pre-eminent hotel (the glitzy upstarts over at Marina Bay Sands notwithstanding), its most prestigious schools, and—at least until around 2005—the business class offering of the world-leading Singapore Airlines.[2] It denoted the very best in provenance and quality: not a bad legacy for somebody who barely graced the island with his presence during his lifetime, and whose name is indelibly associated with a British colonial past that many modern Singaporeans seem keen to play down, if not disparage.

The Raffles story kicked off at that time when Britain was expanding its role as a maritime trading power in Southeast Asia. Its interests centred on bolstering the China–India trade, strategic competition with powers such as the French and the Dutch, and perennial aggravations such as the region's endemic piracy. Raffles was the man responsible for crystallising these interests in the shape of the muddy island of Singapore.

Thomas Stamford Raffles himself led a tough life, at least by modern standards. He was born on board a ship in the Caribbean in 1783. His father, Benjamin, was a merchant captain. There were money problems: Raffles had to drop out of school to find work to support the family, and his father would die in a debtor's prison. Raffles became a clerk at India House, which was the headquarters of the East India Company, and demonstrated a thirst for knowledge that caught the eyes of several colleagues. In 1805 he headed to Georgetown, on the island of Penang, but frequently found that social status and lack of financial means were barriers to full acceptance. However, his effort to learn Malay helped him gain a greater depth of understanding of the world that surrounded him.

In 1818 Raffles had been appointed as the governor of Bencoolen, halfway down the lengthy southeast coast of

Sumatra. However, he believed in the need for a more suitable trading post than faraway Penang, as a vehicle for British interests in the region. The Dutch had begun to establish themselves in the Riau Islands, on the Sumatran side of the Malacca Straits, and Raffles gained the support of the Governor General of India, the Marquis of Hastings, for his search. One option was Karimun, right in the middle of the Straits, just to the southwest of Singapore. It was an island that I circled over in the funereal silence of a Silk Air Airbus while waiting to land at Changi, Singapore's nearby coastline completely lost behind a violent and forbidding floor-to-ceiling curtain of storms. The jumble of townships near the island's ferry port are a minor tourist attraction for Singaporeans and Malaysians looking for cheap shopping and sex.

Raffles discounted Karimun once he came across the more sheltered and larger island of Singapore, with its deep anchorage and welcoming river mouth. On 29 January 1819, he landed on the now-sparsely populated island, at a point now marked by his poly-marble statue, with an inscription declaring that his "genius and perception changed the destiny of Singapore from an obscure fishing village to a great seaport and modern metropolis." In his own words, Raffles promised the Marquis of Hastings back in Calcutta that "What Malta is in the West, that may Singapore become in the East."

The fact that his statue still stands, in a country that has achieved so much since it left colonialism behind, is itself an acknowledgement that a common thread joins modern Singapore to the colony that Raffles founded. There is a common attachment to free trade and global capital, to diversity within a small island, to commerce, and to freeing the sea lanes of hindrances such as pirates. Lee Kuan Yew's influential Dutch economic advisor, Albert Winsemius, was especially keen to promote this link with the British past, sending the message that Singapore was a safe haven for Western capital, while wars and communist insurgencies raged on elsewhere in Southeast Asia. This tipping of the cap to Raffles was also a reinterpretation of the colonial period, aligning it with modern Singaporean values.

When Raffles arrived at its shores, Singapore might have been sparsely populated, but that does not mean it was empty. It already had a long history within the Malayosphere. As well as a scattering of plantations and fishing villages, there was a small Malay settlement at the mouth of the Singapore River, and the island was nominally under the control of the sultan of Johor. Unfortunately for Raffles, the sultan, Tengku Abdul Rahman, had strong links to the Dutch. More promisingly, his older brother Tengku Hussein was aggrieved that he had missed out on the sultanate in 1812, because he had been off getting married at the time of their father's death. The British promptly smuggled Tengku Hussien onto Singapore, agreeing to recognise him as the sultan in exchange for a treaty that allowed Raffles to establish a trading post on the island.

Although the Dutch were annoyed by these developments, their power was waning, and in 1824 they signed the Anglo-Dutch Treaty to divide the Straits into respective spheres of interest.[3] Singapore, with its fortuitous geography and deep-water port, was now firmly in the hands of the British (or at least the East India Company). Back in London, British Foreign Secretary George Canning declared to Parliament that Singapore had made "the British Empire in India complete." It was to be ruled from Calcutta, and was, in effect, "Further India."[4]

In his 1902 book *The End of the Tether*, Joseph Conrad has seaman Captain Whalley remember his first visit to early Singapore: "there had stood a fishing village, a few mat huts erected on piles between a muddy tidal creek and a miry pathway that went writhing into a tangled wilderness without any docks or waterworks."[5] This was all to change as Singapore took off.

Singapore's near-immediate success as a trading post can be seen in the population figures. The Malay settlement had perhaps 150 people living there when Raffles momentously stepped ashore. By 1824 the island had around 15,000 inhabitants, and over 50,000 by 1850. As early as 1830 Singapore was enough of a draw that 7,000 Chinese coolies came during the "junk season," nearly doubling the size of its Chinese population.[6] By the 1830s half of the trade through the Straits was coming through Singapore. British investment had enhanced the island's position within existing Chinese and Malay trading networks. The increase in British influence in China thanks to the Opium Wars and the 1841 Treaty of Nanking boosted Singapore's growth, although its enduring rivalry with Hong Kong also dates back to this time.

The relentless creep of modernity continued to benefit Singapore's geography. Singapore was linked by telegraph to Batavia (modern Jakarta) in 1859, and to Calcutta in 1870. In 1869, the opening of the Suez Canal halved the travel time to London and underlined that the future was coal-powered. Singapore was ideally positioned when Britain began to open up the potential of the Malay Peninsula, mining its mineral wealth and establishing vast plantations of rubber trees. "Into this land God put first gold and tin," wrote Rudyard Kipling, "and after these the Englishman who floats companies, obtains concessions and goes forward."[7] The development of canned food in the 1850s and 1860s increased the value of the Malayan tin mines, while the invention of the motor car ultimately did something similar for rubber. New industries such as a tin smelting works on the island mainly attracted Chinese and Indian labour. Singapore also proved itself to be a useful mustering point for Southeast Asian Muslims, making their *Hajj* pilgrimage to Mecca.

In short, Raffles' vision for Singapore was dead on. The island had few things going for it—sweat, mud, limitless potential for deadly tropical diseases—but, by the stripes of the East India Company's flag, it did have geography. Raffles' talent was strategic, seeing the map rather than the street plan. He recognised the island's potential, then set about laying the foundations for exploiting it. That involved establishing Singapore as a nineteenth-century global trading hub and free port, with the facilities and administrative set-up to outcompete regional rivals and bend the patterns of international trade towards its gravitational pull. Raffles' commitment to free trade fitted with the philosophical direction that Britain was heading in. No taxes were levied on commercial transactions until 1853, and only very small ones after that. This gave Singapore an enormous advantage over rivals (such as Batavia), which were bogged down with bureaucracy, corruption and discrimination. Arguably, its commitment to free trade and non-disruptive administration still mark Singapore out from the rest of the region today.

At first, Singapore benefitted hugely from the dynamism of local Malay trading networks. Larger European vessels docked at Singapore's excellent port facilities, before their cargoes of arms, textiles and opium were dispersed throughout the region on smaller boats. Those smaller boats brought tropical woods, spices and silks back to the hub port.

Curiously, given the continuing headline role that he has in the Singapore story to this day, Raffles barely spent any time in the colony. Instead, running the place was the job of William Farquhar, who had periodic arguments with Raffles about how Singapore should be set up, and how it should be run. Farquhar was determined to utilise revenues from less salubrious sectors of the economy. He taxed gambling, although Raffles was determined to prohibit it.[8] Farquhar also auctioned off monopoly concession licenses for *Chandu*, a smokable form of opium. With these concessions bringing in up to a third of government revenues in the 1820s, it is even probably fair to call Singapore something of a narco-state at this point. For many years these forms of "revenue farming" contributed 40 to 60 per cent of government revenues, and allowed select Chinese businessmen to become very wealthy indeed. In general, the East India Company was quite happy to let the various communities within Singapore organise themselves, while it built the port, contributed to British and its own company's trade, and let the island finance itself.

Raffles himself returned to England in 1824, despite the journey's ill-fated start on board an East Indiaman called the *Fame*. At first the ship caught fire, then sank just off Bencoolen, taking with it 122 crates of everything that interested him, from manuscripts and drawings to animal specimens.[9] Raffles' time in the tropics had extracted an appalling personal toll: he had lost four of his five children and his first wife to various diseases. He also later faced charges from the East India Company in connection with a series of debts. Meanwhile, he suffered from a succession of blinding headaches. On 5 July 1826, just forty-four years old, he was found dead at the bottom of a flight of stairs. He had probably been suffering from a brain tumour or had had a stroke. Notably, the vicar of the local parish church refused to allow him to be buried there: Reverend Theodore Williams' family had made their money from the slave trade in Jamaica, and he vehemently disagreed with Raffles' anti-slavery views.

As Singapore grew, the focal point of the port moved from the wharves of the Singapore River to what became known as Keppel Harbour. This tracked the emergence of maritime steam power, with coal bunkers lining the shore and Chinese workers (organised into gangs according to their clans) carrying the stuff in baskets hanging from their shoulders. Steam power also lessened the seasonal variations of monsoon-dependent sailing ships. Bullock carts were used to carry merchandise into the centre of the city, which remained near the banks of the eponymous river.

Keppel Harbour itself was named after Captain Henry Keppel of the Royal Navy, who played a key role in fitting it with the infrastructure necessary to be a successful port. He had come to the island via the First Carlist War, the First and Second Opium Wars, the Crimean War, and the Battle of Fatshan Creek, where he sank 100 enemy war junks. One of his most notable achievements was ensuring that the harbour facilities were suitable for steam ships. In his diary entry on the 30 May 1848, Keppel wrote that he was "astonished to find deep water close to shore ... Now that steam is likely to come into use, this ready-made harbour as a depot for coal would be invaluable."[10] The importance of his contribution to Singapore was such that he was greeted with cheers and champagne when revisiting the island in 1900 as a ninety-one-year-old. Sir Algernon West wrote about the old man's return, with acting governor Alexander Swettenham and the settlement's leading merchants breaking champagne on a buoy and "cheering the old Admiral to their heart's content."[11]

Arrivals did not only come from China, Malaya, Britain, and South Asia. One of the smallest groups to set up shop was the Armenian community, which enjoyed an outsized impact on life in Singapore. They began to arrive in 1820, wafted eastwards by persecution in Persia and drawn by the trading opportunities of the new boom town. They brought sharp business brains and fantastic names: Sarkies A. Sarkies and Aristarkies Sarkies were the first to arrive, followed by Carapiet Phannous, Mackertich Moses, and two sets of brothers: the Seths and the Zechariahs. Names were often anglicised, so Stepanian became Stephen, and Mardirian became Martin.

The Armenians were responsible for two of Singapore's most celebrated institutions. Martin and Tigran Sarkies, who ran hotels in Penang, were the founders of the iconic Raffles Hotel in 1887. Four-and-a-bit decades before that, Catchick Moses had established *The Straits Times*. He was born in Basra, and had arrived in Singapore just before his sixteenth birthday. He started off as a clerk at Boustead & Company, before striking out under his own steam. In the early 1840s, a friend named Martyrose Apcar had a printing press delivered from England, but was unable to set up a paper thanks to financial problems. Catchick Moses stepped in, and the first edition of *The Straits Times* was published on 15 July 1845.

The front page of the new venture proclaimed that "no pains will be spared to make the Journal of Commerce a correct record of Prices Current and to maintain the accuracy of its Market Reports." There were notices about the Spanish brig *Dardo*, heading for Manila, and the *Anna Maria*, bound for London. Adverts listed goats and billiard tables, ivory card cases, feather fans, cribbage boards, brandy, and genuine Macassar oil. For those with more pressing needs than mere goats and brandy, an entire column was devoted to Holloway's Pills. Some of the illnesses these professed to cure sounded like the ailments I suffered from in the equatorial heat: "King's Evil" or "Weakness, from whatever cause." The column included several testimonies, including one from a William Brooke, who was cured of fifteen running ulcers on his left arm, and ulcerated sores and wounds on both legs.[12]

Unfortunately for Catchick Moses, the new venture did not pay, and he sold it to concentrate on more lucrative ventures such as property. When he died, his *Straits Times* obituary found space to note that he was "always seen in public in frock coat and top hat," but did not mention that he had founded that very paper.[13] The Armenian community remained small but vital, through to the 1970s, with the last Persian Armenian, Helen Metes, dying in 2007.[14]

The Raffles Country Club turned out to be the last bit of genuine greenery that I would see for a very long time. I was close to the epicentre of industrial Singapore, and everything was coated with a layer of brownish grime. There were few allowances made for idiots on foot. When I reached the junction with Tuas Road I found myself having to divert over a kilometre off course, just to find a way through the traffic. The air was laced with chemicals, and I braced myself for the ugliest stretch of my walk across Singapore.

4

JURONG

INSIDE THE INDUSTRIAL MIRACLE

Goodness knows how hard the walk through grimy, industrial Jurong would have been had I attempted the route in reverse. Footpaths disintegrated into patterns of broken concrete and mud pools. Marshy verges were sprinkled with discarded plastic, shards of glass, and indeterminate jags of rust. Promising routes evaporated in junctions with no viable foot crossings. Heavy goods vehicles rumbled past in the bare dawn light, oblivious to any suggestion that a luckless, lone pedestrian might get mangled in one of their half-dozen axles.

If Tuas was forbidding for somebody on foot, Jurong was a no-go zone, designed for heavy industry and all its clanking, belching trappings. It was a tough walk through the industrial heart of Singapore. Hulks of ships were visible from Pioneer Road, like an equatorial Wallsend on Tyne or Sampierdarena in Genoa. Enormous shells of buildings, large enough to swallow a Taj Mahal and still have room for pudding, loomed over the landscape. Compounds were feasts of pulleys and cables, tracks and tyres. A Chinese worker in an ancient nylon Holland football top, his badminton racket strung across his back and a plastic bag of sweet, milky coffee dangling from his fingers, stepped out of a gate, wandered along the verge, then retraced his steps. A pea-green workers' dormitory sat at a junction, its first-floor railings festooned with high-visibility jackets and sarongs. Its windows were taped over with newspapers to afford the night-shift workers some relief from the hazy daylight.

If modern Singapore could be compared to a particularly capable executive car, all computerised wizardry and leather padding, air conditioning and electronics, then Jurong was the humble internal combustion engine. It was the uncomplaining motor that got it to where it is now. The future may have been silent and purring and clean, but without those oiled metal components, explosions and exhaust gas, the present would never have arrived.

In effect, the Jurong story went back to the post-Second World War period, when Singapore was still part of the British Empire. Back then it was a very different place—and a rather different shape, thanks to the Singaporean enthusiasm for turning tropical seaside into viable chunks of physical land.

Land reclamation actually began well before independence, with swamps and mangroves being drained to improve the natural coastline and build the port that was its newly designated reason for being. In 1822, a small army of coolie labourers spent four months turning the flood-prone marsh on the southern bank of the Singapore River into what was to become Boat Quay. Abdullah bin Abdul Kadir, the informal secretary to the British during the project, recorded that "Every afternoon, sacks of money were brought to pay the workmen." Each of them received one rupee.[1] Collyer Quay came much later, built by convicts between 1859 and 1864 in response to booming trade.

The Jurong story, like the broader Singapore story, was not just about economic transformation of an island or a corner of it, but about the transformation of that island itself. After independence the first major shape-shifting project was the "Great Reclamation" along the East Coast, which added more than 15 sq km.[2] Post-independence Singapore continued to sprout land as though on a one-country mission to confound cartographers: there was Punggol and the beaches of Sentosa, the golf courses of Tuas and the installations of Jurong, among which I walked. The petrochemical wonderland of Jurong Island was formed out of seven smaller ones, in a turn-of-the-millennium scheme that cost S$6 billion.

It total, Singapore is now almost a full quarter bigger than at the time of independence: in 1965 it was 581.5 sq km; by 2015 it had reached 719.7 sq km, and was still growing.[3] Adding to the tiny country's stock of physical dry land has not just given it more valuable space, but allowed it to develop specialist facilities, such as container ports, pleasure beaches, and seething industrial landscapes. Around a third of reclaimed land belonged to the Housing Development Board (HDB), which was responsible for putting a roof over the head of 85 per cent of Singaporeans. In its 2013 Land Use Plan, the Ministry of National Development estimated that Singapore would need to grow a further 56 sq km larger, as it copes with a population that may rise by a million.[4] Climate change may also be an issue, as around a third of the island is less than 5 metres above sea level.

I had been able to observe the forbidding skyline of Jurong Island as I chugged along in *SC3139H*, skirting its artificial southeast shore on my way to a spot of angling off the Southern Islands. While it bristled with petrochemical malevolence, the real miracle of modern Jurong actually lay hidden far underground. Workers at the Jurong Rock Caverns first took a lift 100 metres below the earth, to chambers full of bicycles and computers. Below these were two cylindrical vaults, holding 126 million gallons of crude oil. Nine more were planned. This was how a resource-poor island could turn itself, with an impressive combination of determination and imagination, into a hydrocarbon hub.

There is a deeply controversial aspect to magicking water into land. All of the stuff that goes into creating land has to come from somewhere. Some of it is the digging-waste from engineering projects such as the expansion of the MRT transit system, which involves a seemingly never-ending network of enormous tunnels snaking under Singapore. Some of it literally is waste, as with the landfill island of Pulau Semakau. But much of what was being used was sand, which is rapidly becoming one of the world's most strategic and contentious resources.

Sand—or, more specifically, natural aggregate—is the second most-heavily exploited natural resource after water. In this world of binary codes and viral videos, something as simple as sand underpins real on-the-ground economic progress. Up to half of concrete is made up of the stuff, as is as much as 94 per cent of asphalt. One remarkable measure of the astonishing progress made by China is that in the four years up to 2017 it used as much sand as the US did in a century.[5]

Despite its ambitions for founding a twenty-first-century knowledge economy, Singapore is a major importer of sand, and much of it is used for land reclamation. It has the highest demand per capita: around 5.4 tonnes per inhabitant, per year. This has both an environmental and a geopolitical impact: some suggest that Singaporean sand imports have led directly to the loss of twenty-four Indonesian islands, and a rise in tensions over fluid Southeast Asian maritime borders. (Malaysia and Indonesia have banned the export of all landfill materials to Singapore because of rows over territorial infringements.) Continuing high demand, and increasing sensitivity over the impact of supply, have also led to a price explosion. From 1995 to 2001 sand cost around US$3 per tonne. A couple of years later the price was up to US$190.[6]

The quantity of sand that Singapore gobbles up has led to many of its neighbours banning their exports of the stuff. Mysteriously, however, sand from these countries did sometimes still turn up on the island. One investigation found that several Vietnamese exporters spoke openly about their cargoes being bound for Singapore, despite a ban in 2009.[7] It listed forty such vessels in the first two months of 2017, with a total 905,000 square metres of sand on board.[8] The Ministry of National Development has responded to this by saying that land reclamation was for "our nation's growing needs," while noting that it was difficult to be self-sufficient in the necessary materials. It also said that the country was exploring "new and innovative means to reduce our reliance on sand," including recycled excavated materials and polders.[9]

Wisely, Singapore does not take future sand supplies for granted. Like other key commodities such as granite and concrete, the availability of different grades of sand is rigorously tracked. Singapore even has a "Strategic Sand Reserve" in Bedok, so that its appetite for construction cannot be confounded by a troublesome inability to get hold of it.

Jurong does not just represent the industrial side of the Singapore miracle, but something else far less tangible. To understand this, consider the story of a couple of schoolgirls, who might have otherwise passed as novices from a Buddhist convent. They were short and soft-skinned, with a dome of black stubble in place of the regulation Singapore schoolgirl ponytail. Cherry Wong and Leia Lai were not a pair of fifteen-year-olds looking forward to a life of saffron robes and creeping enlightenment; they were simply teenagers, barely able to stifle their grins at the fuss they were causing.

To state the obvious, modern Singapore is not a counter-cultural place. By the usual conformist standards, Cherry and Leia were proper rebels, and almost everyone on the island came to have an opinion about them and their stubbly crowns. At the heart of their rebellion was a laudable action that would make most parents and teachers proud. They, and three friends, had asked their school for permission to shave their heads for the Children's Cancer Foundation. The authorities agreed, so long as they wore wigs until their hair had grown back.

Given that the girls attended St Margaret's Secondary School, such a strict line on uniforms is no surprise. It was the first girls' school in Singapore, founded by a missionary called Maria Dyer in 1842 after she had seen a group of girls auctioned off into household slavery during a Singapore stopover. The school's motto is "Charity, Patience, Devotion," and the principal at the time when the girls shaved their heads said the simple rule for hairstyles was that they could not be "punk, unfeminine or sloppy." Stand outside the school up on Farrer Road and girl after girl, student after student, will step out of the classroom as pristine and orderly as box-fresh dolls.

Unfortunately for the heirs of Maria Dyer, three of the five girls turned up to class the following Monday with their hair as short and bristly as a prize Tamworth pig, with no wig in sight. The school took immediate action, pulling them out of class and marching them to a shop where they each bought a $70 hairpiece. But rather than settle the matter, a social media standoff ensued, and the bald schoolgirls became a national talking point that went to the soul of what it meant to be Singaporean.

On one side were the authorities of St Margaret's Secondary School, and their insistence that rules were rules: the girls knew what they were doing, and ought to stick to what they had agreed. The girls' supporters suggested that this was just another instance of Singapore being unnecessarily stuffy. The girls themselves pointed to doctors' notes explaining that wearing scratchy wigs in Singapore's pitiless equatorial humidity had given the girls rashes on their scalps. This argument seemed to have won the day, and the social media storm died down with everybody believing they had been right all along.

The following November, as glittery pink unicorns and other Christmas oddities started to adorn the malls and temples to consumerism of Orchard Road, I had a coffee with Tong Yee, one of the most incisive thinkers about Singapore's place in the world. His take on the whole saga surprised me. The girls were wrong, he said. "Trust is Singapore's most valuable resource, and we won't survive if we don't recover it." Given that he ran the Thought Collective, which fostered initiative and independence of thought among Singaporeans, this sounded odd. But, he countered, the girls gave their word, then broke it. That simple fact was enough to put them in the wrong.

Back in the 1980s, Tong Yee explained, independent Singapore was still finding its feet. Its PAP government was slowly building the country's economic miracle, and the next step in the plan was to establish a petrochemical industry, down among the mud and crabs on the marshy islands off Singapore's southwest coast. The simple problem was that nobody would invest in the unlikely Jurong Island project. It looked like the whole plan would remain unrealised. But then a major oil company decided that it was, after all, worth risking an investment of several hundred million dollars.

What changed? Other countries do have oil and plenty of other natural resources, Tong Yee answered, but very few countries keep their word. If Singapore said it would make Jurong Island a success, it would indeed be a success, and that counted for far more than any amount of black sticky stuff buried under the ground. The following years confirmed the reasoning of that major oil company, and that is why Jurong Island now bristles with chimneys and flares like the stubbly crown of a stubborn teenager. The schoolgirls were wrong: Singapore might not have much, but can at least keep its word.

This understanding was at the heart of what Lee Kuan Yew and his colleagues in the PAP set out to achieve. They had to make Singapore an attractive place that foreign investors could trust. That meant taking a hard line against disruptive unions and the threat of left-wing radicals, which also pleased the Cold War warriors of the United States.

Singapore's economy faced serious challenges when it became independent. Unemployment was a problem, and in 1962 was above 15 per cent. Many were employed in small-scale craft industries, and a demographic bulge was in the pipeline. Around a fifth of Singaporeans lived below the poverty line. The country relied heavily upon employment through the British military base, which had an uncertain future. Fractious relationships with Malaya and Indonesia had taken away any immediate hopes of building a more integrated regional economy.

Lee Kuan Yew was not the only person responsible for the miracle. Goh Keng Swee, the minister for finance, was at the heart of the push to make Singapore a haven for foreign capital. Albert Winsemius, a Dutch economist, had brought his experience of reviving the Netherlands after the War: the port of Rotterdam had been levelled; vital infrastructure had been destroyed; 80 per cent of factories had been moved to Germany; and the land had been inundated with salty sea water. To Winsemius, Singapore was just another economic development conundrum.

The Dutchman was actually quite bullish about the island's prospects, and in 1963 he published the so-called "Winsenius Report" that explained how it should go about building a new economy.[10] His recipe for Singapore chimed with Lee's. They needed to build upon, rather than reject, the British heritage, and tie the island to a globalised, international future. In an echo of the Singapore founded by Raffles, it would be a free port, with incentives and exceptions to encourage trade, along with substantial investment in infrastructure and education. Priorities included the rule of law, cracking down on corruption, and ensuring that Singapore was clean and leafy enough for highly skilled foreign workers to want to live there. It would be a "Garden City." Rain trees and wild cinnamon trees were planted along with rows of vibrant bougainvilleas. The use of English as a lingua franca was encouraged.

Thanks to its small size, it made sense for the miracle to be centrally planned, through the Economic Development Board. That added technocratic, organisational flair, and valuable recognition of trends that could benefit Singapore. The port was made ready for containerisation, and the Board catalysed the creation of an ecosystem of related industries such as maritime insurance. Singapore took advantage of the Japanese economic take-off, and the growing appetite for more oil products in Northeast Asia. There was no time to rest upon achievements: as its ship repair facilities boomed, there was a push towards higher skills and greater productivity. The Jurong Project, which began in the early 1960s under the guidance of Goh Keng Swee, was a symbol both of Singapore's growing ambition, and its ability to keep its word.

In the late 1960s efforts were concentrated on labour-intensive manufacturing industries that were largely absent elsewhere in the region. Crucially, this created plenty of jobs, many down among the roads and compounds of Jurong. As a small country, however, it was agile, and the guiding hand of government modified the economy in response to developments elsewhere. When shipbuilding took off in Japan and South Korea, Singapore shifted resources into higher-value sectors: in the 1980s this meant investing in extra training and research, and crafting a high-tech strategy. While local labour costs rose, any low-skilled gaps that emerged were plugged with foreign imported labour from South Asia and Singapore's neighbours.

Singapore became globalisation's poster child. Between 1965 and 1987, external trade represented, on average, more than three times the country's GNP. In contrast, the 1984 figure for Hong Kong was 1.67 times GNP, for Taiwan it was 0.89, and for South Korea it was 0.67. In 1987, 79 per cent of all ASEAN's trade came through Singapore.[11]

The miracle did not simply consist of a line on a graph pointing ever upwards. A serious recession hit in 1985 and 1986. Strong growth (of 8.2 per cent in 1984) went into reverse, with serious slow-downs in crucial sectors such as construction and petroleum. The stock exchange closed for several days in December 1985. Wages were very high relative to the region, with a crop of new "Asian tigers" industrialising rapidly. This recession was a real challenge to the government because of two factors. Firstly, it showed just how exposed the little island was to external developments—good and bad. Secondly, it highlighted that the state had simply got some of its choices wrong.

The government acted fast, recalibrating its policies to tack into the wind, rather than be overwhelmed by it. This was the beauty of strong, decisive and responsive government in a small country. Costs and taxes were cut, and money was ploughed into research, education and training. Growth returned quickly, and the recession never turned into a more existential risk. Not only did the miracle continue, but it was a reminder to both the government and the people of Singapore that the biggest risk to their country's fortune was complacency.

5

PANDAN

THE RESOURCE-POOR NATION

A flyover that bridged the Jurong River was the first sign that, 14 kilometres in, I was nearing the end of the beginning. I let a Bangladeshi man and his bike pass me on the narrow footpath, and was thanked with a barely perceptible wobble of his head. Above the riverbanks I could smell human shit, and looked down on a small, shanty-like settlement. A few yards further on, sheep were being driven off a barge, down gangplanks, and into what I assumed was an abattoir. A multitasking scooter rider zipped by, chatting on his mobile and smiling happily underneath a violently green helmet. His T-shirt carried the fitting slogan, "Positive Mind, Vibes, Life." A piglet-sized durian fruit hung from a tree next to a chain-link fence, lovingly protected against pests by its own snug-fitting plastic sheath.

Ahead of me was the Pandan reservoir. Doves picked their way along the shoreline between coconuts that had fallen from a cluster of palms. Ten-storey HDBs—public housing blocks, named after the country's Housing Development Board—dotted the far shore. After being suffocated by chimneys, industrial compounds and a murderously close proximity to the wheels of trucks, I was suddenly blessed with views that reached to the pylons and formidable stands of forest of the Bukit Timah Nature Reserve, 6 kilometres off to the north. Egrets and a wary pterodactyl-like heron picked their way through the flower-speckled reeds on the water's edge. A slight brackish smell was a welcome change from the mind-altering chemical clouds of Jurong.

While Jurong stands for the Singaporean industrial miracle and land reclamation, Pandan represents the resource question that the country has increasingly had to answer. Take water, for instance. Near the Jurong River flyover was a creek the colour of a dead witch's skin, reeking of industrial by-products and sewage. The tiny island is ultra-urbanised, and home to water-hungry industries and leisure facilities, as well as millions of citizens. Despite the staggering amount of rain that can fall from the sky in a single twenty-minute storm, getting enough of the clean stuff to all those millions, their homes and businesses, is far from straight-forward.

Singapore's clean water comes from four sources. First, since 1962 deals have been struck with Malaysia entitling Singapore to 250 million gallons a day from the Johor River. In return, Malaysia gets 2 per cent of this total back as clean water. However, periodic severe dry spells and changing water use patterns have had a dramatic impact on the security of this water: it mainly comes from the Linggiu reservoir, on the Johor River, which in October 2016 was down to just 20 per cent capacity, compared to 84 per cent less than two years earlier. The agreement is due to expire in 2061, and Malaysia has already complained loudly that the price Singapore pays, including rent for the reservoir land and maintenance, is far too low.

The second source is local catchment, including the Pandan reservoir, served by those torrential rainstorms that periodically soaked me to the skin as thoroughly as if a lukewarm bucket of water had been emptied over my head. Planning for this kicked off back in the 1980s, when there was something of a water crisis; much of the bounty of the equatorial skies ran into polluted waterways and was unfit for use. The centre of Singapore is now dominated by reservoirs dedicated to storing this water, creating a deceptively verdant jungly heart. Sea inlets and creeks, including the Singapore River itself, have also been dammed to add to capacity.

Whereas the Malaysian water is testament to Singapore's continuing reliance on a geographical area beyond its own super-limited borders, and the catchment water speaks of a government that has to treat its land resources like a multi-layered jigsaw puzzle, the third and fourth sources are typically technological solutions: desalinated reverse-osmosis water; and "NEWater," which is recycled from whatever gurgles down the pipes and drains. The latter is half the price of desalinated water, and involves technology that is being exported to countries like India and Thailand. With well over 2 metres of rainfall a year, there is plenty of the raw material, if it is collected correctly. Almost a third of the water used at Changi airport is local run-off, used for grey-water purposes such as toilet flushing and fire-fighting (saving S$275,000 a year in the process). All four sources are different responses to Singapore being too small to look after its own rudimentary needs.

The challenge of getting enough clean water from these four sources has potentially serious political implications. Growing urbanisation has made it harder and more expensive to lay down infrastructure such as pipes. Overall costs more than doubled in the decade and a half from 2000 (S$500 million) to 2015 (S$1.3 billion). Consumption is growing. *The Straits Times* has framed the country's unease about water as a consequence of Singaporean success: the water challenge has been met so effectively that citizens have taken it for granted and become profligate (they consume a relatively hefty 150 litres per person each day). The newspaper quoted water expert Asit Biswas' praise for Singapore's public servants' "quality and intelligence," and also noted that water cost only 0.36 per cent of median employed household income in 2014, compared to 0.69 per cent in 2001.[1] Such is progress.

The potential for water-related grumbling was made flesh in February 2017, after Finance Minister Heng Swee Keat's budget speech included a 30 per cent rise in water prices—the first in seventeen years. One MP from the ruling PAP, Lee Bee Wah, told *Channel News Asia* that the hike was designed to build awareness of the water issue. One Facebook user retorted that MPs should have their salaries reduced to remind them of the importance of working hard for a living. Others organised a protest at Speakers' Corner.[2] As Singapore's government largely bases its legitimacy on the efficient provision of public services and putting more money in its citizens' pockets, getting water delivery and pricing wrong can presage real political difficulties for the PAP.

There is also a security angle. Throughout my time in Singapore, water insecurity was a favourite topic of taxi uncles who enjoyed rattling off reasons why the country was doomed. With the country's reliance on either Malaysia or technological solutions, and the costs it will be forced to pass onto consumers who expect their needs to be met by an ever-efficient government, this is one area where the Cassandra taxi uncles are on relatively firm, if slightly boggy, ground. Indeed, water security was recognised as one of the weaknesses of Singapore's fortress role even during the British Empire (if far less so than its modern-day rival, Hong Kong).

With Singapore so chronically short of land, it can come as something of a surprise that it has a thriving farming sector, mostly located a few kilometres to the north of Pandan, in Kranji. Up to the 1970s much of the north of the island was devoted to agriculture, and especially pig farms. Partly this was because pigs were delicious, and partly it was because few things unnerve a nation quite so much as losing complete control over their own food supplies. However, the land used for farming was more valuable if used for other purposes, such as housing or water catchment, and the pig poo was responsible for polluting the Johor Straits. The last pigs were eaten, and the last pig farms were closed.

The farms that remain, up in the far northwest of the island, are tiny, and although they verge on being a Marie Antoinette version of hobby-farming, they are thriving businesses. The noisiest of them is also the most unsettling, filled with what sounds like a dozen washing machines with worn-out ball bearings.

Chelsea Wan's father set up Jurong Frog Farm back in the 1970s, as the pig farms were closing. He worked in the oil and gas industry, but saw an opportunity to provide Singapore with delicious, croaking homegrown protein. The farm that his daughter now works on is now home to 20,000 American bullfrogs, some as big as kittens (but far slimier), and reverberates with an eerie amphibian white noise. The farm welcomes visitors and has a café, as well as a freezer jam-packed with top-quality frog meat. The more sprightly can try to catch the beasts with a net. I have seen plenty of flatbed trucks criss-cross the island carrying baskets full of doomed, jumpy frogs. Chelsea, who styles herself as something of a frog-ologist, tells me that Singapore's achingly hip restaurant scene, with its appetite for novelty, is fertile ground for selling a tasty morsel of amphibian thigh.

Beyond frogs, Kranji also farms crocodiles, beansprouts and goats, all tucked away neatly in the jungle, each making the most of their own little patch of land. There is also a "Koi Hotel," where owners can leave fish—sometimes valued in the tens of thousands of dollars—when they go on holiday. Some even spend good money buying the most promising-looking fish, hoping they have budding grand Koi champions on their hands, and hand them over to the hotels, until they are old enough to take home. Singapore has lots of problems with a shortage of resources, but for the moment it seems to have no shortage of people with money.

6

WEST COAST ROAD

BUILDING THE NEW COMMUNITIES

Jalan Buroh, a highway running around the southern, raised edge of Pandan reservoir, had a more familiar feel to it than the bare, functional thoroughfares of Jurong. Its edges were neatly manicured, the encroachment of equatorial growth kept in check by roving squadrons of Bangladeshi men, wielding strimmers and power saws with regimental intent. Lines of rain trees were pruned into bizarre right angles, their branches festooned with parasitic ferns. The verges were dotted with the pungent plastic detritus of jettisoned hawker-centre meals.

Off to the south, as I crossed the Pandan River, were the cranes and stacked corrugations of the container port. But otherwise, turning onto West Coast Road, I was quite clearly leaving the industrial Southwest behind. Giant concrete HDBs, painted in cream and contrasting shades of blue, rose up around me. They were twelve or so storeys tall, and differentiated only by giant numbers on their ends: 511, 512. There were runs of shops, the Tanglin Secondary School, and covered walkways to shield the locals from downpours and the sun. I saw old folk scrambling for a bus, sheltered seating areas, and sponge-floored play-grounds. Other HDBs clustered in groups, each sporting a distinctive colour scheme: here, shades of green; there, shades of pink. The freshly washed clothes of a hundred families were skewered on ranks of drying poles, poking out from balconies like a domesticated regiment of seventeenth-century pikemen. For my walk, this was the coming of Comfortable Singapore, the utopia of the Pioneer Generation, and the fruit of that hard-scrabble industrialisation.

At the time of independence, the vast majority of Singaporeans lived either in the *kampongs* (villages) or the near-slum conditions of the city. The port that wrung the money out of the island's strategic position was surrounded by clusters of knack-ered old shop-houses, with walls that echoed with noise, air that was overtaxed with smoke and stench, and beds that took their sleepers on shifts. Slums filled the gaps between solid buildings like grime in the crevices of a diesel engine. Rickety huts relied on roofs of attap palms to keep out the downpours. They were propped up above the mud and filth and mosquito larvae on rotting wooden stilts, and were linked by unsteady planked walk-ways that were dank and slippery.

The *kampongs* were dotted between the trees and plantations of the island interior. Tracks became obstacle courses of muddy puddles whenever the tropical skies opened up. Pigs snuffled in garbage piles and toilets were often built over the ponds where villagers kept fish. The "night soil men" who slopped out cesspits were still calling around the island in the 1980s, driving their *sa chap lak meng chia* ("thirty-six-door limousines") from *kampong* to *kampong*.

Given these conditions, finding a more sanitary and functional housing solution on such a cramped equatorial island was a pri-ority for the government, even before independence. Public housing projects had begun back in the 1930s, as the island's authorities wrestled with an acknowledged problem. The Housing Development Board was formed in 1960, and even before the split from the Malay Federation it had transitioned from providing rental properties for the poor to mass owner-occupied housing. There was a strategic motive behind this shift: Lee Kuan Yew believed this particular solution to the country's housing would also give people a stake in the future, a sense of belonging, and a belief in a non-communist future. It also gave the government control over land use, creating useful space in the downtown area for commercial developments.

The social engineering behind HDB provision is explicit. There are ethnic quotas, designed to ensure thoroughly mixed "national" neighbourhoods, rather than "ethnic" ones. (In practice, there is a degree of secondary market self-segregation, as people sell and rebuy to be closer to family and friends.) Up to the age of thirty-five, only married couples can buy directly from the Housing Development Board. As gay couples cannot legally get married, they cannot buy a new HDB. Unwed mothers also struggle. There are discounts for children who buy HDBs close to their parents, which helps them to provide old-age care. Those happy with multi-generational living can apply for a "3Gen" flat.[1] HDBs helped the government shape a new society. They were also used to shape how society behaved: rules governed everything from the mandatory flushing of public toilets to prohibitions on walking around naked at home.

HDBs have become such a foundational element of the Singapore miracle that they even have a museum dedicated to them. The guide promised that I would be "dazzled by the lights and sounds" by my "journey into the world of public housing at the HDB Gallery." This was not the type of treatment that social housing projects routinely get, at least outside of Central and Eastern Europe in that unique window of history between the 1930s and 1980s.

The museum itself was not a particularly easy place to find. A receptionist sent me down some stairs, past a stall promising "Claypot Pig Organ Soup" and a subterranean car park. Through one door was a corridor sporting a colourful and angular mural of jauntily multiracial high-rise living. I turned a corner, and found what I was looking for.

The first set of displays showed how far Singapore had risen in its half-century of independence. It started with a dingy, soot-caked mock-up of a pre-independence kitchen, progressing through a living room from the 1960s, centred around a black-and-white television and adorned with pink plastic bead curtains. A few yards later there appeared images of eager couples pointing excitedly into the future, towards spanking new developments with names like "SkyTerrace@Dawson" and "RiverVista@ KalangWhampoa." As the museum promised, it was a journey "from slums to vibrant towns."

Despite a notable lack of visitors, the museum designers had thrown everything they had at this attempt to explain how high-rise concrete had turned into glitter. Behind every deserted corner there was another 3D display and another audio-visual effect, from life-size holograms to interactive townscapes.

One installation was a giant computer game that allowed up to four players to select a customised avatar, which then navigated the digitised streets of a particular district of Singapore. When an avatar managed to locate a coloured button, players were asked earnest questions: "The Universal Design creates safe and convenient homes to meet the life-cycle needs of the residents. Identify the set of photos which depicts UD features."

I selected an avatar and fiddled with my joystick. When I got the right answer, I was rewarded with an explanation of why I was correct: "Up to 5 per cent of the available flat supply is set aside for applicants under the Third Child Priority scheme. This encourages Singaporeans to have three or more children." It was intoxicating stuff to the competitively minded. If only I had somebody to play against.

The gallery, however, remained stubbornly deserted, and I felt furtive and shifty. My irregular behaviour was probably being scrutinised on banks of CCTV screens, with computerised records being called up on everything from my internet browsing history to my attitude towards eating chilli crab. I left the game unfinished and headed out past the pink bead curtain. I found my way back upstairs where the windows ran with rivulets of rain and where nobody was thinking about Singapore's muddy and soot-caked past. There was shopping to do and all manner of things to eat, mobile phones to be twiddled with, and strangers to walk into while absorbed in an on-screen world.

Despite its disappointing lack of visitors, the place of HDBs in the Singapore miracle was probably as worthy of a museum's attention as any assortment of arrowheads or pottery shards. They were a key part of the solution to building this small island up to its current success story. They gave many Singaporeans their first experience of hygienic, durable and weatherproof housing. They also made the most of the country's limited space, and created flat-pack new communities of the kind that I was walking through. It was fitting that young Singaporeans could even pick up a comic book telling the story of the man known as "Mister HDB," with a front cover showing tower blocks and a stern-yet-visionary Lim Kim San standing in a suit and tie, holding a set of building plans.[2]

HDBs are even integrated with the country's social security system.[3] A portion of a person's Central Provident Fund (CPF), which is built up with cash from both employees and employers, can be used for a deposit. There are also means-tested subsidies that can add up to the high tens of thousands of dollars. Costs tend to be low, or at least manageable: the HDB says the average first-time buyer devotes less than a quarter of household income to mortgage payments. These low costs help to justify the meagre provision of social housing for the very poorest Singaporeans, who must earn less than S$1,500 a month to qualify for help; those who do tend to get tiny flats, however big their family.

There are challenges with the way the HDB system works. Retirees, who draw on their CPF rather than a conventional state-funded pension, are expected to be mortgage-free by the time they retire. This allows them to "right-size" to a smaller flat, freeing up cash. As this has not happened as much as the Housing Development Board hoped, retirees are now allowed to sell portions of whatever remains of their original ninety-nine-year lease back to the government. The lease system itself is starting to cause rumblings of public alarm too, as people become gradually more aware that many ninety-nine-year leases are rapidly shedding value as they steadily count down.[4] HDBs are not necessarily the store of value that many owners and their children, seeing house prices soar, have comfortably—and complacently—assumed. This could spell serious problems for the government, which continues to insist that ownership will revert to the Board once leases expire. Perhaps this is a case of over-complacency on the part of the government: it could undermine the sense of prosperity upon which much of the PAP's legitimacy is built. If Singaporeans ever take to the streets, it is likely to be a furious protest about the money in their pockets, rather than any squeezing of political expression.

Although it has undoubtedly built stability and trust, the success of the HDB system has also been blamed for making Singaporeans risk-averse, preferring to channel money into savings rather than entrepreneurial ideas. It is also open to political manipulation, as any constituency that votes in a non-PAP member of parliament is liable to find itself slipping down the queue for HDB upgrades. A Singaporean teammate at my Wednesday-night football game cited this as an explicit and widely acknowledged reason for not voting for the opposition.

As the government created the new HDB-based communities, however, it lost something. The *kampongs* that dotted the jungle were, by necessity, based around close cooperation. Challenges such as floodwaters, disease, security, and food were dealt with collectively. There were community celebrations, shared interests, and a sense of solidarity. Not only did the new high-rise flats break up these communities, it took away communal responsibilities such as safety and security. There was a concurrent value shift towards individual wealth and self-interest.

The *kampongs* remain the figurative touchstones of the traditional community spirit that has either been lost or recaptured, depending on your experience and sense of optimism. The authorities still talk about designing HDB "vertical *kampongs*," packed with social spaces and rooftop gardens.[5] Local authorities work hard to give communities a focus, with leisure facilities and lots of activities on offer. One that I popped into near Cantonment Road sported a tray of the day's newspapers ("Reading time limit 30 minutes"), and courses for learning beginner-level Korean and making ice-cream cheesecake. One notice advised that "This toilet will be used by hairdressing course students from 9.00 a.m. to 6.00 a.m.," while another warned not to "urinate or spit in public spaces." There was a "balloon sculpture interest group" and notices about public health. Residents were encouraged by the "Big-hearted family awards," and one for an "outstanding mother—a role model for her family, community and society," alongside photos of potentially outstanding mothers from the Malay, Chinese and Indian communities.

The other touchstone of these new HDB-centred communities are the hawker centres, full of bustle and clatter, woks and monosodium glutamate. When they were introduced they were partly intended to ensure better public health, being easier to monitor than true street food stalls. They also fulfilled a socioeconomic role: by providing cheap and quick after-work food, they implicitly balanced out the long hours worked in formal and hierarchical offices; they compensated HDB-dwellers for the tiny kitchens in their high-density housing; they offered a safety net to the poorest in society with their cheap prices; and they provided a mixing place where all classes and ethnicities could mingle over chicken biryani or noodles.[6] Whether in an HDB neighbourhood, a shopping mall or an office block, hawker centres are still the popular touchstone of Singaporean life, and there was universal delight and pride when the Liao Fan Hong Kong Soya Sauce Chicken Rice & Noodle was awarded a Michelin star for its food. A plate of Chan Hon Meng's iconic chicken rice costs just S$2, but you will have to queue.

While there is always room for a paternal hand to guide Singaporeans towards more virtuous or efficient behaviour, others have tried to instil community spirit off their own bat. The CEO of BlockPooling, Moh Hon Meng, told me that most inter-personal interaction in modern Singapore takes the form of grumbling about other residents (70,000 complaints are filed a year, he said, three quarters of which are about noise). He was trying to tackle this epidemic of misanthropy through his community-based social network, designed to encourage sharing and togetherness. He wanted to build interaction through tackling mutual problems, such as dengue fever and flooding, with residents encouraged to lend each other drills and ladders. Less convincing to my ears was the idea of "morning greeters," who would gather for activities like group jogs, where they would cheerfully greet people that they ran into.

Another Singaporean trying to make a difference is former clergyman William Wan. I met him for breakfast in the plush American Club, just off Scotts Road. Straight away I knew that he was different, greeting the serving staff by name and complimenting them cheerfully. Singaporeans are good at being complainers, he told me: "This is no good! This is not right, not up to standard! We're spoiled rotten, victims of our own success." Wan's solution was to make people aware of this, and empower them to change it. When I asked if this meant shaming them, he replied that it was more of a question of guilt. People who behave selfishly are not bad people, he said, but they can improve their bad habits. He chuckled and took another spoonful of oats, bananas and raisins, not forgetting to give the waitress a smile of thanks for his breakfast.

Wan had all the irrepressibility of an evangelical, along with bountiful faith in the goodness of people and the potential of the young. Many societies have people like him, determined to do good. Very few feel the need to set up organisations like his—the Singapore Kindness Movement—dedicated to helping a country's people simply be nicer to each other. He galloped through a whole range of issues. If Christian Singaporeans truly believed in the Sabbath, why did they not give their domestic workers a day off on Sunday? What about putting seatbelts in the back of the flatbeds that carry foreign labourers to their building sites? Why not simply say thank you, and smile more? "Kindness breeds kindness," he said.

The size of Singapore made this more important, he said. "This is not like other countries where you can hide away in a treetop. In the woods in Tennessee it doesn't matter. But we are so small we have to interact. Not every value is transactional. Worth should not just be about money." Was Singapore too materialistic? "In fifty years, we have had an accelerated climb up the pyramid of development," he answered. "But now we're not talking about basic needs like food and clothing. We need to aspire to other things, rather than just material progression." I took that as a carefully couched "Yes."

Although the American Club was only 200 metres from my bus stop, Wan insisted on saving me 200 millilitres of sweat by giving me a lift. He found me a couple of "5 reasons for being kind" leaflets in his Toyota Prius, and then tried to pull out of our parking space. An unblinking lady in a large Lexus cut us off. It seemed a good moment to ask about the country's rather zero-sum approach to driving. "Oh yes!" He paused. "But it's an enforcement issue. That would save lives." That was a very Singaporean comment, reflecting a paradoxical belief that the small-footprint government also had a role in helping to shape society. Just as we approached the gate to turn onto Claymore Hill another car sped up to reach the red light just ahead of us, preventing our exit. "I define everything as a kindness issue," he said as we waited patiently. "Then your job is a big one?" "Oh yes!" He chuckled again. I sensed he was relishing the challenge.

* * *

The first HDB estates I passed on West Coast Road were soon joined by even higher blocks of far glitzier, privately-owned condos. Rows of McMansions, with their porticos and portentous decorative flourishes, clustered in the shadows. Cracks and the mould that crept up walls hinted at the unremitting efforts of the equatorial climate to return all human constructions to the jungle. Both the condos and the McMansions were the homes of the 15 per cent of Singapore residents who did not live in public housing.

It was now 10.00 a.m., and the mercury was rising mercilessly. Despite frequent swigs of water, I was getting very thirsty. Just after the "Bigfoot" Preschool and a spa, I stepped into a ubiquitous 7-Eleven for a can of something cold, wet, and sugary. The heat when I re-emerged after a few glorious moments of air conditioning was quite unpleasant.

I passed a maid, busily white-washing a fence while standing in a storm drain, and a poster advertising a Segway as a green mode of transport. I left the road and strode up a footpath through Clementi Woods Park, where Bangladeshis clad in protective clothing advanced in formation, strimming down the steely equatorial grass. At the top of the hill was the Sakura International Buffet, which seemed to be something of a destination restaurant. Tucked in behind was the Japanese School, founded back in 1912.

There has been an established Japanese community in Singapore for well over a hundred years. The largest Japanese cemetery in Southeast Asia, with 910 tombstones, is just off Chuan Hoe Avenue. It opened in 1891 for Japanese prostitutes (*karayuki-san*), and other residents (the first was a sailor called Yamamoto Otokichi, who settled on the island in 1862). The augmented-reality computer game "Pokemon Go" is expressly forbidden.

The main event in Singapore and Japan's history, of course, was the occupation during the Second World War. As elsewhere in occupied Asia, in Singapore the Japanese earned a reputation for brutality. In modern Singapore, however, their reputation for tidiness makes them landlords' *de facto* number one choice as tenants, whatever their wartime heritage.

This merry and explicit use of racial profiling in housing adverts is something that many Westerners find troubling. Adverts frequently come with notes such as "No Indians" (even if they are Singaporean citizens), or "No PRC" (i.e. mainland Chinese). The 99.co property search website has an "All races welcome" filter, thanks to its co-founder Darius Cheung. He was once told by an estate agent that a landlord was refusing to rent to him because his wife was Indian.[7] The BBC carried the story of a Sri Lankan engineer, Sunil, who secured property viewings thanks to a Western accent, but was then told he could not rent once the landlords met him in person. (Something similar happened to an Oxford-educated Sri Lankan friend of mine.) Sunil was told by one agent that Indians and mainland Chinese were not particularly house-proud. "Many don't clean weekly," she said. "And they do heavy cooking ... a lot of spices that release smells people don't like."[8] This prejudice is something that Japanese house-hunters never have to deal with.

7

NATIONAL UNIVERSITY OF SINGAPORE

TOP OF THE CLASS?

Across the road from the Japanese School was one of the jewels in the crown of the Singaporean education system: the main campus of the National University of Singapore.[1] The campus was slick, leafy and welcoming, peppered with posters and boards bearing buzzwords like "innovation" and "enterprise." A sign pointed the way to the National Wind Tunnel. The site even had a cycle path, a rare concession to the safety of those who risked heat and appalling driving to set off on two wheels. An NUS bus bearing the legend "#engineered for a cleaner tomorrow" scooted along, delivering conscientious students hither and thither.

The atmosphere on the campus was elite, self-sufficient, and deeply professional. It was a credit to the country, and one of the shining stars in its glimmering educational firmament. Curiously, though, after a walk that had so far shown me Singapore's foundations—its place in the Malayosphere, its founding, its industrial miracle and its HDBs—it was here at the NUS campus that some of my doubts about the country's trajectory surfaced.

On the face of it, however, Singapore's education system is world-class, an accolade that isn't confined to NUS and its great domestic rival, Nanyang Technological University (NTU). The 2015 PISA rankings, which assessed the abilities of fifteen-year-old students in seventy-two countries, were a spectacular triumph for Singapore. The country achieved the remarkable triple-whammy of coming top in all three categories: maths, science and reading.[2] Singapore was a touchstone for academic excellence and was studied by a host of other countries as they sought to improve their own schools' performance. The UK, for example, announced in 2016 that half of its primary schools would start to use the Singapore system for maths teaching.[3] Remarkably, these results were achieved with relatively little money: Singapore only spent around 3 per cent of GDP on education, while Britain spent around 6 per cent, and Sweden, 8 per cent.[4]

The Ministry of Education traced the roots of the current system to the late 1950s, when the country was "still reeling from the destruction wrought by World War II."[56] It was a time when schools were centres of violence and communist mischief (especially the Chinese middle schools), which spilled over into the streets, as with the Hock Lee Bus Riots of 1955. The shock of the split from Malaysia in 1965 spurred the government of the newly independent country to rethink the school system; mindful of inter-ethnic friction, it emphasised uniformity in everything from the curriculum to buildings. Ten years later Singapore had laid the foundations for success, and the World Bank classified the country as "Intermediate" rather than "Developing." Then-prime minister Lee Kuan Yew still saw the schools as a vital engine of Singapore's push towards modernisation, confirming English as the language of instruction, and reinforcing the message of hard work and self-discipline.

Recession in the 1980s prompted further reform, aimed at providing Singapore's economy with the skills and raw materials that it needed to push on, deeply rooted in the STEM subjects (science, technology, engineering, maths). A team of teachers spent time studying other education systems and the latest research into learning and psychology. The education budget was increased: in the 1960s and 1970s it accounted for around a tenth of government spending, while by the 1980s, 15 to 20 per cent of the budget was going towards education. Special attention was paid to training the 320,000 Singaporeans who only had primary school education. If Singapore were to flourish, it could only do so by having a better—rather than cheaper—workforce.[7]

By 1997, with the country "One of Asia's four little dragons," a new curriculum was introduced that emphasised citizenship and skills that were appropriate for the approaching twenty-first century.[8] Lessons were aimed at teaching students to really think like mathematicians, rather than just learn how to answer questions. Children learned fewer subjects, but in greater depth.

Teaching standards have also been targeted. It was decided that the starting point of the education system had to be attracting talented people into the teaching profession, then training and motivating them as well as possible. Starting salaries are above the national median, and there is prestige in choosing a career as a teacher. "The culture of Singapore has moved to a place where the profession of teaching is more highly valued by families and parents," says Professor David Hung of Singapore's National Institute of Education. "Two decades ago this wasn't the case. Pay is important. The substantive quality of teachers as observed by the public is important."[9] They are also encouraged towards public and policy work, with a revolving door of secondments allowing the most able to move between the classroom and the Ministry of Education. Class size is not the overriding issue that it has become in countries such as Britain: if the teachers are good enough, and they are given time to prepare lessons, the number of pupils in their classes is not really a concern.

Attracting and training capable people to be teachers might not sound like rocket science, but it was something that too many other countries failed to do. Singapore's top-notch teachers were then able to help children to master the concepts they had to learn, rather than just to sit in lessons, prove a basic level of proficiency, then move on. This approach was particularly useful for mathematics and sciences—areas where other modern education systems have been judged to be catastrophically weak. When you passed by a school entrance, you were as likely to see posters advertising the students' progress in maths Olympiads as in football or tennis.

The entire school day is underpinned by motivational reminders of Singapore's vulnerability. Banners hang in school halls, emblazoned with alarming slogans, such as "No one owes Singapore a living," or "We must ourselves defend Singapore." Classrooms are often bare and distraction-free, compared to the festivals of collage and poster paint found in the UK. School architecture is kept simple: whitewashed, angular concrete, with ventilation through ceiling fans and air bricks, rather than air conditioning. Competition is fierce, and hard work expected. The Singapore miracle, after all, was only achieved thanks to sweat, meritocracy, and high levels of competence in mathematics.

There is, however, a different truth that hides behind the stellar figures. Critics charge that an individual student's success depends too heavily upon just one exam—the Primary School Leaving Examinations, taken at the age of eleven. Success in this single exam means entry into a particularly good school, from which an onward path is charted to good universities and that lucrative-but-stable career in finance that every teenager with dreams yearns for.

In effect, this system places an inordinate amount of stress upon very young children. One survey back in 2000 found that outside of normal school hours children spent between three and eight hours studying each day—from homework to tuition to "enrichment" classes. The same survey found that the biggest fear of ten- to twelve-year-olds was their school exams (36%). This relegated to second place the fear of their parents dying (17%). Getting low marks at school cropped up in third place (14%).[10] OECD research in 2017 suggested that 86 per cent of Singaporean school kids worried about poor grades, compared to an international average of 66 per cent.[11]

There is a very real human cost to this amount of pressure. In 2001 it caused an apparently cheerful primary school student, Lysher Loh, to commit suicide. The ten-year-old had told the family's maid that she hoped she would not be reincarnated as a human, because of the stress of school work. One report, noting the similar suicide of a twelve-year-old the year before, cited survey data that suggested that a third of nine- to twelve-year-olds thought academic pressure made life not worth living.[12]

These problems have not escaped the government's attention, yet have proven difficult to combat. For all the government's insight and wisdom, it is up against the immovable parental drive to see their children succeed. As with other countries at the eastern end of Asia, it is enough to look at the out-of-hours tutorial industry to understand the stakes.

Tan Kah Kee is a spanking new MRT (Mass Rapid Transit— the country's main public transport system) station on the blue Downtown Line, and is packed with uniformed school children milling about in awkward groups. These are not your average school kids, but ones lucky enough to have places at the high-ranking schools that dot this stretch of the Bukit Timah and Dunearn Roads: Hwa Chong Institution; National Junior College; Nanyang Girl's High School; Raffles Girls' Primary School. As they descend the precipitous escalator into the depths of Tan Kah Kee, they—and their parents—are confronted with an advert that covers an entire enormous wall. The advert is for a tutorial college ("Gain confidence in your abilities; Develop critical thinking skills; Ignite your interest in subjects") with a proud

USP that hits you with all the chill of the MRT air conditioning: it opens for lessons at 7.00 a.m. even over the weekend.

The vigour of Singapore's tutorial sector testifies to the pressure kids are under to deliver. With money washing around in parents' pockets, the best tutors can command salaries stratospheric enough to make the eyes of their school-based colleagues water. The fees paid by thirty-two-year-old tutor Anthony Fok's 200 or so students now add up to over S$1 million a year. Phang Yu Hon, who teaches students four lessons of physics for a fee that can reach S$700 in total, includes song-and-dance routines in his classes. In just over the decade, the private tuition industry grew from S$650 million to S$1 billion-plus in 2016.[13]

The money on offer even entices high-performing teachers, with a reputation for squeezing high grades out of their students, to jump ship, a bit like amateur athletes lured into the professional leagues. Fok told *The Straits Times* that he only taught in a classroom for four years before leaving.[14] Tutorial colleges have developed their own aspirational lexicon, from "talent development centre" to "enrichment." While other countries have fly posters for raves and parties, Singapore has them for economics tutors.

Singapore's tutorial industry may not be as intensive or destructive as South Korea's—where there are now tutorial colleges to train children to pass the exams to get into other, top-ranked tutorial colleges—but it is harmful on several counts. For one thing, it is exhausting for the children. It is common to find "No studying during peak hours" signs in Starbucks, to prevent the place being cluttered up by students looking for a spot to do algebra outside of their cramped HDB flats. Children wake up early and go to bed late, with very little free time in between, and an overarching fear of failure. Play and fun, and discovering the world for yourself, are all crowded out, along with the open-minded creativity and inquisitiveness that exploration produces. The fear is that Singapore's education system is often effective, but rarely enjoyable. In acknowledgement of this, the government brought in a new slogan—"teach less, learn more"—along with other measures that gave the kids more say in the subjects they had to study.

Then there is the meritocracy that is so central to Singapore's own success. "A few decades ago, education was a way that poor people could rise," Professor Michael Barr of Flinders University in Adelaide told the *Financial Times*. Now, he said, the costs of competing meant that middle-class tiger mothers with deep pockets were using their sharp elbows to get their kids to the top, at the cost of meritocracy.[15] This is fuelled by the zero-sum nature of the exams, where grading is relative rather than absolute, leading to a private tuition arms race.

For all its garlands and successes, and beyond the human cost of this relentless educational pressure, critics of Singapore's education system have charged that it is simply producing the wrong kind of excellence for a century where a different set of skills is needed. "Here's the problem: content knowledge today has become a commodity," says Tony Wagner, the expert in residence at Harvard University's Innovation Lab. "The world no longer cares how much our students know. What the world cares about is what they can do with what they know." In strict terms, this was actually something that the Singapore system, at its best, was very good at doing: it had top teachers who were very adept at teaching concepts and helping students to apply them elsewhere. However, Dr Wagner argues that unleashing a student's potential for applying education in the real world demands a less tangible soft skill set, which the Singaporean system is not producing.

Part of that skill set was initiative. As I followed my walking route through the NUS campus, along Lower Kent Ridge Road and past the University Hall, I was struck by a simple sign. It told students how to cross the road. These were not primary school children who needed prompts from overly sensible cartoon characters, but students at Asia's best (or second-best, if you ask NTU students) university. "When in doubt," it seemed to say, "instruct, rather than risk a non-optimal choice." This mollycoddling was no route to fostering soft skills.

Another Singaporean problem was common to several East Asian countries. Singapore had achieved its high rankings on the back of a system that focused too exclusively on high-pressure exams. "High performance among countries in Asia is not indicative of increased capacity for innovation," warns Dr Wagner. "They are test-driven countries." Parents take a couple of years off work before the PSLE to help tutor their children. The kids had "only one life. They go to school; they come home; they have tutoring; they go to sleep at midnight or later, then get up at 5.00 or 6.00 a.m. and start all over." This intense, monotonous study regimen, he says, sits badly with a premium on the types of creativity and curiosity that come from enjoying learning. Not only are these the areas that computers and artificial intelligence will be least likely to replicate, but they also instil a love of knowledge and education that will be crucial for those expected to engage in life-long learning, who will need to use their initiative and consolidate their expertise throughout a fluid and challenging career.[16]

These issues were playing on the mind of Bobby Jayaraman, a fund manager and ex-management consultant, when he wrote an article for *The Straits Times* that called for a rethink in education.[17] He argues that high international test scores are mainly due to Singaporean students being relentlessly drilled in heuristics that only allow them to negotiate specifically delineated problems. This, he says, cuts out any actual thinking, understanding, or the ability to deal with problems intuitively. Language tests are presented as abstract grammatical constructions with multiple choice answers, without any real discussion about books, flexibility or creativity. Essays could be gamed by demonstrating taught-to-the-test flowery vocabulary, rather than using one's imagination.

The strict regimentation of learning might help explain why Singaporeans display a very low interest in reading books, other than self-help books, relative to global averages. One survey found that just 40 per cent of Singaporeans had read a book in the previous year, compared to around 70 per cent in the US. Miniature S$10 "ticket books" have been launched to combat the lack of interest in anything beyond the shortest internet articles or social media pieces.[18] In a world depressingly full of people staring at tiny screens, Singapore is notably worse than most—so much so that one McDonald's fast-food outlet offers phone lockers to customers to encourage them to talk to their families while dining. A McDonald's survey apparently found that two-thirds of Singaporean parents used their phones during mealtimes.[19]

This matters in Singapore more than in most places because, as Lee Kuan Yew noted, people are the country's "only available natural resource."[20] Educating large numbers to be scientifically and mathematically literate was vital for its breakneck economic rise. Now, as Dr Wagner suggests, countries are discovering that other less tangible attributes are crucial as they enter the age of the knowledge economy. Indeed, Singapore's successes so far had raised it to the point where such a knowledge economy could be the only place left to go. But, as Mr Jayaraman noted in his article, the current education system is hindering Singapore's ability to ascend to the next stage of growth. Instead, it seems to be a factory that churns out mid-level workers for multinational corporations, sprinkled with the odd genius. Professor David Hung has expressed concerns that the country's system may not be producing the "talented innovators and mavericks" that flourish in knowledge economies.[21]

This need for the education system to match a twenty-first-century information economy was echoed in a speech that Linda

Lim Yuen-Ching, a high-flying professor of strategy, gave at the Methodist Girls' School strategic planning retreat. She told the gathered educators from her alma mater that Singapore had to embrace the challenge of what wonks called a "VUCA" world: full of volatility, uncertainty, complexity, and ambiguity. The steady, safe and lucrative careers that many of Singapore's best and brightest aspired to would be "competed or technologically disrupted away." The school, she said, would need to break the conventional mindset and teach kids to think differently. "Diversity is an asset and empathy a necessity, as we work and play among people who are very different from us." She also brought some hard truths to the retreat. Despite its successes, neighbours such as Indonesia associated Singapore with conformity and a lack of entrepreneurship. One American banker had told her that the reason foreigners would always be needed on the island was simple: "Singaporeans all think alike."[22]

Adrian W.J. Kuah, of the Lee Kuan Yew School of Public Policy, has also pitched into the debate. His concern is that Singapore's high-pressure education system means that children never have the time for creativity or innovation. In his view, time had to be found for iteration and exploration, failure and experimentation. But hope is not lost, for Kuah does see some signs that the country is waking up to this, not least in the decision by the Nanyang Girls' High School to start school forty-five minutes later each morning.[23] When an education system even co-opts children's sleep hours, you know it cannot be much fun.

8

NUS SPORTS FACILITIES

SCHOOLED BY SCHOOLING?

Across from the sign at University Hall telling young adults how to cross a road were NUS' sports fields. They were just as splendid as the rest of the campus, down a bit of a slope from Lower Kent Ridge Road. It looked as though very few expenses had been spared in kitting the place out with the spaces and equipment needed for running and jumping, kicking and throwing.

As the last chapter suggested, Singaporean children do not have much time for sports. When they do, there are apparent ethnic divisions in the activities they choose to partake in. The stereotype has it that Indians play cricket, Malays play football, and Chinese children stare longingly out of the window while doing yet another maths exercise. This is, of course, a generalisation, but it contains an element of truth.

Either way, Singapore was never going to be a sporting superpower. It is tiny, with very few people to throw at sporting success. The climate is also forbidding, as I discovered every Wednesday evening on my five-a-side football pitch. Even in the dead of night my clothes would be wringing wet within seconds

69

of kick-off, with mosquitoes eager to attack any flesh that stopped moving. Every so often we were disrupted by electric storms so severe that I once found myself cycling back along footpaths where the water suddenly came up to my knees. Sporting interest in Singapore is usually limited to cheering on the more successful European football teams on television.

In 2016, however, something changed, and a curious wave of sporting euphoria swept the island. The occasion was the Rio de Janeiro Olympic Games, and arguably no country in the world enjoyed them quite as much as Singapore. The reason for this was a certain chiselled sportsman, Joseph Schooling, who won a gold medal (the country's first ever) in the 100-metre butterfly. In a country so small that its sporting achievements rarely extended beyond a footnote on Wikipedia, this was extraordinary.[1]

Almost immediately, Schooling became a high-profile national celebrity, sought out by everyone from the government to Singapore Airlines. The latter managed to take a celebratory photo with the athlete himself, who was almost entirely crowded out at the back by a scrum of executives and women in SIA's iconic "Singapore girl" outfits, sparking a "Where's Schooling?" meme on social media, in the style of *Where's Wally?* Leafing through a copy of *Today* in a doctor's waiting room, I found that every second photo featured the square-jawed Adonis, shaking hands with luminaries, letting schoolboys try on his medal, and promising that he would compete in four events at Tokyo 2020. His Eurasian ancestry even led to a sudden flurry of articles about this little-recognised demographic group, while others debated whether he would still be forced, like all other young men, to do National Service.

A couple of articles also pointed out something quite uncomfortable about the Joseph Schooling phenomenon: it was most un-Singaporean. "Joseph Schooling is an outlier. And will remain as one for quite a while," says Bermont Lay. Schooling's parents had sent him abroad to give him the best chance of flourishing, selling their million-dollar house to fund this. A typically risk-phobic cost-benefit analysis would have been to raise the alarm at such a move. "If the Schoolings were more pragmatic and living in an HDB flat," Lay muses, "their son might have become a fully-certified swimming coach in Singapore instead."[2]

* * *

Getting Singapore's education system right is crucial for its success—even its viability—as a country. This is not just a question of training the best workforce for the economy, as the country continually sheds skin after skin and reinvents itself and its place in the world. It is also about the glue that holds the social fabric of Singapore together.

Meritocracy is enshrined as the guiding principle at the heart of Singaporean society. In part, this dates back to the split from Malaysia, which eschews meritocracy in favour of offering a leg-up to its Malay population. Singapore's potentially volatile ethnic mix is salved by its commitment to meritocracy. In large part it is also the ideology of necessity in a small, resource-poor country, squeezing the very best out of the limited human resources at its disposal. Its education system is informed by the belief that the country simply cannot afford to let anybody's talent go to waste, whoever they are. It is determinedly colour-blind, race-blind and religion-blind.

Singapore certainly does its best to nurture and reward its brightest stars. It hands out generous publicly funded scholarships to brainiacs, paying for them to study at the world's best universities. They are then summoned back home and thrown into public service. Administrative Service officers are assessed each year, and mercilessly culled if they haven't made the grade. Those that survive are paid the kinds of sky-high salaries that, in the UK for instance, drag people away from public service and towards careers in high finance. Politicians are also generously rewarded for spurning the CBD corner office and applying their talents to "the greater good." Prime Minister Lee Hsien Loong takes home a whopping pay cheque of US$1.7 million (and that's after a 28 per cent pay cut was brought in a few years back), while the US president picks up well under half a million.[3]

A third important function of meritocracy is that it gives people the impression that everyone starts of on an equal footing. This is extremely important for societal cohesion. It gives the state legitimacy by making the disparate segments of its citizenry feel that they are all treated the same. But what if it became clear that this apparent commitment to a level playing field did not always translate into true meritocracy? The academic Michael Barr argues that Singapore's "twin myths" of meritocracy and multiracialism disguise the predominantly Chinese patronage networks that crowd out entry points to the country's networks of power.[4] Another study, by Professor William Keng Mun Lee of Lingnan University in Hong Kong, suggests that educational differences only account for a small part of the income gap between racial groups. Professor Lee's analysis is that Chinese economic and political domination has led to a form of discrimination, with Malays and Indians being segregated (perhaps subconsciously) into lower-paying jobs and occupations.[5]

The myth of educational meritocracy does not just reside in the fact that access to the best tutors is limited. Living in an area chock-a-block with good schools, such as near Tan Kah Kee station, also makes a difference, and such an advantage can come at a forbidding financial cost. A flyer once came through our letter box, advertising a "two-storey bungalow" in Bukit Timah. The agent was pictured receiving various awards, and the text was peppered with capital letters ("ALWAYS ENGAGE A CONSISTENT PRODUCER & AWARD ACHIEVER"). The bungalow's location, it noted (and highlighted in a sudden splash of lurid pea-green ink), gave any buyer an "unfair advantage in close to proximity to Raffles Girls' Primary!" Gaming the meritocratic system through having millions in the bank could just as easily be achieved within the main education system as through out-of-school tutoring.

If you asked a Singaporean about this, they would either mutter or laugh that it is all down to *kiasu*. This is the quality of being afraid to lose out to somebody else, and is associated with selfishness and disregard for others, along with over-caution and fear of failure. Sometimes it is embraced: one online forum for ambitious mothers and fathers, focusing on everything from sleep patterns ahead of big exams to teaching pre-schoolers, is called www.kiasu-parents.com. Some even say that the country's *kiasu* focus on achievements is the fuel that powers the Singapore miracle. Many others are slightly ashamed at how it underpins the national psyche, supposedly making Singaporeans small-minded and mean (and ungenerous drivers). Either way, *kiasu* is accepted as a fact: one survey found that *kiasu* was the top value or behavioural trait that Singaporeans thought best described their society.[6]

"It's a bit of a national joke, right?" remarked Kuik Shiao-Yin over a coffee in the Food For Thought café on Queen Street. "But I sense it is a joke that nobody really enjoys." Ms Shiao-Yin is one of Singapore's NMPs (nominated members of parliament), appointed by the president and not affiliated to any party. She is also the creative director of The Thought Collective, a social enterprise that tries to unlock creative thinking among young people. She noted the ways *kiasu* manifests itself in all sorts of Singaporean behaviours. "Sometimes people just join a queue without knowing what people are queueing up for, because they fear they will lose out. Or, in school, kids hide books in the library to make sure that no one else finds the book."

In part, said Ms Shiao-Yin, *kiasu* comes from the endless reminders about the country's size and vulnerability. "The fear and vulnerability and scarcity mindset are not entirely bad things," she reflected. Singapore should not take its success for granted. "The thing about miracles is they don't come twice. You don't squander a miracle." But though she understands its uses, she has also been outspoken against *kiasu*, saying that it should now be dispensed with. Vital qualities such as innovation, productivity, collaboration, and generosity, are, she told Parliament, "wholly dependent on a person's desire and drive to generate greater worth and real value to share with the world. And *kiasu* culture doesn't give a damn about generating or sharing worth and value." This, she said, prevented the emergence of genuine entrepreneurs, rather than "copy-and-paste" businesses like "bubble tea shop[s] ... hipster coffee joint[s] and cat café[s]."[7]

Such public comments have attracted a fair measure of criticism, and Ms Shiao-Yin acknowledges what she calls the "benign" version of *kiasu*, as well as the "malignant" one. However, she blames *kiasu* for the government's current lack of ambition, and the way so many Singaporeans are content with risk-free jobs, leaving foreigners with more daring and initiative to become the leaders and captains of industry.

Again, this concern goes back to the lack of room for manoeuvre on such a small island. Singapore's size has undoubtedly helped its government create a world-class education system that is an integral—and necessary—part of its miracle. But moving on to the next stage for a country already at the top, with others snapping at its heels, is far more difficult than getting there in the first place. The country now needs a new approach and to shift emphasis to different, high-technology aspects of its economy. It needs a reaffirmed sense of boldness and ambition from its politicians, along with qualities like initiative and innovation from its people. That is a challenge for its feted education system that will require it to step far beyond what it already does so well. It stands Singapore in good stead that its education system is blessed with excellent educators and an enviable approach to STEM teaching. However, on this small island in Southeast Asia, once again the story is not about the effectiveness of the miracle up to this point, but how on earth it can be adapted and revamped to keep that miracle alive in the future. High levels of mathematical competence will not be enough.

I looked over the glorious NUS playing fields and the running track, and noticed that nobody was using them. Maybe that was simply because it was now mid-morning, and getting very hot. I took a swig from my water bottle, and continued.

9

NATIONAL UNIVERSITY HOSPITAL

A NEW TYPE OF STATE

Having walked 23 kilometres on legs a full four-and-a-half decades old, I was reassured to see my next landmark loom into view. As I approached the National University Hospital, a smartly dressed man leaned out of his Honda Vezel, cleaning his bare feet with wet wipes. A cigarette was clasped daintily between his middle and ring fingers. Outside NUH itself, a patient with Arab features stood in a dressing gown, smoking a fragrant, stick-like pipe, which was inlaid with gold leaf and sported a tiny bowl.

The hospital itself was familiar to me from visits with my son, and was rightly renowned for the quiet efficiency of its medical care. During my handful of years in Singapore I was given the chance to visit several of the country's medical facilities as a largely reluctant patient. Various malfunctioning body parts were patched up professionally, leaving me grateful and impressed. If I had to be medically misfortunate in any country in the world, I would be tempted to choose Singapore.[1]

Despite the near-constant improvement in global health outcomes and technologies, this claim is based on the travails of health systems elsewhere as much as on Singapore's apparent successes. The US system is full of gaps and ruinously expensive. Britain's is based on a near-fetishistic worship of avoiding visible financial transactions. Others, more prosaically, are simply failing to cope with a demographic bulge of older patients with chronic illnesses. In comparison, Singapore manages to achieve good outcomes quite cheaply. It is no wonder the world studies it.

Singapore's astonishing rise from sweaty equatorial island to pint-size public policy superpower can be seen in health metrics such as infant mortality rates. In 1908, the rate of infant mortality in Singapore stood at 347.8 per 1,000 live births (60 per cent of these dying in the first three months of life), compared to around 100 per 1,000 in the US; by 2015, Singapore had a rate that was half that of the US. Back in its early years, Singapore's medical system was a product of its early demography, and nursing on the predominantly male island was a job performed by convicts (still in chains). In 1885 French nuns from the Convent of the Holy Infant Jesus stepped in. Obstetric duties were often performed by traditional Malay *bidans*—midwives.

In December 1926 a Scottish woman called Ida Simmons arrived on the island, on a mission to improve infant mortality and maternal health. She promptly learned Malay and travelled to *kampongs* in the depths of the jungly interior. Her own personal impact was reflected in the bald figures: in 1927, the infant mortality rate was 263 per 1,000 live births; when she retired in 1948 only 57 per 1,000 babies died in their first year.[2]

Singapore's current medical system is tied in to its overall system of social security. At its core is the Central Provident Fund, a compulsory employment-based savings plan. Up to the age of fifty-five, workers put 20 per cent of their wages into their CPF account (the figure falls after that age), along with a 17 per cent top-up from employers.[3] This provides for three things: 1. An ordinary account that looks after things like housing, insurance and education; 2. A special account aimed at retirement; 3. A Medisave account for medical expenses and insurance, which is capped at S$52,000. Workers can also pay into Medishield Life for catastrophic illnesses (most do), and there is also Medifund, which operates as a safety net for when other accounts are depleted.

This system results in a mixture of private and public hospitals, each carrying a different tier of care. If you opt for Class A, for instance, you get a private room but have to pay for everything. If you choose an open ward with a shared toilet (Class C), then the government will pay for up to 80 per cent. Although overall costs are low, especially in comparison with the US, competition between hospitals has led to some significant price inflation. In response, the government now mandates the proportions of different wards available, makes providers seek approval for expensive technologies, and controls other variables such as doctors' salaries.[4] It is a very Singaporean system: efficient, market-based, but with a very effective state ultimately in control. It may be two-thirds private, but you can also characterise it as four-fifths public provision, including targeted Medifund money, eschewing the system of—in the words of former finance minister Tharman Shanmugaratnam—"wasteful and inequitable" universal benefits.

Singapore's healthcare strategy is emblematic of its broader approach to public policy, with a technocratic small-state system backed up with just enough coercion to keep people in line. It has something of the Mary Poppins about it, as John Micklethwait, editor-in-chief of Bloomberg News, and Adrian Wooldridge of *The Economist* suggest: "not just a wonderful nanny, but a very bossy, perhaps slightly sinister one."[5] They point to one of former prime minister Lee Kuan Yew's best quotes: "We decide what is right. Never mind what the people think."

As Prime Minister Lee Hsien Loong remarked during a speech at the 2005 Administrative Service Dinner, civil servants in Singapore practise "public administration in laboratory conditions."[6] They are inventive and results-orientated, and not over-constrained by ideology. As in the laboratory, however, experiments in Singapore are commensurate with its size, which means they can be hard to replicate at scale. According to the economist Tyler Cowen, it is debatable whether Singapore's health system could ever be a durable model for other countries, because, "It's easier to monitor quality in a small, Confucian city-state with high levels of expected discipline."[7]

This concern about the replicability of the Singapore public policy experiment has not stopped others from flying in to Changi airport to learn from the way the island does things. Interest has been especially sharp as evidence grows that Western social security schemes have been teetering under the weight of unresolved pension liabilities, demographics, and perverse incentives. To the PAP the Western welfare state was not just potentially unsustainable, but it was also a drag on dynamism and personal responsibility. In 2010 Prime Minister Lee Hsien Loong noted that Europe was discovering that its much-touted sense of solidarity, thanks to its generous welfare system, meant that it was living beyond its means. He was not the only one to have noticed this, but he spoke from the authoritative position of leading a country with a claim to having a better system.

The leaders of large, rapidly developing countries have seen little attraction in aping the Western model, thanks to its expense and poor incentive structure. Singapore's system was not only more frugal, but it also tied neatly into a semi-authoritarian political system. The architect of China's economic take-off, Deng Xiaoping, paid Singapore a visit as he was laying out the plans that would revolutionise his country. He explicitly saw it as a role model (and a link between Beijing and the wider world). After retiring from public life in Singapore, former senior politician Goh Keng Swee spent time advising China. Chinese ministers meet twice a year with their Singaporean counterparts, and four times a year the mayors of fifty Chinese cities arrive for courses in city management.[8]

Even within the limited confines of its own borders, however, the Singaporean system has its challenges. It may not have the massive exposure to pension and health risks that are surfacing in the ageing West, but it does have to deal with the country's own alarming demographically induced changes. In 2014, the country's fertility rate was just 1.25.* Globally, an average fertility rate of 2.1 is needed for a population to sustain itself from one generation to the next. In contrast, Japan, thought to be nursing its own demographic time bomb, had a 2014 fertility rate of 1.42.[9] The rate in South Korea is admittedly even worse, at 1.20. A South Korean parliamentary committee has calculated that, all other things being equal, the last of their citizens will die in the year 2750.[10]

Meanwhile, average ages have risen precipitously, from 26.6 in 2005 to 40.7 in 2015. The United Nations said that Singapore would become a "super-aged society" by 2026, with a fifth of the population already past their sixty-fifth birthday. By then, the core labour force between the ages of 25 and 49 would already be in decline. There were already fewer than five citizens within this age range for each Singaporean aged 65 and over, compared to more than ten in 1990.[11] Some have even suggested that the welfare system has contributed to this problem, by incentivising Singaporeans to have fewer children.[12]

The country's technocrats will justifiably back themselves to tinker in the laboratory and find effective ways to adapt the country's systems to these challenges. Their task will not be straight-forward, for they will have to integrate their solutions into other

---

* The rate reflects the average number of children that each woman has during her lifetime.

complex dynamics, such as Singapore's ebbing and flowing labour market, and its place within an evolving, global knowledge economy. They will then have to revise and rework their solutions, constantly adapting to whatever the outside world throws at Singapore. Small size may be good for laboratory-based solutions, but it means you have little control over the wider environment in which you operate, and almost no wiggle room if you get your technocratic solutions wrong.

* * *

"When I first came back to Singapore after twelve years in Europe, I realised there were no beggars," Koh Seng Choon told me, his voice slightly raised above the hubbub of a busy Serangoon hawker centre. "There are no homeless people, no disabled people. Singapore must be utopia!" The country may not quite be utopia, despite its cheerleaders, but Koh's observation about the lack of poverty or disability on its streets seemed to me to be accurate.

There are plenty of people living relatively tough lives in Singapore. Take, for instance, the low-skilled migrants from the Philippines, Indonesia and Bangladesh. Or the hunched septuagenarians who silently collect trays at hawker centres, having failed to provide for their own old age. Yet poverty is generally noticeable by its absence. The authorities, true to their belief that hard times are often the fault of the person involved, emphasise the importance of personal responsibility in Singaporean society.[13]

Koh's observation about the lack of disabled people on the streets, however, is more complex. Occasionally I saw wheelchair users at pedestrian crossings, selling forlorn single packets of tissues, but that was it. Koh said this absence was partly an "Asian" thing, where people with disabilities tend to be enveloped and cared for by their extended family, and so are not as visible as in other cultures. Some might view that as the by-product of a society based around family networks and the concept of "face," but others might simply call it shame and prejudice. Either way, like many other Singaporeans whom I met in my years there, Koh took on personal responsibility for changing the way the place worked. "I guess we still have a lot to learn about people with disabilities," he said. "They can do things if only they're given a chance."

Koh's way to give disabled people a chance in Singapore is to teach them a trade, and that was why we were having our conversation in a Serangoon hawker centre. This centre, which he called Dignity Kitchen, is not like the hundreds of ostensibly similar ones dotted around the HDBs and office blocks elsewhere in Singapore. It sits an escalator ride up from a wet market full of fish heads and sea cucumbers. But beyond the concrete walls and the smell of frying Oriental morsels, there is something tangibly different about the place. It is not quite as busy as most hawker centres, and there is a palpable air of eagerness, of readiness to serve, that feels different from the usual professional short-order nonchalance. Staff behind stalls track visitors with their gaze, not viewing them as the next S$4 for a plate of *bee hoon*, but as a fundamental test of their ability to contribute.

"We take someone who's challenged and train them in three basic skills: food preparation, cooking, and then service support," said Koh. That, he said, was quite complicated. On the one hand it meant teaching people with different physical, emotional, and mental challenges to work, say, on a stall selling fishball noodles or *kolo mee*. Koh had designed a one-handed roller for curry puffs, chopping blocks for the blind, and an automated noodle cooker for one man who suffered from cerebral palsy. Different tasks on some stalls are completed using gloves in specific colours. Koh found that one young man with Down's syndrome loved to complete exact tasks, so he arranged for 120 chicken wings to be laid out with the ingredients and implements in a precise way, every day.

However well Koh and his staff train people and come up with inventive, engineered solutions that address any disability, the entire enterprise also relies upon the public meeting them half-way. At the coffee stand, for instance, customers get the attention of the deaf staff using vibrating buzzers and a handily placed mirror, before communicating what they need by using simple sign language. Customers in Dignity Kitchen also had to be prepared for slightly longer wait times. A dish might be ready in twenty minutes rather than six. Counting change, said Koh, could be quite an involved task. But the customers needed to exhibit more than just patience, and that was part of what the whole enterprise was aiming for.

"The biggest challenge is empathy," said Koh. Just as he wants to teach his trainees a trade, he wants to teach the Singaporean public some sympathy and understanding. This is not easy. "Because my people are very slow, I decided one day to give them badges with labels like 'Blind,' 'Deaf,' 'Mental.'" However, Koh's idea was not successful, with sales falling off a cliff. "People see the word 'Mental' and nobody buys," he explained. Drawing attention to the workers' disabilities also led to insensitive comments. "Some guy even said, 'Who's mental enough to come up with this mental idea?' The guy selling to him cried! If you don't buy, then don't buy, but don't pass a remark like that." He shook his head and smiled ruefully. "After two weeks we decided enough was enough. People were asking me if they could take the badges off. I agreed, and you know what? The next day, sales pick up! Same people who wouldn't buy before. Empathy is definitely the biggest challenge."

Koh does not just aim to help one specific group of disabled people, but a wide range of people who are disadvantaged in go-ahead Singapore: the physically challenged, people who have been badly injured in car accidents, teenage mothers, battered wives, and those with mental illnesses or disabilities. The list of setbacks and disabilities is also a list of the areas where Singapore's ultra-lean state and largely Confucian society may fail a tiny minority of its people. As ever in Singapore, this can be measured against the absolute good that the state and society achieves, but it is sobering nevertheless.

It was time for lunch. I asked Koh what his favourite was. "*Long mee*. Noodles with a lot of fatty stuff. It's not healthy but it's my favourite. I love the fatty stuff, like pig's tail." As he spoke he glanced over his shoulder, as though checking for somebody. "But my wife says it's no good for my cholesterol." He gave a nervous giggle, and cast his eyes hungrily over the feasts promised by each of the stalls he was calling into being.

10

ONE NORTH

FUSIONOPOLIS AND THE NEXT ECONOMY

If Singapore ever launched a space rocket, it would have a good name for it. Across the Buena Vista Flyover from NUH I could see one of the crucibles of Singapore's push to become a leading knowledge economy, and it was peppered with names that gave voice to these ambitions: Fusionopolis, Galaxis, Innovis, LaunchPad@One North, and BASH (Build Amazing Start-ups Here). They were names that could come from the mind of a six-year-old boy on a sugar high in a Transformers factory.

I knew One North fairly well, having spent an enjoyable few months as a newsroom-based TV reporter for Fox Sports News Asia (tagline: "Where sport goes BOOM!"). During dinner breaks between reports on women's golf and football transfers, I wandered around, taking in the construction projects, the gangs of tech workers earnestly discussing work, and the futuristic names. I saw mock-ups of the swish new Mediacorp Campus, where Singapore's state broadcaster was due to be moving. It all looked very space-age.

If Singapore's economy is to move forward while holding on to its current lofty position and all the bells and trinkets that implies, then it will rely on One North being more than just an admirable collection of Buck Rogers names and forward-thinking companies. One North and the smart economy will have to become the mainstay of the Singaporean economy. That will not be easy.

Part of the answer is to become a "Smart Nation." Luckily, an initiative with exactly this name was introduced in 2014, with the stated aim of improving the quality of life for the country's residents as they faced challenges such as an ageing population and increasing population density. To Peter Ho, then the head of Singapore's civil service, this was not just a case of exploiting technology to improve lives, but of innovating at the systems level, combining tech with policy and planning. The ambition could be big, he said, but some projects could be small. This might include robotic helpers that prepare meals for the elderly, or complete routine administrative and healthcare tasks. Above all, this involved empowerment, as too much top-down control would "kill the spirit of innovation that is central to a Smart Nation."[1]

The government has encouraged the financial sector to branch out into fintech (financial technology). The Monetary Authority of Singapore has a room called LookingGlass@MAS, where young men who look somewhat scruffier than the average financial regulator scrawl buzzwords on whiteboards. The MAS has a "sandbox" approach to fintech, whereby regulations are relaxed for small-scale experiments, allowing innovations to be tested in safe conditions. By 2020, MAS plans to have US$158 million invested in developing fintech, which it hopes will complement and strengthen a traditional financial sector that accounts for well over a tenth of GDP. The keyword for fintech in Singapore is "enabler" rather than "disrupter": there is no sense in killing a golden goose in the name of progress.[2]

Some of the push towards being "smart" is provided by the country's concerning demographics and its labour market shortages. The "Smart HDB Town Framework" includes ideas like using motion sensors that can alert carers if an elderly person topples over. One initiative involves a fleet of peculiar bright orange security robots. Their job is to patrol, using a battery of cameras and sensors to manage tasks like monitoring rogue car number plates. The company involved, Ademco Security, explained that they had failed to attract enough Malaysians to work as auxiliary police officers, despite more competitive pay levels, and see robots as a way of filling the gap.[3]

The island already has a long track record of encouraging innovation in transport. At one extreme it has been trying to use aromatherapy to entice people to junk their cars in favour of sweet-smelling buses. This ploy, straight out of Singapore's technocratic innovation playbook, involves pumping a scent with hints of rose and peppermint into the buses owned by Tower Transit.[4] Meanwhile, the island's Electronic Road Pricing scheme charges cars according to where they go and how busy the roads are, and it has been copied in cities from London to Stockholm.

Naturally enough, the country has tried to plug itself into the self-driving car revolution, setting up the Committee on Autonomous Road Transport in Singapore. One study suggests that replacing all the country's human drivers with robots could cut the numbers of vehicles on the roads by 80 per cent. (My own feeling is that replacing the country's human drivers with robots would also make the roads 80 per cent safer).[5] Such innovative attitudes to the shibboleth of car ownership are music to the ears of visionaries like Kishore Mahbubani. "This is where Singapore needs to have leaps of imagination. I've been arguing that we need to be the first country in the world with zero car ownership," he tells me. "We are small enough, and don't need to own cars. Why not create the first carless society—with access to cars, but no need to own them?"

The prognosis for becoming "smart" seems to be good. In one 2016 study from the computer company Dell, Singapore ranked third in the world (behind San Jose and San Francisco) for its "future readiness": having the right people with the right skill sets; having infrastructure to support new technologies; and providing opportunities for businesses to innovate and grow.[6]

Singapore also has plenty of clever people, both within government and without, looking ahead to see what the future holds. One of these clever people sat down with me for a chat and a cup of coffee at the National Gallery, their beaming smile complementing a firecracker of a brain. They were a key part of the prime minister's strategic planning unit. "The Singapore government has thought about the future in a systematic way for quite a while," they assured me. I had never doubted that.

Like Professor Lim Yuen-Ching, the strategist spoke a lot about the "VUCA" world of volatility, uncertainty, complexity, and ambiguity, along with a tumble-drier-full of horizons, narratives, budgets, and impacts. "VUCA problems don't have any precedent. The feedback loops are very long. It's not like I try something, get a feedback loop, and can then adjust." Instead, the job involved scanning for what might be "the next candidates for problems," with a relentless focus on what these scenarios meant for the here and now of current strategy-making.

"What keeps your team up at night?" I asked. "China–US relations. And de-globalisation." The latter was more of a rising sentiment than a phenomenon borne out by firm numbers, but it was very worrying for Singapore's globalised economy.

These concerns, however, are merely future trends the team is trying to decipher. If I were in their place, what would keep me up at night is the near-impossibility of keeping the Singapore ship on track. The more I looked at future trends, the more I would panic at the prospect of negotiating them in this tiny country with no wriggle-room, politically or economically, for making strategy based on misinterpretations of the future. "Being too far ahead is the same as being wrong," I was told.

And even small mistakes had an impact. "You get it wrong and that's it. You lose a lot of your legitimacy there."

This reference to legitimacy seems to be a particularly important point. Building a "smart" city, infused with strategic responses to trends barely sensed by mortals, is certainly a step forward. But it is also potentially disorienting, and there is a constant risk of either being wrong or having to constantly shuffle one's feet in anticipation of whatever is coming down the track. Beyond all the signals and strategies, this strategist's far-sighted operation was surely only as good as the more basic building blocks of Singaporean legitimacy, such as good health-care and an MRT transport system that works. It is an unenviable balancing act, whatever the clever branding. On the way from its evolution from Garden City to Smart City, Singapore will have to work hard not to become Dizzy City.

11

KENT RIDGE PARK

WHEN SINGAPORE WAS *SYONAN-TO*

On Science Park Road I was tasked with finding a footpath that sneaked through a gap between the buildings lining the street to my right. I wanted to double-check the map on my phone, but few things were as aggravating in the revolting Singapore heat as having to fiddle about with my reading glasses, which slipped off my sweaty nose as drops of liquid obscured my vision. I wiped my bare eyes, saw a likely footpath, and took it.

The way curved to the right, and I saw a long flight of stairs rising ahead of me, covered by a snaking roof of red tiles. My path headed left, down broad steps that kept pace with a straight, narrow channel of gurgling water. Trees lay thick on either side. For a hundred metres I enjoyed the relatively cool air of the forest, and the feeling that I was walking where people should be walking: in something resembling nature, rather than industrial Jurong or a giant version of a city-planning computer game.

Kent Ridge Park made my hike feel like a stroll, at least until one particularly steep yellow-painted flight of steps. A sign warned me of what not to do if confronted by monkeys, including feeding them (on pain of a S$5,000 fine). The track soon joined Vigilante Drive, which afforded a spectacular view of the container port, beyond a landscape of pastel-coloured condos rising through the trees. An awkwardness of Singaporean youngsters loitered around the minibus that had disgorged them a few minutes earlier, uneasy in the open air.

A rising feeling of discomfort from my right foot prompted me to sit down, gingerly unlace my shoe and remove my sock. I was faced with the slightly less spectacular view of an entire little toe that was turning into a single, weeping blister. I reckoned that I was still a few kilometres off halfway on my walk, so this was bad news indeed. I patched it up with the rudimentary blister repair kit I had packed before dawn, and spent a few seconds reflecting on the pain ahead. Then, heartened by the simple beauty of walking on a wide, undulating path through thick clusters of trees, I set off again. I distracted myself by pondering whether the sloping path would be suitable for a four-year-old with a scooter: would he glide along with a grin on his face, or run out of control before being launched into thickets festering with snakes and plate-sized spiders? I decided to return with him to find out, after recovering from having that pesky little toe amputated.

Ahead of me, just after a swanky hilltop condo called The Peak (where apartments cost the best part of S$10 million), was a white-washed colonial bungalow with beautiful proportions and a rhomboid lattice of white bars over its windows. The bungalow was the site of the Bukit Chandu War Memorial. It commemorated the battle of Opium Hill (the literal translation of Bukit Chandu), where 1,400 soldiers of the 1st Malay Regiment held off 13,000 Japanese soldiers in February 1942.

The action was part of the successful invasion of Singapore by the Imperial Japanese Army. For the British this was a calamity (Winston Churchill called it the worst disaster in British military history); for the citizens of modern Singaporean it was a deeply formative experience that set them on the path to independence, and gave them a lasting reminder of the island's vulnerability.

The British (and the Royal Navy in particular) had seen the security of their Eastern empire through the lens of a "Singapore strategy," shaped by the growing naval power of Japan. Even when it was latent in the 1920s, the British and Americans recognised Japan's threat to trade with China. Admiral of the Fleet Sir John Jellicoe visited the region to assess options, but decided that the practical approach to defence was to build a base and hope to give it the necessary resources if it was endangered.

Britain's idea was essentially that they would be able to move two-thirds of its fleet to the East to respond to a direct danger, using Singapore as the fulcrum. This depended on maintaining or securing some form of security in the Western hemisphere first. Earlier thoughts about having Eastern efforts focus on Sydney were dismissed; although it was more vulnerable, a fortified Singapore would help to safeguard Malayan assets (it provided half the world's rubber, and a third of its tin), and represented a crucial strategic link between India and the Pacific. Singapore, as ever, had geography on its side.

The outbreak of war with Germany put this strategy to the test. At first, France was seen as the key to balancing the Italian navy in the Mediterranean, allowing the Royal Navy to concentrate on the Atlantic. But the fall of France in 1940 made things very difficult. If the Axis powers, which now included Vichy France, could control the Mediterranean and make inroads into the Black Sea, they could access the oil of the Middle East and Romania, and have a direct route to the Soviet oil fields too. When Britain found itself at war with Japan after the attack on Pearl Harbour in 1941, the southeastern corner of Asia, from Hong Kong to British Malaya—including the island of Singapore—and Indochina to Indonesia, looked very vulnerable.

Britain also had to think about the Indian Ocean. It provided a link to the USSR through Iran, a degree of protection to the eastern Mediterranean, and the ability to access India, along with other imperial assets stretching down to Australia and New Zealand. Any hope that the Americans would step in and move assets from Pearl Harbour to Singapore were always forlorn, as the Americans could not afford to leave Hawaii—and their west coast—exposed.

This perilous strategic situation may have concerned the more sober minds in Whitehall, but most residents viewed the island as something of a fortress. It boasted five of the heaviest guns (15 inches, or 38 centimetres) deployed in the British Empire, and had four aerodromes. But when war with the Japanese came, Singapore proved to be less of an impregnable stronghold than a deeply vulnerable concentration of British assets and hopes. There was no way it could repel air attacks without being able to enforce a perimeter of more than 400 kilometres. The fall of the Philippines took away any confidence that US air power could provide some of that cover.

As the situation worsened, the British had the option of drawing down the vulnerable forces in Singapore, in favour of safeguarding India and Australia. They chose not to. The foreign secretary, Anthony Eden, decided to move a battleship, HMS *Prince of Wales*, to the island in the hope that it would deter the Japanese. But Britain's efforts were stymied by lack of forces (especially planes), bad coordination, and the hard reality of the war.

The man in charge of the defence of Singapore was Lieutenant-General Arthur Percival. Photos of him looking slight and buck-toothed, clad in tropical shorts, long socks and pith helmet, have the unfortunate effect of reinforcing perceptions of weak and ineffectual colonial leadership. In mitigation, he had predicted the importance of forward-defence in Malaya back in 1937, and well understood the challenges he faced once war had broken out: vulnerability to air attacks, inadequate air and sea forces, and a fairly inexperienced army. Not everybody was as concerned. Governor Sir Shenton Thomas reportedly told a code clerk called Molly Reilly that no Japanese would ever set foot in Malaya.[1]

The Japanese soon went about proving the governor to be more than a little over-confident. They landed high up the peninsula, on the Malay and Thai coasts, in early December 1941, and began working their way south on a swarm of bicycles. "The eyes of the Empire are upon us," warned General Percival, as the Japanese advanced towards the Johor Straits. Despite Hermann Göring's warnings that it would take "eighteen months and five divisions" to reach the Strait, it took just two months with only three divisions.[2]

One of Singapore's defenders was an American airman from the dairy farms of Minnesota, Arthur Donahue, who had volunteered for the Royal Air Force. "Everything hung on Singapore," he wrote. "If it fell, the enemy would be able to conquer the Dutch East Indies, which would give them rubber, tin, and oil that they needed to continue the war." He and his comrades cheered when they heard they would be part of the island's defence: "We all wanted action, and now we had drawn the jackpot!"[34]

Another defender was John Baptist Crasta, from Kinnigoli in India (a town where "nothing has [happened], or ever will happen"). He arrived in Singapore from Bombay in early 1941. For him, the place was a "dreamland" of amusement halls filled with dancing and Malayan pageantry, and Chinese prostitutes who covered themselves in make-up and lined up for selection by the punters. The Japanese aggression apparently came as something of a shock to him.[5]

There was nothing surprising about Japan's choice of target. The Japanese saw Singapore as the necessary next step in their quest to secure the resources and territory that their imperial economy demanded. Taking the island would deny the Allies a strategically vital base, and allow them to move against the Dutch East Indies and its oil reserves.

With the enemy now sitting ominously across the Johor Straits, Singapore itself waited anxiously for the inevitable assault. The ill-fated HMS *Prince of Wales* and the battlecruiser HMS *Repulse* had both been sunk by long-range torpedo bombers in late 1941, resulting in the deaths of 840 men. These losses had shocked Britain, and confirmed that Singapore was utterly exposed. Thomas Kitching, the chief surveyor, wrote to his sister Brenda in typically stoic fashion: "Singapore is bound to have a packet of bombs, with inevitable casualties which must be dealt with." He spoke of blackouts, a charity screening of *Goodbye, Mr Chips*, and rising tensions over putting up friends and colleagues who had been displaced from Malaya or been bombed out of their homes on the island.[6]

On 8 February 1942 the first Japanese soldiers landed on Singapore, concentrating their attack near what is now the Woodlands border checkpoint, in the northwest of the island. They had used the jungle to screen their preparations, clearing bush for amphibious attacks while feasting on some of the local estuarine crocodiles.[7] That day, Thomas Kitching wrote that, "it seems incredible that 15 miles away 100,000 men are waiting to kill each other, armed with every conceivable engine of destruction." The next day his diary gives voice to his dismay over the costs of subscriptions to the Royal Singapore Golf Club and Singapore Swimming Club. A few days later, he hides bottles of spirits in his office in defiance of an order from the governor to destroy them.[8] In some ways, life went on as normal.

The fighting on the island lasted a week, with many instances of heroism and fortitude such as the Malay Regiment's defiance at Bukit Chandu. However, faced with inevitable defeat, and low on both water and ammunition, Percival agreed to surrender. By then the front line was a couple of hundred metres from the location of my old house (which did not exist at the time), on a steep ridge now occupied by the National Junior College and

Raffles Girls' Primary School. The Japanese had always viewed this area, Bukit Timah, as key, since it was on high ground with control of the reservoirs and key road junctions.

The surrender was signed further up the Bukit Timah Road, behind the glorious art deco façade of the Old Ford Factory, all square-shouldered angles and panes of opaque, emerald-green glass. The factory had only been built in 1940, and was Ford's first car-assembly plant in Southeast Asia. The humiliation was completed by the Japanese insistence that the spindly Percival walk to the Factory, accompanied by a white flag as well as a British one. The gaunt and shame-faced British officers at the signing ceremony stood in stark contrast to the bullish, crew-cut Japanese, led by Lieutenant-General Tomoyuki Yamashita.

On the now-silent battlefields, the Japanese cut off the hands of dead comrades at the wrist, before burning their bodies. The hands were to be sent to the soldiers' families for burial. Some Japanese wrote home about trying the asparagus and cheese the British had left behind.[9] This bastion of the great British Empire, complete with strange foodstuffs, and Thomas Kitching's hidden drinks cabinet, had fallen—and fallen to an Asian power, rather than a European rival. Winston Churchill was right to register his shock and disorientation at just how easy it had been for the Japanese.

Many of the British civilians had been evacuated (to the chagrin of the non-British they left behind). Thomas Kitching's wife, Nora, had a near miss at the docks during an air raid, but was then taken on board a Chinese river steamer, called the *Kuala*, on a stretcher. The next day, on the fourteenth, the *Kuala* was hit. A passenger called Mrs de Malmanche had just finished breakfast when she heard the "ear-splitting crash" of a bomb hitting the bridge and engine room. The order to abandon ship came, and the Japanese continued to attack those in the water.

Mrs de Malmanche survived after being washed onto a rocky beach. Nora Kitching was killed.[10]

The British and those allies who failed to escape faced a grim future of incarceration. They were told to assemble on the Padang with ten days of clothing, before being marched off to the prison in Changi. Other soldiers ended up in hell holes in the Philippines, Burma, or Japan itself. Thomas Kitching was interned in Changi Prison, not far from where the western runway of Singapore's much-admired modern airport stands today. The prominent post-war politician David Marshall was also in Changi, before being sent to Hokkaido in Japan. He worked in a coal mine alongside several hundred British and Dutch, and a few Americans, in Hakkodate Camp 1B. At one point he was too weak to continue mining and was moved onto an airfield that was being constructed. He later said that another winter of sub-zero temperatures would have killed him.

Meanwhile, the Japanese occupiers began to govern the island that they called *Syonan-to*, or "Light of the South." It lay at the strategic heart of their "Co-Prosperity Sphere." Sketches of Singapore were distributed to Japanese soldiers to celebrate their victory. The entire country was shifted by 1.5 hours into Tokyo's time zone, and the Japanese calendar was adopted (1942 suddenly became 2602).

The fate of the civilians left in occupied Singapore depended in large part on their race. As an Indian John Baptist Crasta was told by the Japanese that the common enemies of "Asiatics" were the Anglo-Saxon British, as they canvassed for volunteers for Subhas Chandra Bose's Indian National Army.[11] Bose had been shipped over from Germany via submarine. He addressed cinema audiences, spoke grandly of his ambitions for a Brit-free India, and even reviewed a military parade alongside the Japanese prime minister, Hideki Tōjō. Crasta would survive the war, unlike a great number of his comrades, despite years of starvation and brutality as a prisoner in Papua New Guinea.

The Japanese attitude towards Singapore's Chinese community was less constructive. They saw it as a source of potential resistance, not least because of Japan's continuing war in mainland China. In trials after the war, lawyers for Japanese defendants argued that they had expected to encounter guerrilla warfare, enflamed by communist agitators. These fears were no doubt reinforced by widespread looting after the island's fall, and the large quantities of arms and ammunition that had been left behind by British and ANZAC troops.[12] The result was Operation *Sook Ching*, which was an attempt to eliminate opposition within Singapore's Chinese community.[13]

On 18 February 1942, Chinese males aged eighteen to fifty were ordered to report to screening centres. Although the *Kempeitai* military police had lists of suspects, the screening was also arbitrary. Pre-dating the Khmer Rouge's search for intellectuals in Cambodia, they considered both spectacles and soft hands to be evidence of education, and therefore of anti-Japanese sympathies. The screening itself was brutal, with frightened Chinese huddling in groups before being forced into lines at bayonet point. Bodies were dotted around. One man, Goh Sin Tub, remembers being pushed into a tent where a screening panel passed judgement. "This included some strange men who had their faces hidden behind hoods and spoke only in whispers but did a lot of pointing with their fingers." A man who had made the mistake of reporting to a centre wearing military-style boots was immediately taken away by the Japanese. The lucky ones were given slips of paper or stamps on their arms or clothing, to confirm that they had been screened. Goh's father was detained, but managed to dart into a drain rather than climb on board a waiting truck. "For myself," remembers Goh, "*Sook Ching* was the purge of my childhood innocence. It was my first encounter with evil."[14]

The country's future leader, Lee Kuan Yew, reported to Jalan Besar Stadium with a family friend and rickshawman, Koh Teong

Koo. They stayed overnight in Koh's dormitory cubicle, which was within the barbed wire compound. When he tried to leave he realised that something sinister was going on, and was able to return to the cubicle to hide. He stayed there for a day and a half before getting past a checkpoint, complete with a rubber stamp certifying that he had been screened.

Those selected were taken away in lorries to execution sites. Japanese estimates are that around 5,000 were killed. Singapore's Chinese community estimated that the figure might have been as high as 50,000, including those who died during the entire campaign in Malaya. The Chinese community in particular was to remain the object of scorn, suspicion, and violence throughout the occupation. The repression was also cultural. Chinese schools were closed, and only reopened in 1943, with all students expected to learn Japanese for fourteen hours each week.[15]

After the war there was an attempt to account for the repression. Seven *Kempeitai* and Imperial Army officers were tried for the *Sook Ching* atrocities in 1947, guarded by men of the British Seaforth Highlanders regiment in front of a crammed Victoria Memorial Hall. Under cross-examination, Lieutenant-General Kawamura Saburo claimed that he would have been shot if he had gone against orders, although he also said he thought those orders were justified.[16]

Also involved in the trials, as a prosecution witness and interpreter, was one of the occupation's more equivocal figures. Mamoru Shinozaki's appearance was that of a bespectacled bank clerk: he had a clipped moustache and neatly combed hair, a weak chin, and a head that seemed to melt into his collar. Shinozaki had been part of Singapore's Japanese community before the war, working as a journalist and press attaché at their consulate. He was also a spy, and had been involved in collecting intelligence on the Chinese community.[17] The British interned him on espionage charges, but after the invasion he was appointed as a senior official in charge of education, and later welfare.

Shinozaki was certainly entangled in some unsavoury aspects of the occupation, notably the inspections that led to the *Sook Ching* massacres. His autobiography, however, emphasises more benevolent activities, such as his deliberate storage of food in a convent so that the nuns would have access to it. He also maintained that he had decided to help those at risk from the *Kempetei*, for instance by protecting thousands of Singaporeans through issuing them with special cards from the "Special Foreign Affairs Officer of Defence Headquarters."

Another controversial project that Shinozaki was involved in was the resettlement of civilians to the Malay peninsula. The most important of these was based on the edges of Bahau, a small and unremarkable town in the state of Negeri Sembilan. Along with the Catholic bishop of Singapore, Adrien Devals, he set up a community that the Japanese called *Fuji-go* ("beautiful village"), for Singapore's predominantly Eurasian Catholic community. Both Shinozaki and Devals had championed it as a way to relieve pressure on overcrowded Singapore. In December 1943, the first "settlers" met at the Cathedral of the Good Shepherd, and embarked on a train journey to their new lives in the north.

Fuji-go was something of a Swiss Family Robinson project. Most of the early arrivals were young men, and each family was allocated 3 acres—although at first the jungle had to be cleared so everybody lived communally in sheds. It was far from prime agricultural land, with malaria a constant threat. On the plus side, food (of a sort) was relatively plentiful: there were *bangkwang* (Chinese turnips) and *kangkong* (water convolvulus). Beyond filling stomachs, however, the diet was lacking in nutrition. Lizards and snails were roped in to provide a bit of protein. The harshness of the conditions took its toll; 500 or so died in the first eighteen months. Bishop Devals himself lost a leg to gangrene, and died in 1945. As they needed exit permits to leave Bahau, residents smuggled out warnings to their relatives telling them not to come, despite newspaper adverts exhorting them to resettle.

Shinozaki was arrested by the returning British, and once again charged with espionage. However, he was released, found work as an interpreter, and provided evidence against other Japanese who had been accused of war crimes. Some contemporary newspapers allege that this was an attempt to win favour with the British so that he could stay in Singapore. In his autobiography he said the British began treating him well because so many civilians vouched for his behaviour.

One who spoke well of Mamoru Shinozaki was Herman de Souza, who had worked with him in the education department. Much later, he recounted to his granddaughter, Fiona Hodgkins, that Shinozaki had told him simply: "I had great ambitions... But when the British interned me in this place I had time to think, and I have now only one ambition ... to do good to people ... Doesn't matter who they are."[18] Fiona Hodgkins also relates a 1946 letter to *The Straits Times* from her great-uncle, P.F. de Souza, who noted: "I do feel that Shinozaki's public spiritedness and achievements—at a time when we who were there were subjected to all kinds of degradations—characterise him as a great humanitarian and a great gentleman."[19]

As it happens, Shinozaki was deported from Singapore in 1948, after being deeply associated with what happened in Operation *Sook Ching*. His autobiography and other accounts that he gave of his time in Singapore have been heavily criticised as self-serving and misleading. Others maintain that he is, in that disagreeable formulation, "Singapore's Schindler." Moral clarity is unusual during an occupation.

The Japanese used Singapore as a repair base for its navy, but, as the war did not necessarily proceed to their advantage, the island's economy began to suffer. Violence and boorish behaviour from the Japanese soldiers stationed there was commonplace.

When Australian commandos destroyed several oil tankers in Keppel Harbour in late 1942, a local driver called Joseph Francis was arrested, suspected of passing a radio transmitter to POWs. He was held and tortured for six months. His health never recovered, and he died in May 1945. Not long after, the Japanese lost the war.

John Baptist Crasta returned to Singapore in November 1945, but found that the gaiety he had been struck by on his first visit had entirely vanished. It was, he wrote, not even a tenth of the place it had been before. Shops and eateries had vanished, and although people still visited attractions such as New World Amusement Park, Crasta thought this was more out of habit than enjoyment. Prices were high for whatever was left in the shops: a packet of Capstan cigarettes now cost S$4. Poverty and misery, he concluded, were the Japanese legacy. Even those who had managed to save a bit of money faced privation, as the "banana dollars" that the Japanese occupiers had introduced were cancelled by the returning British administrators.[20]

The psychological impact of the war was huge. The British Empire's great eastern fortress had crumbled in the face of an Asiatic military power, raising questions in their minds about the viability of maintaining a global imperium. The non-British residents of Singapore learned different lessons. One Malay woman, Aisha Akhbar, called the British "gods with feet of clay" after the Japanese had been defeated. Not only had they failed to protect Singapore in 1942; their return in 1945 was marked by a festival of drinking, swearing and whoring.[21] The racially differentiated treatment under the Japanese also had a pernicious impact. That the Chinese community was treated harshly, in comparison to the Malays and Indians, was quietly noted. Some mixed their anti-colonialism with a dose of communism.

Many people felt dissatisfied with the peace. Although the rubber and tin boom helped the Malay economy, with a knock-on effect in Singapore, the island's infrastructure was still a mess, and post-war Britain was a shadow of its former self. The Suez Canal, so central to Britain's trade with Asia, took a long time to be cleared of shipwrecks. Slow economic progress led to widespread resentment of the British. The well-educated Chinese elite felt themselves ever readier to take on governing roles for themselves.

The war was a formative experience for Lee Kuan Yew. Not only did it expose British weakness, and foreshadow a redrawing of the world map in favour of independent countries, but it demonstrated that Singapore was vulnerable, even when protected by an apparently mighty empire. This informed his view of how the country's security should be organised: instead of simply trying to repel aggressors, it needed to make itself an unpalatable target. "In a world where the big fish eat small fish and the small fish eat shrimps," he said much later, "Singapore must become a poisonous shrimp."[22]

A war memorial to the civilians killed now stands at the junction of Bras Basah and Beach Road, consisting of four obelisks. In 1967 the Japanese government paid reparations of US$17 million to Singapore in loans and grants, following the discovery earlier that decade of a mass grave containing several hundred bodies. Tomoyuki Yamashita, the "Tiger of Malaya" and the mastermind of the fall of Singapore, was hanged in 1946 in connection with atrocities committed in the Philippines.

12

HYDERABAD ROAD

END OF EMPIRE

The hairpin path down through the undergrowth of Bukit Chandu was an unwelcome and jolting reminder to my joints that it was going to be a long day. At the foot of the path lay more greenery. Off to the right was Hort Park, where I would be able to use the toilets and peel off my damp T-shirt to swap it for a bag-fresh replacement. Ahead, rising slowly up a sweeping bank of indestructible tropical grass, was a slice of equatorial England.

I climbed the hill and stepped past a couple of bollards onto Canterbury Road. It was like passing through a time warp to emerge somewhere half anchored in an age when real men rather than hipsters sported moustaches, and where the sun had never set on the British Empire. The streets tracked graceful arcs that seemed purpose-built for Edwardian spinsters on cast-iron pushbikes. Beyond Canterbury Road there was a Winchester, a York and a Cornwall, and then the short and purposeful Berkshire. They were dotted with grand "Black and Whites," most topped with red tiles, but one or two sculpted out of icing sugar in art deco style. There were outhouses for servants, kids' scooters left in driveways, and neat wooden decks standing proud around the edges of swimming pools, all fenced off by lush approximations of privet hedges. I could see ceiling fans rotating half-heartedly through the primly divided windows, as though acknowledging defeat in their task of stirring up the heavy, tropical air. Singapore's Black and Whites are still referred to as "bungalows," but most are grander than the image of single-floored dwellings that conjures up. They have an upstairs and a downstairs, high black-beamed ceilings and cavernous rooms, ripe for entertaining and fortifying one's body against the equator with over-strong cocktails. A second hand is needed to count the number of bedrooms.

The buildings are, like most of Singapore, owned by the state. One by one they have been methodically refurbished, before leases are auctioned off to those with five-figure sums to throw around every month.[1] Some ended up gracing the pages of *Expat Living* magazine, complete with stylish women chirruping about the furniture they picked up for a song in Bali, and how they lost a pet rabbit to a python. A remarkable number of others did not seem to shift at all, which might be an economic indicator hinting at the shrinking financial packages available to expats. Very few seemed to attract Singaporean citizens into all that snake-riddled nature.

Many Black and Whites were built by plantation owners, or in clusters of "home county" streets for well-to-do Edwardian Brits. Up next to the Seletar air strip, a few acres of prime sweaty jungle had been turned into central London: Lambeth Walk and Maida Vale intersected with Piccadilly. There was a Battersea Road and a Regent Street, a Baker Street and a Mornington Crescent. Hyde Park Gate looped around The Oval, before being joined to Seletar Aerospace View by Park Lane. It was presumably just like home, but with the Aga on full blast and cobras in the water closet.

Despite these splendid reminders of picnics and empire, an imperial posting to Singapore was not necessarily something to be envied. In Joseph Conrad's *End of the Tether*, Captain Whalley walks into the half-built world of early Singapore, finding a "slummy street of Chinese shops" and "patches of jungle-like vegetation." It was a place where non-Europeans disappeared from the streets after business hours, as though expecting to find tigers who hoped "to get a Chinese shopkeeper for supper."[2]

The heat was something that Rudyard Kipling found difficult to deal with when he visited. He said it was the heat of the orchid house: "a clinging, remorseless, steam-sweat that knows no variation between night and day." Kipling found very little to his taste in the colony ("I want to go home! I want to go back to India! I am miserable"). He wrote about the British that he found there ("the spinster fresh from home, and the bean-fed, well-groomed subaltern with the light coat and the fox terrier. On the benches sat the fat colonel, and the large judge, and the engineer's wife, and the merchant-man and his family..."), suggesting that there was much lounging and loafing going on. He noted that working days only began at 11.00 a.m., and ended as soon as anybody could get away with it. Partly, this was due to the inexorable climate. "Yet no one talks about the unhealthiness of Singapur," he wrote. "A man lives well and happily until he begins to feel unwell. Then he feels worse because the climate allows him no chance of pulling himself together—and then he dies."[3] That was not quite my experience of the Singaporean heat—at least not the last bit—but from the moment I arrived, parts of my body started to physically rot, recovering with indecent speed within a couple of weeks of leaving. I never left the house without water, several spare T-shirts, and a plastic bag for quarantining the ones that I took off, sodden with sweat. My spectacles sometimes simply slid off my nose. Like Kipling, I hated the climate, and I shivered with second-hand discomfort when I imagined how my Northern European predecessors had coped with their bodies visibly rotting in front of their eyes.[4]

The Black and Whites also represented something that many early colonials had to do without: family life. By the time they started being built in the early twentieth century, the city itself was growing up, with more of the facilities needed by European families. The Suez Canal opening, and the speeding up of transport links in general, had also contributed to others coming to settle with their husbands and fathers.

One side impact of this was the closing down of many of the brothels that served Europeans in 1927, with families now reunited and "going native" far less common.[5] Prostitution had been a feature of Singapore, as so many early arrivals—British administrators, Chinese merchants, Indian convicts—had been male. The brothels were also racially stratified, thanks to public health concerns rather than morality. This, it was hoped, would stop "Asiatic diseases" crossing the racial divide. Many of the prostitutes catering to resident Europeans were the Japanese *karayuki-san*; those for tourists and sailors were often Malays and Eurasians; Southern Chinese women were usually the prostitutes that catered to coolies.[6] By 1882, a third of the female population of Singapore were prostitutes.[7] A refuge was established through the Office for the Preservation of Virtue, equipping women with the domestic and language skills needed for a life outside the sex trade. It began as a single-room enterprise in a hospital in Kandang Kerbau, but soon expanded to take in 120 women, before being forced to move to a bigger site on York Hill.

In between the Berkshires, Yorks, and Winchesters, one road stood out. I followed Canterbury Road to a T-junction, then turned right, the park laid out below me to the right. This was Hyderabad Road: not quite England, but to those who laid these streets out in those days of empire, not quite not England either.

Singapore has had a Subcontinental tinge since the days of Raffles, the East India Company, and "Further India." There was an acute need for manpower on the Malayan plantations and in the ports, especially after the British abolished slavery in 1833. The majority of South Asians came as "assisted labourers." If they were indentured they worked for five years for fixed wages (the contract could then be renewed). This system was abolished in 1910 after condemnation of the harsh conditions, which included extended indebtedness and poor living conditions. Another system, called *Kangany* (from the Tamil word for overseer or superior) was developed in the late nineteenth century, mainly for the coffee and rubber plantations on the peninsula.

While many Tamils came from the south (especially the Madras area) as "assisted labourers," Singapore also drew in educated Indians, including Ceylonese, Tamils and Sikhs. There were Parsee and Gujarati businessmen from north India. Others accompanied British officials and soldiers, for instance as sepoys and servants. Through the twentieth century professionals, such as lawyers and doctors, arrived.[8] Some, including Professor Kishore Mahbubani's forebears, came after the partition of India in 1947.

Many also came as prisoners. The first convict shipment was the brig *Horatio*, which arrived from Bencoolen in 1825 with a cargo of eighty men in chains.[9] Raffles himself had introduced a humane but productive system for using their labour, and the newly established Singapore was also hungry for their muscles. They carried soil from Bras Basah and Pearl's Hill to reshape the centre of the new town, cleared the jungle (and its tigers and snakes) in Bukit Timah, and built St Andrew's Church in 1862. First Class convicts were considered trustworthy, and given license to move freely. Third Class ones were used on building projects, while those of the Fifth Class had to work in heavy chains, often after attempted escapes. The Sixth Class was populated by the very old, very young, and women. In 1873 the last remaining Indian convicts were shipped off to the Andaman Islands and India, with First Class ones allowed to remain in Singapore. Some of the more skilled were able to establish notable careers afterwards: Babajee from Bombay, who had worked on the plans for buildings such as St Andrew's, became the island's first native draughtsman, and a convict called Hammapah became a land broker.[10]

Citizens of South Asian origin now make up a sizeable chunk of the island's permanent population, and have been prominent in roles ranging from diplomacy to entrepreneurship to high politics. I had the honour of a visit from one of the older members of the community, who drove over for a cup of tea one sizzling afternoon. Raghavan Raveendran exemplified everything that had helped Singapore's Pioneer Generation move mountains. When I met him he was in his very late eighties, but spry and bubbling over with character and purpose, brandishing a sheaf of newspaper clippings. He had not been born in Singapore, but came over from Kerala in 1950 as a young man looking for opportunities. His initial two years, working as a surveyor for the Public Works Department, soon turned into six. After returning to India to get married, he came over to settle permanently in Singapore, and worked on projects that laid the foundations for the miracle, including Changi airport. He still spent his time constructively, championing the causes of integration and doing creditable public works. It was on the backs of people such as Raghavan Raveendran that Singapore's miracle was built, and I see few signs that younger generations of citizens have a similar appetite for hard work in the name of the public good.

There was also a sizeable South Asian chunk of Singapore's population that was not permanent: that army of hard-working labourers who seemed to disappear from sight and mind, living parallel lives far away from the villages and towns that they still called home. They were the ones who were responsible for building up so much of Singapore, while chopping down the endlessly spreading undergrowth with their shears and saws and strimmers. The gangs arrived at daybreak and sweated until it was time to scoop up some pungently flavoured rice dish on the edge of a pavement. They then stole twenty minutes of equatorial shut-eye like the scattered, prone victims of a nerve gas attack, before more work and a dormitory bed.

The relationship between these pods of workers and the island's permanent residents tended towards mutual ambivalence. But it would be wrong to characterise Singaporean attitudes as universally uncaring. Money had been raised for several migrant workers who found themselves in desperate straits, injured, for instance, or left unpaid by their employers. I traded emails with one student at Nanyang Technological University, named Kenji Kwok, who spoke of wanting to combat xenophobia and break the stereotypes surrounding migrant workers. He mentioned recent cases uncovered in *The Straits Times* where Bangladeshi cleaners had slept in foul surroundings in bin collection centres.[11] Pieces regularly appeared in the media, encouraging simple gestures such as smiling, to make these South Asian Stakhanovites feel more welcome.

Relations, however, could be strained. Back in 2013, they reached something of a nadir, when an apparently drunk thirty-three-year-old construction worker called Sakthivel Kumarvelu was ejected from a bus, before being fatally run over. This sparked what became known as the Little India riots, the worst such public disorder in Singapore since the 1960s. Several hundred other migrants attacked cars and an ambulance, and threw beer bottles at the police. The bustle and colour of Singapore's Little India was replaced by angry, fearful faces lit by the flickering lick of flames and police lights.

Although Prime Minister Lee Hsien Loong initially said that the culprits would feel "the full force of the law," he was careful afterwards to remind Singaporeans not to say bad things about migrant workers in general. This sensitivity is no surprise, given that race relations in general are such a sticky subject on the island. It might be too easy for troublemakers to draw a line between themselves and different communities of South Asian descent, whether they be migrants or citizens. The migrants themselves already lived on the margins—between the flatbed trucks and building sites, the dormitories and leafy highway verges—but real alienation from a suspicious population would not benefit anybody. Their sweat is just too important for the fabric of the city state, as was restoring the peace and harmony that underpinned a crowded island of different races and vastly different incomes.

It says something about these barely spoken truths that the Little India riots did not lead to an aggravated spiral of suspicion between migrant workers and Singaporeans. Small changes to public order regulations were introduced in Little India itself. There was to be no more enjoying a cheap beer in a public space. Public urinals appeared, so nobody had to wander around an HDB block or dark alley trying to find somewhere to pee. Street lights and CCTV cameras appeared, alongside a police station, smack-bang in the middle of the riot zone. Otherwise, life goes on. Off-duty workers turn up in their finest shirts, chatting away to their friends and co-migrants, while shoppers pick up gaudy material and packets of the most fragrant spices. The shops sell gold of the yellowest hue, the food is delicious, and the five-dollar prostitutes, hidden away in Little India's back alleys, continue to do a roaring trade.

* * *

Singapore's post-war years now feel like the prelude to the inevitable, especially in the light of the Japanese invasion. In 1959, Singapore was given autonomous status, but against a security-conscious backdrop, thanks to continuing concerns about the creep of communism and occasional street fighting. The chief minister, the anglophile Lee Kuan Yew, was determined to draw on Singapore's British heritage rather than simply cast it off in the name of self-determination. This was wise, as modern Singapore is still able to point to its durable foundations on the rule of law and the English language. But the relationship with the colonial past is also antagonistic.

"Growing up in a British colony we were made to feel like second-class citizens," said Professor Kishore Mahbubani, with the wry chuckle of somebody who has seen the long term play out. "The British were always smarter and better than us." He marvelled at how things have changed. "To go from that feeling where the Asians are inferior to living in a world where the Asians believe that they're now superior to the West, it's quite amazing. If you haven't experienced that cultural inferiority you won't understand how far the journey has come."

I left Hyderabad Road through a side gate, entering the Vineyard restaurant in Hort Park, where—crucially—I finally had the chance to pee and change into a new T-shirt. I was now well over 20 kilometres into my walk, which meant that I was nearly halfway.

13

SOUTHERN RIDGES FOREST WALK

BATTLING THE JUNGLE, TAMING THE PAST

After Hort Park and the grand Black and Whites of Hyderabad Road, I took to the air. From the gently arcing foot bridge over Alexandra Road and a spaghetti junction of ramps, I was able to rattle along part of the 18-metre-high raised steel walkway known as the Southern Ridges Forest Walk.

This particular stretch lifted me high above the dense jungle surrounding the old Gillman Barracks (now a cluster of arts studios and creative spaces). Off to the left, another run of rather less imposing Black and Whites lined Preston Road, backing right up against the jungle. As spaces opened out below me, I could see the birds and butterflies of the equator, flapping and fluttering between flowers and branches and leaves. I passed small groups of both locals and tourists, some dressed as though on an expedition to find the source of the Blue Nile. I was forced to choose between a zigzag of switchbacks up to Telok Blangah or a shortcut of steps, and took the latter: my muscles were getting sick of the constant jarring of shoe-on-concrete.

Being up on the raised walkway was a small joy. Not only did the air move about me, as though imitating a breeze, but the flexing steel put a literal bounce in my step that afforded my legs and feet some measure of relief. The HDBs of the urban sprawl were never quite out of sight, and some patches of that jungle below looked as though they had a regular trim. But being surrounded by the natural world was a welcome reminder that the day's endeavour was really just a picturesque walk across a tropical island.

The raised walkways are a remarkable construction, and the type of thing that only a particularly rich and well-thought-out country can do. Indeed, Singapore does this type of thing extremely well. It has a network of "Park Connectors" that link up the island's pockets of green space, opening up the great outdoors for citizens on foot or wheels and with a bit of energy to spare. Not too far north of the walkways are the splendour of the UNESCO World Heritage Site Botanic Gardens, showcasing what it is possible to do with orchids, sealing wax palms, and a horde of oblivious water monitor lizards. There are other carefully curated green spaces, including the strangely surreal Alice-through-the-looking-glass Gardens By The Bay.

Typically for Singapore, these spaces are not just there by accident; they are an integral and well-planned element of the Singapore miracle. The Botanic Gardens date back to the age when Britain was pinching Brazilian rubber tree seeds and setting up plantations in Malaya. The island's surprisingly green centre is packed full of reservoirs and forests, and part of the solution to the water scarcity problem. Leisure areas like East Coast Park are there as a pressure valve for the jam-packed high-rise citizens of the island. The fancier green areas, including the Botanic Gardens and Gardens By The Bay, help brand Singapore as a Garden City. As Margie Hall of the Singapore Nature Society told me during a radio interview at the Botanic Gardens, "management personnel would not want to move here if it was not such an attractive place to live." So much greenery was, she said, mainly an economic decision. Lee Kuan Yee (known as LKY) himself had explicitly spoken of creating a garden city.

But although these world-class facilities were in themselves an unalloyed good, they also hinted at the slightly troubled relationship that Singapore had with nature. The walkway that I was bouncing along was symbolic of a desire to tame nature, and keep it at arm's length—just right for a selfie, but not quite close enough to be troubling. It suggested a transactional nature-as-leisure-facility relationship. To overgeneralise, many Singaporeans tend not to feel comfortable with the red-in-tooth-and-claw natural world.

"They've definitely lost touch with nature," remarked Margie Hall. She spoke of the insulating effect of living in unnaturally clean high-rise apartments, and noted that Singaporeans tend to be far more worried about germs than others. "If you take out a group of school children to a nature area, they practically refuse to touch anything. That recoil from natural things is a problem." Carl Baptista, the co-founder of Pollen Nation, suggested that *kiasu* played a part in this attitude to nature: why take the risk with that funny-looking insect when you could simply kill it?[1/2]

This has both an educational and an economic implication. Many education experts argue that the skills needed by highly developed economies in the twenty-first century will come from a far less regimented approach to schooling. Not only does the natural environment provide stimulation, space for exploration, and a more involving sense of risk, but it helps children link classroom concepts to the world beyond their school walls. There is a tangible link between children recoiling from the natural world and Singapore's future ability to flourish as a modern economy.

From up on my metal vantage point I spied several mitigating arguments in the dense greenery. Curious luminescent silky reflections hinted at lairs that were maintained by eight-legged monsters. There would be snakes, and some of those snakes would be angry if you disturbed their serpentine ways. In places it was impossible to tell where the floor of the jungle was, so lush and deep and downright scary was the undergrowth. The bushes throbbed with itching, crawling, scratchy forms of life. Nature in Singapore was not bucolic; it was capable of devouring a pasty Western body and spitting out the bones. I may have had the heart of a country boy, but I was quite happy keeping this particular bit of country 18 metres away from my bare legs.

Taming, or at least controlling, nature has always been on Singapore's agenda. Making sense of the Singapore River's muds and marshes was one of the first priorities of the country's early administrators. The heat is oppressive and unremitting. Air conditioning is a godsend, and it is hard to imagine how any work was done without it. Building high-rise HDBs out of concrete and extending the shores of Singapore have been integral to the Singapore miracle. Myriad signs on building sites and playgrounds are a constant reminder that the fight against diseases like Zika and dengue continues. Back in early Singapore the dangers could be more flesh-and-bone. In 1843, tigers devoured 300 of the island's inhabitants. Alfred Russel Wallace spoke of one that was captured in an anti-tiger pit in 1854. The last one, a 2.6-metre beast that weighed over a hundred kilos, was killed in the 1930s after a reign of terror among the villagers of Chua Chu Kang. The tigers may be gone, but wild boars are sometimes spotted snuffling about in the north of the island, and gargantuan estuarine crocodiles still visit the shores along the Johor Straits.

Ironically, some of the most famous figures to have graced Singapore's early years were avid naturalists. Raffles, as we saw earlier, gave his name to the *Rafflesia* plant, which looked like it was sewn together from flaps of red meat and teenager's skin, while smelling like the end of civilisation. Alfred Russel Wallace was also very active in the region. He has gone down in history for having independently established the theory of evolution, despite failing to beat Charles Darwin in fully describing it. Singapore's Natural History Museum has several of the items that he picked up in the region, including a stuffed orangutan with the face of a desiccated Tutankhamun. The museum also boasts a large gibbon with an expression fit to scare small children, collected by William Farquhar, and a sun bear from Raffles himself, that looks like it has been chewing on an air pump.

Singapore's attitude to the past has something of its arm's-length attitude to nature. The place is so relentlessly modern that very few tendrils of bygone days make it up through the concrete. Those that do are either relics like the Black and Whites, or are to be suspected of feeding some narrative or other about the present.

The colonial "mud-flatism" narrative, for example, whereby British Raffles was seen to be arriving in a pristine, untouched land, before creating a new Jerusalem out of clay and jungle, is now considered misguided. This myth placed too much emphasis on the colonial period laying the foundations for modern Singapore. Instead, due recognition has to be paid to Temasek and Singapura, and the island's much longer history within the trading routes of the Malayosphere, Southeast Asia, and Asia itself.

Similarly, while some deference had to be paid to colonial-era Singapore, it is also important to note that British rule primarily served British interests, treating the Asian inheritors of the island (whoever they have been) as culturally inferior. It was really the genius of Lee Kuan Yew, allied to a sense of vulnerability and a hefty dollop of hard work, that forged Singapore's triumphant, fragile miracle. Time itself is fleeting and is seen through the lens of the present and future—something to be tamed in the service of continuing success. History, like nature, is best viewed from a steel walkway.

This controlling, arms-length approach to both history and nature can lapse into carelessness or even disregard. Take, for instance, the vast, unkempt swathe of snake lairs and under-growth called Bukit Brown. My first brush with the history of the area was on a Saturday morning trip to the glorious waterside boardwalks of MacRitchie Reservoir. A small sign next to a bus stop on Lornie Road spoke of Japanese war graves being moved because of a new development. The existence of these graves was not a surprise: we were just a grenade's throw from Sime Road, the scene of fighting during the Japanese advance over the island. Its barracks had morphed from an RAF command and control centre to a British prisoner-of-war camp, then a landmark above the sweeping golfing fairways of the Singapore Island Country Club. I had also spotted the odd old Chinese grave nestling in the undergrowth, squatting like a miniature tiered altar, circum-scribed from behind by a semi-circular stone halo.

The new developments promised by the sign were obviously well underway. A fence of steel sheets was being dug into posi-tion along the sides of Kheam Hock Road. I could make out the familiar Singapore splutter of diesel engines jerking back into purposeful life. The development, however, was doing more than just shifting around a few half-forgotten Japanese war graves. It was churning up swathes of the largest Chinese cemetery in Southeast Asia, along with what passed for Singapore's version of pristine-ish nature.

One man who is doing more than most to draw attention to the historical cost of this development is a fifty-something phar-macist called Raymond Goh. I met him among the shrines and graves of Bukit Brown one Saturday morning, already drenched with sweat after rushing there on my bicycle. Mr Goh had founded a society called the Asia Paranormal Investigators with his brother, a decade or so earlier, and this had led him to the Bukit Brown cemetery site. They started leading tours for like-minded Singaporeans who wanted to know more about the past, and were happy enough to do it without air conditioning.

On one of his tours, Goh spotted an inscription relating to the Qing Emperor Daoguang, who ruled for three decades in the early- to mid-nineteenth century. "I said, 'Oh my god!'" he told me, "'How can such things exist in modern Singapore?' That got me very excited and I decided to find out more about this place." That was not easy: the whole vast expanse was overgrown, and only gave up its secrets with a leafy snarl. Luckily, Goh had a bucketful of enthusiasm on his side. "The earliest tomb that I discovered was from the 1860s, but there are relocated tombs dating all the way back to 1826. Those first tombs were from the first pioneer generations!"

In total, for those who are spider-tolerant and carry an anti-snake stick, there are 100,000 tombs in Bukit Brown to discover, or maybe even twice that. "We do encounter snakes, especially with those graves that have been untouched for fifty or sixty years," said Goh, climbing blissfully through the thick jungle greenery towards a tomb that seemed to exactly fit his description. "Cobras, sometimes. That's why I always bring a stick." He waggled it in the air, giggled and ploughed on. Goh's enthusiasm, and that of his friend AJ, was infectious. They were like two young boys showing off their new presents on Christmas morning, rolled white towels wrapped around their necks to soak up the sweat.

Bukit Brown's graves reek of history and the insistent creep of nature. Dates often relate to political upheavals back on the Chinese mainland, with the inscriptions noting the deceased's ancestors' village and members of the extended family. Fearsome ants patrol up and down miniature statues, while some graves are busy being gobbled up by the roots of trees. Lichens add vivid greens and rusty reds to the weathered and cracked stone. Some of the incense boxes at the base of the tombs are evidently still in occasional use. Goh jabbed at one with his stick, explaining that these honoured the earth deities that protected the graves.

Now, however, that protection was faltering. "I have a map here," said Goh, unfolding a large sheet of paper. "We are in Block One, around here. But this grey area, here, is a new road. It cuts across the cemetery, slices it into two." His voice rose as he spoke. "It is the physical dissection of this. You can hear the machinery at work, right?" The diesel roar in the background was just as insistent as the high-pitched, bloodthirsty whine of mosquitos.

"We're a bit of a nation lost in transition," AJ chipped in. "There's so much history here that we didn't know about. We know about Raffles, and maybe about the Japanese occupation. But all these pioneers, they sailed down from China. They see all the lights in the Singapore harbour, and they know they've arrived." He lamented, "There's so much history here, and they want to put a highway through this place. It is sad. It's very, very sad."

The four-lane highway was certainly no mindless show of faith in concrete. It was being built to reduce local congestion, with a promise that the new layout would even allow for better access to the oasis that is MacRitchie Reservoir.[3] Although the developers were trying to minimise the impact on the cemetery, this still affected thousands upon thousands of graves. Meanwhile, a new MRT line is being planned that might involve a tunnel underneath these forested areas.[4] The reaction to both projects demonstrates a growing—if limited—public sensitivity to both history and the environment. But on such a tiny island, development sometimes means making unavoidable sacrifices. In Singapore's stark utilitarian terms the congestion-cutting benefits for the many probably do outweigh the soft-spoken, sweat-soaked exasperation of the occasional Raymond Goh or AJ.

"It was during that rebuilding, from 1965, that everything was forgotten. I heard there were even plans to erase Chinatown!" Goh had the quiet optimism that attaches itself to men and women who instinctively think of the greater good. I saw this in several people in Singapore, where the initial barrier to speaking one's mind is higher than in Western countries, and requires a steeliness of character. "But then when their lifestyle gets better, people start to remember and ask why they are destroying this place that is linked to the past. Singapore is waking up!"

In another fifty years, I asked, what would become of Bukit Brown? Would it be bulldozed, covered in jungle, or restored?

"At that time, it will be a Bukit Brown heritage park. People will come, remember their history, remember their roots. Reflect on the greenery, and interact with nature, touch the stones." Goh smiled. "That's my hope. I call this an open-air classroom. You learn things the books don't teach you, stories from beyond the grave."

No more than 200 metres away, another flatbed truck pulled up, and a half-dozen more workers jumped off, hard hats already firmly strapped to their heads. The clanking and banging and the roar of engines would go on until sunset, even on a Saturday. I was even more drenched with sweat than Goh and AJ, and my white European legs were dotted with red, bleeding insect bites. Bukit Brown was an extraordinary place, but Goh, dubbed the "Tomb Whisperer" in the local media, was a man of rare tastes. I could not imagine many other Singaporeans sharing his desire to stomp around Bukit Brown on a Saturday morning, enjoying the throb of crickets and the warbling of birds, deciphering inscriptions and thwacking cobras. When Singapore celebrates its centenary in another fifty years, my bet is that the area will have a lot more concrete.

I have few complaints about this. After all, Singapore cannot afford sentimentality without a purpose. Its appreciation for history and nature will always be curtailed by its lack of physical space. Accepting constant and disruptive change is sometimes the price for remaining fit for purpose.

In an attempt to make sense of Singapore's attitudes to the past, I had taken to listening to an excellent series of podcasts from the historian P.J. Thum. They were full of provocations, insights, and references to *Pirates of the Caribbean*. Professor Thum himself was quite a character: he was an Olympian, the first Singaporean to swim the English Channel, and something of a dissident historian. He had also contributed to a recent book, *Hard Choices*, that spoke frankly about Singapore's need to take them.[5] By reputation, P.J. Thum did not entirely embrace the PAP narrative about the Singapore miracle.

I met the professor at the Crown Bakery, on Bukit Timah Road. The location itself was enough to spark conversation about just how disruptive Singapore's constant churn and change was. His grandparents had bought a house just around the corner, back in the 1950s. The Bukit Timah of that time was a long way from the comfortable, hilly suburb of expats and millionaires that it was to become. Back then, its roots as a tiger-infested plantation district were still plain. It flooded regularly, and Professor Thum's grandparents' house was raised above the ground to guard against the waters. On one occasion, a dead body floated past their front door. Now, if there was a flood it would be a Ferrari drifting down the road. In Singapore you could expect several such dramatic reinventions within a lifetime.

Did such flux mean that the past was forgotten too easily, with people desperately scrabbling to live in the present? I mentioned the house my family lived in, a bare kilometre away. It was part of Singapore's first privately built estate, a neo-colonial suburb of wrought iron and concrete airbricks. Its whitewashed walls had barely been modified since the estate was established in 1969. But that meant that it had character in spades, a large garden, dodgy air conditioning, and the occasional rat venturing into the kitchen. This rough-and-ready quality also meant that we were able to secure it for a relatively cheap rent, as very few Singaporeans (or expats) would ever want to live in a property that was so exposed to equatorial nasties. The house next door, a carbon copy that was painted in two-tone blue, was home to an old lady and her Filipino helper. The lady's family were trying to sell the house (for a price in the millions), and when that happened demolition would be the next step.[6] A new structure would rise in its place, and there would be no garden worth the name. Angles of concrete and marble and glass would push to within an inch of the edges of the property, maybe with a poor excuse for a swimming pool that served no purpose other than looking good in photographs. It would be ugly, sanitised, and speak in a loud voice about status and wealth. The past would be gone. In any other country, I suggested, such lovely houses, on an estate that plays a historical part in the country's social history, would have some sort of preservation order. But not here.

This was all part of the balance that the government is seeking to find, answered Professor Thum. He lived in Oxford, a city with one of Britain's biggest disparities between house prices and wages. This, he argued, was because its historic buildings have been so well preserved. Such a commitment in as small and crowded a place as Singapore would lead to horrible distortions, and the government would lose some of its control.

He then suggested that the fiftieth-anniversary celebrations for Singapore were also a distortion, with 1965 being something of an artificial line drawn in the island's history. Instead, the "current" history of Singapore was informed by two particular things. Firstly, the economic crisis of the 1970s, which led to the government re-imagining everything from the economy to the education system. Secondly, the global political re-ordering of the 1980s, including the triumph of neoliberalism, the neutering of organised labour, and the dismantling of post-war welfare systems. This had allowed Singapore to become the booming international finance centre that it was today, Professor Thum explained, although he was not particularly complimentary about the society that had been achieved.

This is not the only part of the PAP's Singapore narrative that Professor Thum has cast doubt upon. He is particularly well-known for arguing that an internal security action known as Operation Coldstore was in reality a ruthless and calculating attempt by the PAP to destroy the political opposition. Coldstore was mounted in early 1963, when the PAP was jostling for power with left-wingers, and Singapore was facing a low-intensity war with Indonesia known as the *Konfrontasi*. The operation's ostensible aim was to contain the threat posed by the Communist United Front, which at that point was increasing in influence, thereby opening up the possibility of a post-colonial Singapore joining the Federation of Malaya and staying firmly in the pro-Western and anti-communist camp. But Professor Thum has argued that the real purpose behind the action was driven less by security and the need to prevent communist infiltration than by politics, first and foremost the destruction of any credible left-wing electoral threat to Lee Kuan Yew's PAP.

The reason why this pre-independence operation has become quite such a bone of contention, or so it seemed to me, is that it paints the PAP as slightly sinister in its unflinching will to power, talking about national interests while looking after its own. The implicit message of those who question the operation's motives is not as much an attack on the Singapore miracle as a warning that, in their view, the PAP—whatever its undoubted successes—fundamentally distrusts democratic politics. For those who do not fully endorse the results of Singapore's relentless rise as a beacon of globalised capitalism, Professor Thum included, it also suggests that other economic and political philosophies will be ruthlessly suppressed. In April 2018 the academic appeared before the ominous-sounding Select Committee on Deliberate Online Falsehoods, accused of possible involvement in "a coordinated attempt, with foreign actors involved, to try to influence and subvert" Singapore's parliamentary process.[7]

These slightly dissident interpretations of the past took on a more popular form with the publication of the most extraordinary book about Singapore for years, just as the country was turning fifty years old. More remarkably, *The Art of Charlie Chan Hock Chye* is also an inadvertent case study in the art of stealth marketing.[8] The book is a stunningly inventive visual feast, charting the life and lowly cartooning career of the eponymous hero. It tracks him through a childhood in colonial Singapore, across the years of Japanese occupation and post-war street fighting. It sees his talent bloom, as the city state gains independence and the Singapore miracle takes shape. For all that talent, however, Charlie Chan fails to make the waves that his talent deserves.

The same is not true of the unassuming, bespectacled artist and author who created the book. Before *Charlie Chan*, Sonny Liew's career had been admirable, without being stratospheric. Then the book showed just what he was capable of: jaw-dropping artwork and deft characterisation, allied to clever storytelling that shrewdly weaves a path through complex real-life events and flights of fancy. Lee Kuan Yew appears as an alien and a mouse-deer, and later a chairman who throws the writer of the company newsletter into the janitor's cupboard. There is an ill-conceived superhero called Roachman. It explores government censorship, and charts both the comic-book artist's growing politicisation and the awareness of his own failure. It has also sold like hotcakes.

Other than the brilliance of the graphic novel itself, the main reason for this was a sudden burst of inadvertent pre-launch publicity that Singapore's National Arts Council gave the book when it decided to withdraw a grant of S$8,000 that it had awarded to Sonny Liew, just after the book had already been printed. The senior director of NAC's literary arts sector, Khor Kok Wah, said that this was because "The retelling of Singapore's history in the work potentially undermines the authority or legitimacy of the government and its public institutions, and thus breaches our funding guidelines."[9] Whatever the reason, the result was that Mr Liew's book got plenty of attention. And when people saw the extraordinary visual re-imagining of the Singapore story that had so displeased the NAC, they understandably loved it. Half of the original print run of 1,000 had sold within days. It made the *New York Times* and Amazon bestseller lists. *The Economist* called it a "touching, thoughtful meditation on Singapore's relentless progress." In 2017, Sonny Liew won three Eisner Awards (the Oscars of the comic-book world), and would probably count that forfeited S$8,000 as the best money he has ever spent. The authorities, meanwhile, were given a lesson in how not to control the messages of history. Some older and more traditional heads may have questioned why the book was allowed to be published in the first place. As *The Economist* noted in its review, "One wonders if Lee Kuan Yew would have been so lenient."[10]

14

MASJID AL-AMIN

WRESTLING WITH RELIGION

After crossing the organic wood-clad curves of the magnificent Henderson Waves Bridge, I reached the edges of Mount Faber. If I had continued along its ridge I would have passed something called the Bell of Happiness, before arriving at the start point of a string of cable cars, swaying vertiginously out towards Sentosa. Instead, I ducked down a footpath on the northern edge of Mount Faber, leading to a set of damp, winding concrete steps. Descending these was the first time on my walk that I had felt real pain, juddering down, step by step, feeling the strains and vibrations working their way through my lower limbs. It was time for me to take a proper break, give my legs a breather, and gulp down more sugary sports drinks.

The Masjid Al-Amin (Al-Amin Mosque) was at the bottom of the footpath as it emerged from the jungle onto Telok Blangah Way. It was not one of Singapore's most evocative buildings, looking a bit like a 1990s-era out-of-town supermarket. I checked my phone, found a convenience store a few hundred metres ahead, and picked up my feet.

I took my rest on the edge of Bukit Purmei Hillock Park, near a bench where three Filipina domestic workers were busy chattering, each looking down at her phone. Every minute or so, one would raise her eyes and regard me with something of suspicion, as though I were a spy sent to make sure they were occupied with chores.

The paper map that I had sketched out before setting off was now slightly the worse for wear: worn at the edges, and unpleasantly damp. The next segment of my route seemed unnecessarily complicated, tracing an arc around Bukit Teresa Road, before joining Kampong Bahru Road as it cut across the very same AYE toll road that I had left way back in Tuas. Not only was this complicated, but it added a few hundred unwanted metres. I poured fresh water into the bottle I was carrying, tore the foil on a packet of ibuprofen that I had just bought, and resolved to cut out any unnecessary yardage.

I found a shortcut through the HDB blocks ahead, cursing slightly at yet another jarring flight of steps. That brought me out just next to a salmon-coloured Taoist temple called Tan Gah Beo, just a few metres from the trim, whitewashed walls of the Church of St Teresa. Within a few hundred metres I could have also visited the Silat Road Sikh Temple or the Danish Seamen's Church. I made a quick note on my phone that this should clearly be the section of my journey to discuss the vexed and explosive issue of religion in Singapore.

Religion is ever-present in Singapore, in an odd and circum-scribed way. With some, you see religion in the way they dress. Once a week, you can watch the Filipina ladies heading off to church in all their Sunday finery, sometimes wearing matching T-shirts bearing the names of their Catholic or evangelical churches across the front.[1] On a Friday, you might catch a mosque emptying. Hawker centres often have a small shrine hidden around a corner, and pavements are scattered with incense and offerings during the Buddhist "Hungry Ghost" festival.

The basic state policy regarding religion is that it is a private matter, and should be kept that way. Few things have such potential to cause cleavages between the various communities on such a crowded, multi-ethnic island, and there is a widely respected public taboo against discussing it too openly.

I had only ever heard two religious matters being openly discussed in Singapore. Surrounded, as the country was, by many, many millions of Muslims, one of these concerned the danger that some form of radical Islam might take hold among some of Singapore's own Muslims. This could either take place in the Malay community, which might be exposed to religious currents from Indonesia or Malaysia, or among the country's South Asian migrant labourers.

The government is clearly vigilant. Cells of radicalised mischief-makers are occasionally uncovered in the dormitories of Bangladeshi workers. One Muslim preacher, named Nalla Mohamed Abdul Jameel Abdul Malik, was convicted of promoting enmity between different religious groups in 2017. During a Friday prayer at the Jamae Chulia Mosque on South Bridge Road he had intoned (in Arabic) "Grant us help against the Jews and the Christians." Apparently the words came from a non-Quranic text of Indian origin. He was fined S$4,000 and deported back to India. Singapore's Ministry of Home Affairs reiterated that such phrases are unacceptable, even if found in the Quran.

The other religious issue that received public attention was the jaw-dropping scandal surrounding an evangelical group based at the City Harvest Church. In truth, this owes little to interest in religion, and almost everything to an unfolding, real-life soap opera involving millions of dollars and dreams of pop stardom.

The City Harvest Church story centres upon its founder, Kong Hee. He was found guilty of embezzling the best part of S$50 million from the church, all in the name of his wife's hopes of becoming a global pop phenomenon. Sun Ho already had a bit of a name, warbling in Mandarin. This, however, was evidently not enough. What she really, really wanted was to conquer the English-speaking world too. There was a hitch: to become the next Miley, Britney or Madonna did not come cheap, but Kong Hee obviously thought the stratospheric price of stardom well worth paying.

Rather than rely upon the vicissitudes of the fickle music industry, Kong Hee made sure money was made available to facilitate Sun Ho's rise. Millions were spent on music videos, including large fees for more established stars and their sprinklings of stardust. In the video for "China Wine," she gyrates enthusiastically alongside Wyclef Jean, with plenty of non-religious bum-shaking going on in the background. "I asked her what does it mean?" raps her more established co-star. "She said in China, we know do di dutty wine, so mash dem a mix it with di China wine." In another she is busy doing the vacuum cleaning, while singing about killing her philandering husband (played by the supermodel, Tyson Beckford).[2] Unfortunately, the money for these sterling ventures came from funds that had been earmarked for a new church building, with more money misappropriated to cover up the original theft.

At the original trial, prosecutors spoke about the sums involved being "in line with Shakira's marketing budget and less than the budget for Beyonce." The defendants maintained that they were hoping to use pop music to attract more followers to the church. Whatever the lure of Sun Ho's stardom, the church's congregation started to slip, once it became obvious that it was the subject of a criminal investigation. Putting the lie to the old adage that "there's no such thing as bad publicity," Sun Ho's own career has also failed to take off in a fashion commensurate with the sums invested in her talent. Whether this was because of the court case, or for some other reason, will be decided by history.

The oddest monument to religion in Singapore is a theme park that thrusts visitors into the darkest vision of Chinese hell.

The Haw Par Villa complex sits up on a concrete slope just above an MRT station of exactly the same name, and is the type of thing that makes the vengeful God of the Old Testament seem like a softie at heart.

The first part of the complex is—literally—a tour through hell, complete with multiple dioramas that are populated with figures torturing each other in all sorts of grotesque ways. Helpful signs explain the abuses that are being perpetrated. In the Third Court of Hell, sinners have their hearts cut out for the crimes of ingratitude, disrespect to one's elders, or escaping from prison. Tomb robbers are tied to red-hot copper pillars and grilled, along with drug addicts and those who have urged people to commit crimes or fomented social unrest. In the Sixth Court, cheating and cursing are punished by being thrown onto a tree of thorns, while those who have misused books, possessed pornography, or wasted food, are sawn in two with an evil-looking blade.

I mentally notched up the punishments that I might have racked up, and gulped. I pondered how multiple sins would be dealt with. What if somebody had wasted some food, then robbed a tomb, before escaping from jail? Would the miscreant be sawn in two, with both halves then tied to the red-hot copper pillar, before their heart was torn out? And what if somebody was disrespectful to their elders while in possession of porn? Teenagers of the world beware: Haw Par Villa does not host the type of hell where mitigating factors are given a fair weighting by a forgiving judge.

Helpfully, the brightly coloured figures are always big enough for the pain etched on the wrong-doers' faces to be clearly visible. And there was plenty of pain to go around. Some unlucky chaps were being impaled on hills full of spikes, or slowly dismembered by a blue-skinned goblin, or crushed under a rock. Once punished, sinners were led to the Pavilion of Forgetfulness (or in some cases, presumably, carried in a bucket), where an old lady called Meng Po would hand them a cup of magic tea to help them forget their past lives.

Beyond the multi-roomed vision of hell, the horrors of Haw Par Villa became less coherent and more whimsical. One display had a number of animals in leisure gear pointing cameras and guns at a couple of giant crickets. Another showed an old lady drinking milk out of the bared breast of a well-endowed mother figure, while a baby lay crying on the floor. Hallucinogenic fantasies from Chinese folklore were given intricate and nightmarish form in plaster and concrete and paint. Pig-headed creatures danced while maidens bathed, and a rat-headed man in a sharp suit and two-tone shoes answered a telephone. Turtles drank a mug full of something warming, with a deer sporting a shirt and tie. A bellow of angry, colourless giant apes clambered around on a tree trunk, bringing back my own childhood nightmares of *2001: A Space Odyssey*. Elsewhere a steam ship sank into a turbulent sea, bedecked with colourful pennants, while something resembling a sturgeon chomped dead-eyed on a passenger. There were grim battle scenes and wild dancing, and I imagined that everything carried a moral for well-tuned visitors to ponder. Somewhere, hidden away, there might have been a statue of a sweating, middle-aged Northern English man, walking far too far in weather that was far too hot, on legs that were obviously far too old.

15

KAMPONG BAHRU ROAD

THE MALAYAN SKINHEAD

While Haw Par Villa was a psychotropic trip into the imagination, much of contemporary Singapore is altogether more regimented and sober. It is relentlessly, unflinchingly modern. Remnants of the past tend to be shuffled into the long shadows cast by glass and steel edifices, while the forces of progress and modernity march confidently onwards. But there are plenty of historical scraps if you know where to look. Some, like the Black and Whites of Hyderabad Road, have been revamped and recast as niche upscale monuments to a lost age of gin-addled colonials complaining that their *punkah wallah* was not working the ceiling fan fast enough. Scattered around the more central parts of Singapore are rows of ornate shop houses that were somehow passed over. Many are seedy, full of curry houses and KTV bars.* Others are deep in the process of creeping gentrification, as wealthy urban hipsters realise their dreams by converting them

---

* "Karaoke TV"ars. Some patrons end up doing far more than singing along to favourite hits while drinking expensive bottles of whisky.

into iconic homes, full of internal balconies and *Peranakan* design flourishes.[†]

As I rounded Kampong Bahru onto the traffic-laden New Bridge Road, a run of non-gentrified shop-houses on the right marked the beginning of what I considered the heart of Singapore. There were the Sparkly KTV lounge and the DDD Club. Some windows were blacked-out, or carried the silhouettes of dancing girls, while others advertised expensive cognac (to be bought by the bottle) and unusually branded beers. Siam Secret (which sells Thai food rather than something more exotic) nestled next to the Strength Venue gymnasium, and an office that specialised in commercial aviation leasing. A man studied his laptop and nursed a flat white in an artisanal café, while a sturdy pipe a bare metre from his seat pumped sewage out of the building's septic tank. I ran my eyes across the clientele at a place selling cheap Indian food on the corner, to see if I could spot a familiar face, but Taufiq Yussef was not there. He was probably at work a few doors along, upstairs at the suitably hipster DeepCuts barber's.

Taufiq was one of the most interesting people that I had met in my years in Singapore. He is a Malay, and a Muslim, and had evidently spent a lot of time thinking about what he was, and what he was not. Now, he is a barber, and an inveterate sharp dresser. Not too long ago he was also a skinhead.

"[Growing up] you face teenager problems and you just want to feel you belong," he explained to me. Interviewing Taufiq, as I had originally done for a BBC radio piece, was a pleasure. He is mild-mannered, youthfully innocent, and eager to please. This sits uncomfortably alongside my ideas of what a skinhead is.

[†] *Peranakan* refers to descendants of the Chinese who arrived in the Malay archipelago between the fifteenth and seventeenth centuries, forming a community in Singapore that was distinct from later Chinese arrivals.

Back when I grew up in the Northeast of England in the early 1980s, skinheads were the tough lads who hung around the back of the school gym in their bomber jackets and oxblood Doc Martins, sharing packs of Benson & Hedges and scowling at people. The subculture also had its music, and a political edge that could be as unpleasant as the scowls.

"You liked this kind of music, and you want to belong. A little bit of reggae, a little bit of ska, and some political ideas that after a bit of growing up I now feel are stupid to believe in," said Taufiq. "Everyone believes in silly things when they're younger," he added quickly. Instead of White Power, some skinheads were into Malay Power, and wore brown shoelaces in their Docs instead of white ones. Although he said he did not know any like this, Taufiq's group were certainly racially aware Malays. The group even included what he called "skinbirds," girls who continued to wear the hijab while dressing like the boys.

Alienation in Singapore's Chinese-dominated society played a part. "If you look at it from the US point of view, the Malays are like the Mexicans or the natives of America; the Chinese are just like the white people coming from England or Ireland; the Indians are just like the blacks." As Taufiq saw it, the different communities in Singapore continued to follow different paths. "The Chinese like to play basketball; the Malays play football; and the Indians, cricket. The Chinese do play football, but they often have their own leagues, sometimes teams from companies. It's very hard for you to get a team you find randomly and find different types of people in one team."[1] For the teenage Taufiq and his young friends, being a skinhead was a defiant way of proclaiming their own identity.

There had been some violence on the fringes of Singapore's skinhead movement. Taufiq remembered a newspaper article about skinhead football fans beating up supporters of the Myanmar national team, but again said that this type of thing was not part of his own experience. There was also friction with local punks, who seemed to be following their own path to defiance and identity.

For Taufiq, sitting there in DeepCuts, wearing immaculate patent-leather loafers and a carefully ironed green striped shirt, being a skinhead had been more about style and belonging than about aggro. "I like the fashion," he admitted. He said that those, like him, who became skinheads mainly for the Levi's jeans and Fred Perry shirts were called "trendy wankers" by the others.

Fittingly, Taufiq's time as a skinhead started to draw to a close during National Service, when everybody else had to get their heads shaved too. It sounded like it had been a formative experience for him. He spent a bit of time in the detention barracks, after being caught helping a friend pass a physical test. But he also found a direction for his sartorial awareness, deciding to become a barber and being introduced to his current boss.

After his return to civilian life, that boss sent Taufiq to train in the Dutch city of Rotterdam. He says he did not know what to expect, having read about a backlash against Muslims following an influx of refugees from Syria. Happily, he says this rumour was a "ghost," and there was no backlash to be seen. Then he fell in with some of Rotterdam's own skinheads, and—in his own words—felt nervous, "because in Singapore we don't have any neo-Nazi skinheads."

At one point, Taufiq felt pressured to accept a beer from one newly made friend, but after declining umpteen times on the grounds of religion, the other man relented. The two started talking, and spoke first about their shared love of skinhead music, and then about Islam. The man's girlfriend said there was hostility to Islam in the group because they did not like people coming to Rotterdam and imposing their way of living on the Dutch. Taufiq seemed to be happy with this explanation, and spoke fondly of the couple, who even defended him in an argument with another

Equatorial Edwardiana: Black and Whites are where the families of the imperial elite recreated suburban Surrey almost 11,000 km from home.

The building blocks of a new society: HDB blocks were an integral part of the reorganisation of Singapore.

A high-rise cure for inequality? The towers and sky gardens of the ground-breaking HDB Pinnacle@Duxton rise 50+ floors above prime real estate.

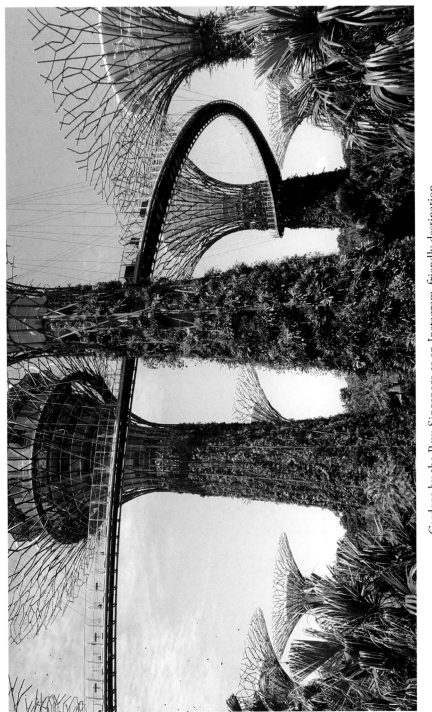

Gardens by the Bay: Singapore as an Instagram-friendly destination.

Looking out across the container ports and Sentosa, to the Straits and the jungles of Indonesia.

The endless whirring toil of containerised globalisation.

Haw Par Villa: where hallucinogenic fantasies from Chinese folklore are given intricate and nightmarish form in plaster and concrete and paint.

AJ and Raymond Goh in Bukit Brown: "I call this an open-air classroom. You learn things the books don't teach you, stories from beyond the grave."

Taufiq Yussef: from Malay skinhead to sharp-dressing, deep-thinking barber.

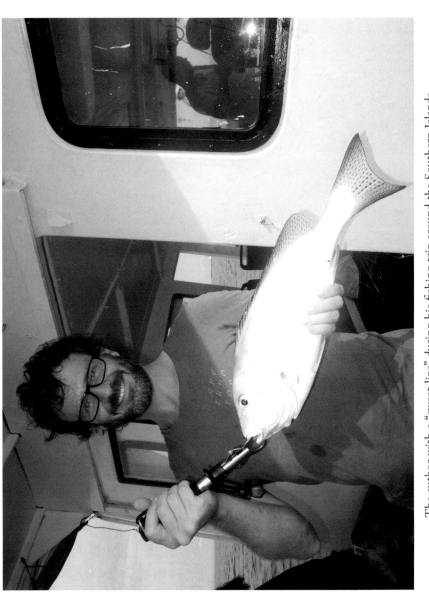

The author with a "sweet lips" during his fishing trip around the Southern Islands.

skinhead, who was less accepting about not drinking beer on Islamic grounds. Taufiq showed me a cherished photo of this Dutch friend of his, stuck on the edge of his barber's mirror. He told me that when he returned to Singapore he tracked down his friend's band, The Firm, on YouTube. According to the video, they are Rotterdam's finest "Oi" band, and play their gigs in front of a knuckleduster logo and the legend "Hated, Feared, Damned." Taufiq's new friend goes bare-chested on stage, which allows the crowd to see his swastika tattoos. But that Taufiq, with his innocent charm and modest good nature, had won over this intimidating man did not surprise me.

Taufiq the barber is now a different man, not least because his hair is carefully sculpted and shiny with hair products, rather than bristling with defiance. He has also learned to embrace Singapore. "You always think the grass is greener on the other side," he said. Back in Rotterdam he had been asked what he loved about his home, and found it difficult to come up with an answer. But when he complained about life in Singapore, he was chided by new friends from the Netherlands, South America, the United States, and Korea. "Every single thing that I said is bad in Singapore is worse in other countries. I came back here, and felt bad because I'd looked down on my country."

So, looking back, was Singapore a strange place for a youth subculture like the skinhead movement to take root? "In Singapore you won't easily be exposed to things," he said, reflectively. The globalised city bobbed about on currents that arrived from elsewhere, on Instagram and a taxi uncle's radio. There was K-pop and Star Wars and Cristiano Ronaldo underpants. Countless hairless legs were adorned with baroque tattoos, but they were Beckham-esque fashion accessories, rather than Lemmy-esque statements of "fuck-you" rebellion.

But Taufiq said that skinhead culture was disappearing. "You only see them at gigs. There are a few old-timers, who are still in bands and stuff." He had lost touch with most of the skinheads he used to know, and the ones he was in contact with were no longer skinheads. "You can live that culture, but for me there's so much more to be than to be a skinhead."

Some of Taufiq's passing observations about Singapore are pertinent to questions about its long-term health. Discounting authentic rebellion, there is little room for mavericks or counter-culture. The invocation of Asian values of family and education can seem like cover for an overly conformist society, heavily circumscribed by exam results and filial piety. Failure and shame sit on the flip-side of the same coin.

Certainly, Singapore does need cohesion. That tiny dinghy on whipping, hostile seas might have capsized during its first uncertain decades without it. But perhaps it now needs something more subtle, as it tries to develop a cutting-edge knowledge economy fit for the mid-twenty-first century. Entrepreneurship depends on iteration, trial and error, and learning from failure. None are particularly encouraged by Singapore's system.

Taufiq's story was also relevant because it spoke about a tangible form of ethnic alienation within Singaporean society. The teetotal Muslim skinheads and beheadscarved skingirls buzz-cut their hair and laced up their boots to express their rebellion against a Chinese-dominated Singaporean conformity, while consciously cleaving to their own Malay and Muslim heritage. Taufiq's comparison between the Malays and Native Americans reflected both a claim to being the indigenous inheritors of the region, and their current relative deprivation and disenfranchisement. Singapore must continue to work hard to make everybody feel like the system is working for them as much as for their neighbours. As I peeled off onto Neil Road, passing the gorgeously ornate sky-blue façade of the *Peranakan* Baba House, I caught a glimpse of a cluster of fifty-storey behemoths that spoke to the same questions of inequality and fairness.

16

PINNACLE@DUXTON

THE INEQUALITY CHALLENGE IN FIFTY STOREYS

Just before Neil Street crossed Cantonment Road, I passed Ji Xiang Confectionery, little more than a hole-in-the-wall at the base of an enormous peach-and-cream-coloured HDB. Its fame belied its humble physical presence. Its business is vibrantly coloured globules of shimmering, patterned sticky sweetness, made of glutinous rice flour, coconut milk and sugar. Singaporeans come from far and wide to buy a beautifully presented tray, with traditional treats tasting of peanuts or corn, yam or salted beans. Personally, I find them hard to like: overly sweet, overly gelatinous, and designed mainly for getting stuck in between one's molars. They are a gummy reminder of the gulf between my life as an expat and the lives and tastes of the many Singaporeans who queue up endlessly at the confectionery.

Life for ordinary Singaporean citizens is built around the three pillars of the island's social contract: the air-conditioned subterranean MRT transport network, the humble hawker centre, and the high-rise HDB. As the country's inhabitants busy themselves with getting incrementally richer, there is an expectation that these three basic aspects of life—transport, food, and housing—will be reliable and affordable.

This contract, however, feels less robust than it used to. Paradoxically, as Singapore has soared to the top of international measures of wealth, a large chunk of its people has felt relatively less well-off. Bundles of S$1,000 notes have not prevented the global inequality debate washing up on its coddled shores. That debate is particularly explosive in Singapore, in part because the island is apparently so rich, but also because the country is built upon such explicitly meritocratic foundations.

A slew of reports of those at the top of the financial heap flaunting their cash has contributed to this tension. In April 2017 a local restaurant owner, Gary Lim, was alleged to have taunted a taxi driver about wealth, after the driver said he could not accept one of Lim's S$1,000 notes. "Look, I have so much money, I can't control myself," he was caught saying on video. "You can't do big things. You know why you are a taxi driver? Because you can't do big things." Social media did the rest. Lim's restaurant was given an online licking, bombarded with a fusillade of outrage. A suitably chastened Gary Lim tried to defuse the situation by offering taxi drivers free meals at his restaurant.[1]

However, the restlessness over perceived inequality is not just about crass behaviour by some of Singapore's super-wealthy. It also concerns the three pillars of that social contract—transport, food, and housing—and how they represent a glass ceiling on the aspirations of a people who have been told they have achieved true affluence.

First, take transport. The MRT works pretty well, and the buses run on time. When you disembark, you tend to have a covered walkway to protect against biblical showers, all the way to the front door of your HDB or the local wet market. Getting around is also cheap. Compared to other rich cities, even taxi fares are a bargain. Citizens may gripe about the mechanical gremlins that undermine the smooth running of MRT trains, but most have not struggled to work against the character-building headwinds of public transport in London, let alone dipped their toes into rush hour in Jakarta or Bangkok. Locals may grumble, but public transport is cheap and efficient, if over-air-conditioned, and ride hailing apps like Grab and Uber have removed the Russian roulette of taxi rides.[2]

Not all expats have shown their appreciation for the public transport system. Take the case of an unfortunate Brit called Anton Casey. He found the buses dirty, and bewildering for his young son. He was uncomfortable with some of the more peculiar habits of taxi uncles. However, rather than take on board Mr Casey's constructive criticism, the people of Singapore hounded him out of the country, and his employer sacked him. Unfair? Not a bit of it.

Anton Casey was a prime example of a globally reviled species. He was not just a banker, but—in the words of a fellow finance worker quoted in the *Daily Mail*—a "pillock."[3] He and his son were only on public transport because his Porsche was temporarily off-road. He put a photo of the bus ride on social media with the caption, "Daddy, where is your car and who are all these poor people?" He complained that he was going to have to wash off "the stench of public transport." He labelled a taxi uncle a retard. As details of his gilded and rather smug life emerged—including his marriage to a former Miss Singapore—the red mist descended, and the metaphorical pitchforks came out.[4] A grovelling apology after a hasty (economy class) escape flight to Australia did little to quell the anger. The second decade of the twenty-first century has scant sympathy for bankers, even in finance-loving, open-for-business Singapore. Especially if the behaviour of the banker in question fits a caricature that could have been drawn up by a red-flag-waving Marxist agitator.

The behaviour of Anton Casey focused attention on one of the great, nigh-unbridgeable divides in Singapore: between the masses on public transport, and the minority who own their own vehicle. A study by Deutsche Bank found that a midsize car that might cost US$24,000 in America or Britain would be US$90,000 in Singapore.[5] When you see a Rolls Royce or Ferrari passing by—as happens with remarkable frequency in some parts of town—you can bank on it costing the owner the better part of a million, and sometimes far, far more.

Expat bankers are not the only ones who receive opprobrium. Wealthy and entitled Singaporeans also scoot by in McLarens and Aston Martins, with all the brotherly compassion of hyenas. The greatest weight of public ire is perhaps reserved for the regional super-rich, from places like mainland China and Indonesia. The flames of this anger have been fanned by incidents such as a fatal crash in 2012, involving a Ferrari and a taxi. The Ferrari 599 GTO sped through a red light on Rochor Road at 178 kph, smashing broadside into a taxi. The taxi driver and his passenger—a Japanese woman—were killed, along with the sports car's driver, Chinese national Ma Chi.[6]

The system underpinning car ownership in Singapore is based on the Certificate of Entitlement. In effect, the COE is a ten-year road license for car ownership, which is transferred with the vehicle if it is sold. When the car is three years old, it has seven years left on its license, and its value is reduced commensurately. After ten years the licensed car loses its right to be on the streets, however fancy and expensive it is. It is then shipped off for sale elsewhere.[7] The ten-year licenses are auctioned off every year, and prices have gone through the roof. Back in January 2009, a Category B COE (for cars above 1600 cc or 97 kW) cost S$200; on 8 November 2017 this price had risen to S$57,414. This sum actually represented a saving compared to the thunderingly high peak price of S$96,210 in January 2013.[8]

On one hand the COE has controlled the number of cars on Singaporean roads. Traffic jams are rarely serious, and certainly nothing compared to the festivals of exhaust fumes and marauding scooters that choke other rising cities of Southeast Asia. In one index compiled by the navigation company TomTom, Jakarta was ranked the second most congested city in the world, Bangkok third, and Singapore fifty-fifth.[9] On the other hand, as only 11 per cent of Singaporeans have their own set of wheels, car ownership is an increasingly visible glass ceiling for most Singaporeans.[10] In Singlish terms, it is a case of "Look, but confirm cannot touch."* Singaporeans certainly have good transport services, but when a VW Golf represents an unobtainable and unthinkable luxury in one of the world's richest countries, aspirations morph into frustrations.

The next pillar is food. Wet markets and the ubiquitous hawker centres are the main vehicles for putting food in the bellies of most Singaporeans. You can *chope* a choice table with a packet of tissues, feast on chicken rice, *chai tow kway*, or a nourishing plate of live bullfrog porridge, and have your tray collected by a seventy-year-old who failed to save wisely for retirement, all for a matter of pennies.† Beyond these, food can become ruinously expensive, and the thought of a meal out with alcohol causes beads of sweat to form across even the most air-conditioned of brows. I have seen small punnets of (Japanese) strawberries selling for S$70 in supermarkets, have sipped S$20 pints of beer guiltily, and treated the discovery of a decent bottle of wine for less than S$40 as a staggering coup. These are prices that distort reality and shock visitors. It is true that many of those treats apply to those with expat expectations of food and drink, but even so there is a significant step up between what a typical citizen can afford, and what the minority treats itself to.

* Colloquial Singaporean English is known as Singlish.
† *Choping* is an informal reservation system whereby restaurant-goers stake their claim to a seat by leaving tissue packets at the table, which some foreigners find extremely aggravating at busy times.

The third pillar is housing. Some 85 per cent of the population lives in public housing (although usually as owners of ninety-nine-year leases), while the wealthy few enjoy private housing resembling upscale holiday resorts, with infinity pools and names like Cape Royale and Nassim Regency. The Reignwood Hamilton Scotts condominium has a car elevator that allows you to park your spanking-new Lamborghini inside your fifteenth-floor apartment, visible both to guests in your sitting room and the poor schmucks on the number 171 bus. The Interlace is a jumble of thirty-one otherwise innocuous six-storey Lego blocks: more of a stack than an interlace, to be honest, but that is splitting hairs. Either way, this striking, massive cluster-stack that won the 2015 World Building of the Year award has the style and cachet that a four-square concrete HDB can only dream of.

Private owners do not just get to live in architectural fantasies and Instagram holiday complexes; they have also benefitted enormously from galloping price inflation. Singapore's safe-haven status has contributed to this, with hot money flooding in to the property market from other parts of Asia, where the rule of law is slightly less reliable and currencies fluctuate like monsoon winds. The bank accounts of those lucky enough to own property have thus been boosted by millions (some swiftly regurgitated in Porsche and Ferrari dealerships). HDBs have also risen somewhat in value, but their lease owners are firmly on the other side of the glass ceiling.

This is inequality of a different sort to that experienced in the West. In Singapore, people are—apparently—living the dream. In fifty years it has gone from jungly post-colonial island to one of the richest countries on earth: the IMF listed Singapore third in the world by GDP per capita in 2016, behind Qatar and Luxembourg, but ahead of places like Brunei, Norway and the United Arab Emirates.[11] The country has achieved this without digging up vast quantities of hydrocarbons, or offering kleptocrats zero-tax ways to hide whatever they have stolen from their people. The typical Singaporean has financial security and a level of material wealth far beyond their parents' dreams. Real poverty is rare.

And yet, the typical Singaporean is angry. That gap between what the masses can expect and what the small numbers on the other side of that impenetrable glass ceiling are enjoying seems unbridgeable. Constant messaging about their world-leading education system is harder for Singaporeans to swallow when so many of the top jobs still go to expats and a gilded layer of citizens, who then enjoy the cars, condos and restaurants that average people cannot afford. There is also a generational element to this feeling of inequality. For the Pioneer Generation, jobs, prosperity and security were the features of a utopia worth striving for. But the younger generation that bounces around the glitzy shopping malls of today, glued to their miniature screens, has never had to deal with the same hardships. They expect much more, but bang their heads against the reality of that glass ceiling.

Findings such as those by the Economist Intelligence Unit's cost-of-living survey, which in 2017 named Singapore as the most expensive city in the world for the fourth year running, usually appear in the local press with semi-official disclaimers about expat appetites for wine and condo-living.[12] During the 2014 Budget debate in Parliament, Deputy Prime Minister Tharman Shanmugaratnam pointed explicitly to supposedly expat-specific expenses such as "imported cheese, filet mignon, Burberry-type raincoats, four best seats in a theatre, three-course high-end dinners for four people."[13] The implication was that for Singaporeans, life is not expensive, at least if they are happy with public transport, hawker-centre food, and an HDB flat. I am not sure this message resonated with citizens to the extent that Shanmugaratnam had intended.

Not only is there an apparent glass ceiling for these three staples of the social contract, but belief in the mechanism that underpins Singaporean society—meritocracy—is faltering. "The quality of a people determines the outcome of a nation," Lee Kuan Yew once noted. "It is how you select your people, how you train them, how you organise them, and ultimately how you manage them that makes the difference." If you are good enough—the message goes—you get the job, backed up by the ethos that in such a small nation there is no room for wasting talent.

However, even without the wealthy expats and the mega-rich Asians, studies confirm the impression that Singaporean society is only fluid up to the point it reaches an increasingly impermeable top stratum. Although 85 per cent of the population lives in public housing, one study found that those living in private properties, or studying at the top universities, are much better connected to that small minority of people in the same position as themselves than they are to others.[14] The privilege of those at the top is increasingly being reinforced by the social circles in which they move, while those outside the top feel excluded. Such dynamics are not uncommon in the modern world, but they are particularly destructive in a country as small as Singapore, with such a public commitment to mobility and meritocracy.[15] One survey suggested that 60 per cent of young people have considered moving abroad in their search for work opportunities and affordable living.[16]

Concerns about the fracturing of Singaporean meritocratic culture were heightened by a strange episode that surfaced in the media a couple of years after Lee Kuan Yew's death. It took the form of a feud, centred on a clause in Lee's will, stating that the family home should be demolished after his death. This was partly due to privacy issues, but also because of his laudable fears that a personality cult might otherwise develop around him. After all, despite the extremely high regard in which most Singaporeans hold their former leader, there are no streets or statues honouring his memory. LKY may have been a great man, but this should not confer an advantage to his family.

Lee's house itself is a lovely (if decaying) five-bedroom bungalow in a prime spot on Oxley Road that used to be plantations.
(Newspapers estimated that the plot would now be worth north
of S\$20 million, simply because of its location.) The question of
what would happen to the house hit the headlines in a quite
sensational way in 2017, when the two siblings of Prime Minister
Lee Hsien Loong alleged in a statement that their brother was
"driven by a desire for power and personal popularity [that was]
inextricably linked to Lee Kuan Yew's legacy." As such, he had
resisted their father's belief that the house should be demolished
(once his daughter Lee Wei Ling, who looked after him in his
old age, no longer lived there), in the hope of using it to burnish
his own image. They also alleged that their brother was trying to
establish a political dynasty, and stated that "We do not trust
Hsien Loong as a brother or as a leader."[17] Prime Minister Lee
explicitly denied these charges in Parliament. He said his son had
no interest in politics, and joked that if he needed the house to
exploit his father's "aura" even after thirteen years as prime minister, "I must be in a pretty sad state."[18]

Whatever the veracity of these claims and the prime minister's
rebuttal, the mere fact that this squalid squabble surfaced in
public is extraordinary. It has continued to rumble on, largely
through Facebook posts. There is a very real risk that it will
further undermine citizens' faith in the disinterested and meritocratic nature of political power in Singapore. This has implications for public faith in the disinterested and meritocratic nature
of society itself, and in the legitimacy of the political class.

The anger about perceived inequality is having an impact on
public and political life, with the blogosphere and social media
allowing Singaporeans an often-novel medium for venting their
frustrations. There has been increased animosity from some
towards foreigners, whether expats or domestic workers, labourers or Asian "Rich Kids of Instagram." The Western expats take

the best jobs, so the complaints go, and the domestic workers clutter up public transport (try taking the 174 bus between Bukit Timah and the Filipino multipurpose hang-out of Lucky Plaza on a Sunday). A third of the island's day-to-day population is non-Singaporean, and balancing interests between the three pots—citizens, highly skilled expats, and low-skilled migrants— is no easy job.

The Singfirst website (with the tagline, "Fair Society, Strong Families and Esteemed People") notes that, "For the past 50 years, Singaporeans have become secondary to the relentless pursuit of economic growth." It explicitly blames the "elitist" policies of the PAP for turning Singapore "into a highly divided society with extreme inequalities of wealth and income between the rich and the poor and a shrinking middle class squeezed in between." The list of complaints goes on: tax rates are designed to encourage foreign multinationals and their expat workforce; cheap low-skilled labour, on the other hand, depresses wages and leads to overcrowding; the island has become too expensive for the locals; National Service requirements disadvantage Singaporean men. There is a real need, it says, to dissociate Singapore's entire model of growth from "multinational corporations and foreign labour."[19] Meanwhile, successful applications for "permanent resident" status for foreigners (giving them a raft of advantages, without full citizenship) have fallen dramatically. The requirement to "show adequate local integration," and the role of committees of local people in assessing each application's merits, led to a 76 per cent failure rate in 2016, compared to 30 percent in 2009.[20]

In political terms, the fall-out from this rising disquiet has been dramatic. In the 2011 general elections, the PAP's support fell from 75.3 per cent to 60.1 per cent, and the PAP presidential candidate won only 35.2 per cent of the vote in a field of five. There were further PAP by-election defeats in 2012 and 2013. In

Singaporean terms, this qualified as an earthquake. In the words of Gillian Koh of the Institute of Policy Studies, as Singapore has edged towards a "winners and losers" society, this has translated into the type of politics "where people have less trust in the established political institutions and political leaders because they think that it's the establishment that has done them in."[21]

The governmental response has been to consult, and to push money towards those on smaller incomes. Its analysis reflects that of governments elsewhere, which recognise a divide between those who feel more able to embrace the challenges of an open, globalised economy, and those who desire more protection. In Singapore's case those on smaller incomes are called "heartland-ers." There have also been initiatives to ensure that Singaporean citizens are first in the queue for available jobs. According to something called the "Fair Consideration Framework," this includes measures to "strengthen the Singaporean core in the workforce."[22] In 2016, the minister for manpower, Lim Swee Say, said there was a two-pronged approach to doing this. First, 100 companies which had not made reasonable efforts to strengthen the Singaporean core would come under closer scru-tiny. Twenty per cent of those identified had subsequently improved, but the others still remained under Mr Lim's steely gaze. Secondly, those exhibiting exemplary fair and progressive human capital practices were given "differentiated treatment."[23]

On a purely anecdotal and personal level, expat friends of mine suddenly found that they were frozen out of competing for jobs, no matter how stellar their qualifications and how evident the lack of local talent in their sector. As we pulled on our boots for our Wednesday-night football games, my friends from Britain, the Netherlands, and Australia all decried the hoops they were being forced to jump through in recruiting for their own com-panies. After two or three wasteful and expensive months, they said with a rueful shake of their heads, they almost always ended up having to bring in somebody from abroad anyway.

Meanwhile, at a more quantifiable level, there has been a sudden reversal in the numbers of non-resident Singaporeans on the island, after many years of increase. In 1970 foreign workers made up 3.2 per cent of the population; in 2010 they made up 34.7 percent.[24] In 2008 their population increased by around 190,000, or almost 20 per cent, compared to a 1 per cent rise in the numbers of Singaporean citizens. Although this was a bumper year, there were steady increases each year (often in double-figure percentage terms) up until 2012, just after the fateful election. The rate of increase then fell steadily. In 2017, numbers decreased by a hefty 27,000.[25]

These figures often represent skilled workers that are in high demand, not just in Singapore but across the world. The Indian IT trade industry body Nasscom said it had seen a sharp drop-off in visa acceptances.[26] In 2017, their president, R. Chandrashskhar, said there were fewer than 10,000 Indian techies employed in Singapore; they used to issue almost that number of permits every single year.[27] This is despite a continued rise in demand for IT workers: adverts for people with those skills grew by 30 per cent in the fourth quarter of 2016.[28]

Although it is easy to seek out parallels for this kind of immigrant-sceptic regimen, Singapore's size makes this drop-off a bigger deal than elsewhere. The US under President Trump may restrict access to Green Cards, but it is still the US, with hefty internal resources at its disposal. Some might also condemn the UK, as the Brexit noose draws tighter, for cutting its nose off to spite its face over EU immigration, but the country still has 60 million people and an enormously varied economy. Not so, Singapore. It is, remember, that dinghy adrift on the open sea of globalisation. If it needs an extra shipmate to fix a sail or add navigational expertise, it cannot necessarily find it among the dinghy's native population. Its miracle was explicitly built upon the backs of multinational companies and highly skilled and internationally mobile workers. The balance between the needs of its labour market and the interests and feelings of its citizenry—given voice in a new age of social media—is a difficult one for the government to get right.

Part of the answer has lain in Singapore simply pretending it is bigger than it is. In effect its hinterland for its labour market extends in several concentric circles beyond its borders: the first takes in daily commuters from places like Johor Bahru, just over the Malaysian border; the second takes in workers in the factories that are, in effect, lower-wage extensions of its domestic industries, in particular in Batam and other neighbouring Indonesian Riau Islands. Beyond that, there are the foreign domestic workers (FDWs), from Indonesia, the Philippines, and Myanmar, and the manual workers from Bangladesh and India. There are higher-skilled workers from places like India, for instance in the heavy industrial jobs that Singaporeans now shun. Then there are the expats, at the top end of the skill spectrum, from across the entire world.

Changing the balance of this labour market mix is not straightforward and requires a guiding governmental hand that feels disconcertingly statist. Highly skilled expats and the multinationals and financial institutions that hire them have been at the forefront of Singapore's determined drive up the economic value chain, so restrictions on their numbers can have a very real impact on the viability of its high-end economy. At the other end of the skills range, to restrict the number of FDWs that could come into Singapore would be highly contentious, as their unheralded labours are crucial for keeping Singapore functioning on the home front. However, as the political economist Linda Lim has pointed out, economic planners also have to calibrate the demand side of the labour equation, to ensure that incentives do not go to the sectors that favour foreign workers.[29] This includes construction, where the supply of foreign workers (and the reluctance of Singaporeans to follow a career in the sector) has led to persistent low wages and low productivity.[30] Similarly,

the easy import of FDWs means that a professional service sector, including ones that help care for an ageing population, has
never been established. Professor Kishore Mahbubani shares the
sentiment that the easy foreign labour supply has a distorting
effect on the economy and could exacerbate social pressures. "It
became a kind of opium," he told me. "You take in foreign workers, and the foreign workers increase your GNP very easily. But
then it creates social problems. When you try to get on the train
in the morning, the MRT is full."

The Filipino and Indonesian governments have played their part
in protecting the rights of their migrant workers. In 2016,
President Jokowi announced that he wanted to improve standards
for FDWs from Indonesia, by giving them better training, certifi-
cation, regular hours, and dormitory accommodation. Needless to
say, he also wanted the 125,000 Indonesian FDWs in Singapore to
be treated better.[31] The Filipino government has also made it clear
that conditions for its workers need to be safeguarded.

It is to be hoped that this message gets through to the minority of Singaporeans who treat their domestic employees abomi-
nably. In March 2017 Lim Choon Hong and Chong Sui Foon
were sentenced to jail for starving their maid, Thelma Oyasan
Gawidan, a forty-year-old Filipina woman. In just fifteen
months, on a diet of white bread and instant noodles, her weight
dropped from 49 kilograms to 29 kilograms, before she escaped
to a migrants' refuge. In another case, an agent complained to a
prospective employer that one particular FDW was finding it
hard to get a job, because she insisted on two days off each
month: "Is she here to work or enjoy a holiday?" the agent asked.
One hard-working FDW who lived near us worked seven days a
week, every day of the year. That included Christmas Day and
Easter Day, despite the crucifixes and symbols of Christian devotion that hung on the family's walls.

* * *

Just beyond Ji Xiang Confectionery, across Cantonment Road, an interesting public policy experiment towered up into the sky. Seven speckled blocks, each the dimensions of a fifty-something-storey domino, were threaded together by two high-rise belts of shrub-encrusted "skybridges." Collectively, on a plot not much larger than two football fields, they comprised the world's tallest public residential building. The Pinnacle@Duxton contains 1,858 swanky apartments, thousands of shiftable lightweight concrete walls, and the hopes of the Singaporean government.

The Pinnacle project was part of the fight against the growing perception of inequality, and was designed to show to the Singaporean citizen that even public housing can be aspirational. Anyone, within a daily ticketed limit, is allowed to take the lifts up to the fiftieth-floor skybridge to catch awe-inspiring views that stretch across Singapore and to Indonesia (the bridge halfway up is reserved for residents). The skybridges are, in the best Singaporean tradition, not merely walkways but true gardens—so much so that there are signs prohibiting camping—and gambling. A double set of railings keeps people behind a set of tracks that are used for window-cleaning bogies, and vertiginous oblivion.

In August 2010, Prime Minister Lee Hsien Loong gave his Independence Day address to the nation from the fifty-first floor of the Pinnacle@Duxton. Fittingly, it was a speech that emphasised that the government's goal was "for all Singaporeans to enjoy the fruits of growth." He tipped his hat to "valid concerns" about immigration, while talking up the provision of services, including swankier HDBs.[32]

The supremely swanky Pinnacle@Duxton is indeed almost everything that its designers hoped for. It demonstrates that a humble HDB need not be humble at all, but can smash through that glass ceiling that separates the 85 per cent who live in public housing from the Jet Set. This it does admirably. However, the project also unwittingly reinforces the idea that some Singaporeans have been unfairly rewarded by the lottery of life. More than 5,000 people paid the S$10 application charge for a flat in the complex when it was first built. The lucky ones were not allowed to sell up for the first five years of their occupation, but since then many have made handsome profits, perhaps reflecting unrealistically low initial sales prices for such a prime and prestigious site. In 2004 a five-room flat cost the new owners between S$345,100 and S$439,400. In 2016 one of them sold for S$1.12 million. This was an HDB record, although at least ten other Pinnacle@Duxton flats had already made it into seven figures.[33] In effect, noted one property analysis website in 2015, getting a flat in the complex was akin to winning the lottery.[34] As symbols go, this hardly serves to emphasise the innate fairness of Singaporean society.

Pinnacle@Duxton may be Ground Zero for sprucing up the Singaporean social contract, but elsewhere entire districts have been built to match the shifting expectations of the city state's people. Take the Punggol area, in the north of the island. It has been redeveloped as a tropical resort wonderland, where swanky new HDBs like Northshore Cove rub shoulders unashamedly with full-force private condos such as A Treasure Trove. The blurb for the "new executive condominium" of Twin Waterfalls speaks of waking up "to a view of a tropical paradise, every morning" in the "charming waterfront town of Punggol." There's a Wild West-themed Punggol Ranch, with concrete chalets painted to look like wagons, and a horse statue clad in ill-fitting sheets of fake turf. You can arrange a horse ride at the Gallop Stables and play a game called "soccer golf." The hungry can head to destination restaurants such as House of Seafood and Leong Ji Signatures, just past two murky green teardrop-shaped pools where turtles raise their heads to the sky and gasp for air. Citizens wobble unconvincingly along the boardwalk on hired bicycles, stopping every few dozen metres to adjust the volume of the music blaring from cell phones. Punggol Beach, where hundreds of Chinese were massacred by the Japanese during Operation *Sook Ching*, is now covered in curiously rounded stones. What was Serangoon Island, just off the Punggol shore in the Straits of Johor, has now been rebranded as Coney Island. It is a very measured attempt to update the social contract for a generation not used to the uncertainties faced by their parents. The message is that it is not just the lottery winners of the Pinnacle who can see their Instagram aspirations realised: the resort lifestyle is for everybody, including both the annoyed and the complacent.

17

CHINATOWN

74.3 PER CENT OF THE POPULATION

The meanders of Neil Road led first to a building site and then to the Buddha Tooth Relic Temple and Museum. Despite its Tang Dynasty styling and layer-upon-layer of roofing, the temple was only opened in 2007, as a complex catering to both locals and tourists. As such, it was a fitting introduction to Singapore's somewhat sterilised, visitor-friendly Chinatown, which stretched out along the edges of South Bridge Road.

Chinatown was demarcated in Raffles' Town Plan of 1822, in keeping with the British attempt to give each geographic and linguistic community a distinct area. Its original name was *Niu che shui* or "bullock water cart," named after the carts used to supply fresh water. By 1836 it was the largest district thanks to 13,700 Chinese settlers, and a seething and chaotic quarter. Now, in an echo of the Buddha Tooth Relic Temple and Museum, it is a rather sanitised tourist magnet, full of spick-and-span shop houses, and stalls laden with red-and-gold keepsakes.

Most of those early settlers came to the Straits as coolies, carried down from China by the trade winds of the junk season.

Some were "free," which meant that they had paid their own way and were free to find work for themselves. In contrast, "credit" coolies were indentured and worked under binding contracts. They were brought to Singapore in the holds of ships, and kept there while the crew sold those contracts on. Some ended up in coolie holding stations, which have their modern-day analogue in the maid agencies dotted around the island's less-glitzy malls, with their benches of wary-eyed young archipelagic women.

There was plenty of work for these unskilled labourers across Malaya and the Straits Settlements, from pulling rickshaws to stevedoring, although fluctuations in supply and demand could mean sudden collapses in wages. There was a surge in demand from the 1870s, as plantation agriculture and mining took off in Malaya (and convict Indian labour was brought to an end), met by a large increase in immigration from southern China. The coolie trade began to die out in the early years of the twentieth century, and indentured labour was abolished in the 1914 Labour Contracts Ordinance.

Chinatown was governed indirectly through community leaders. This led in turn to the establishment of mutual aid societies, based around clans. The first secret society, *Ghee Hin*, grew out of one of these. In the 1820s it provided jobs, security, and accommodation, while also helping the police by turning in those who broke the law. As it grew, *Ghee Hin* began to control pepper and gambier plantations and the rice trade, while also developing interests in prostitution and opium.

This increase in power and wealth began to attract the attention of rivals. These included ambitious splinter groups, along with new Teochew and Hakka arrivals. In March 1846 these new rivalries broke out into violence, with the "Huey Funeral Disturbances." When a 6,000-strong funeral procession for the *Ghee Hin* leader Ho Ah Yam was diverted towards Telok Ayer, it was confronted by up to 3,000 armed members of rival society

Ghee Hok. In 1851 the "Anti-Catholic riots" broke out as *Ghee Hin*'s control of the plantations was challenged by members who had become Christian. *Ghee Hin* members attacked plantations in Kranji and Bukit Timah, before the Christians retaliated. Within a week, almost 500 lay dead and twenty-seven plantations were damaged. Another 500 were killed in the 1854 "Hokkien-Teochew riots" that began with a trivial dispute over rice prices, before escalating into fights with spears and sticks on North Bridge Road.[1]

Violence was not just confined to the secret societies. In 1876 the British tried to regulate the remittance business, setting up the Chinese Sub-Post Office to collect all China-bound letters and remittances for a fixed price. This undermined a lucrative (and monopoly) business for the societies, and Teochew merchants started spreading rumours that it was aimed at hurting the entire Chinese community, along with offers of rewards for those who decapitated Post Office staff. Riots broke out, leaving several dead.

The secret societies were very much an issue at the time of Rudyard Kipling's visit. He noted that the Straits Settlement Council was trying to tackle them, when a riot brewed up over the seemingly innocuous issue of clearing over-hanging verandas. "A Chinaman must have a secret society of some kind," he wrote. "He has been bred up in a country where they were necessary to his comfort, his protection, and the maintenance of his scale of wages from time immemorial, and he will carry them with him as he will carry his opium and his coffin." Kipling also remarked on how the physical presence of the Chinese had come to dominate the island. "I knew I had touched the borders of the Celestial Empire when I was thoroughly impregnated with the reek of Chinese tobacco, a fine-cut, greasy, glossy weed..."[2]

Inevitably, the authorities began systematic efforts to monitor and control the societies. In 1877 it set up a Chinese Protectorate that forced them to register. This was not welcomed. The first "Protector of Chinese," William A. Pickering, was attacked by triads in 1887. Two years later, a Societies Ordinance was introduced to abolish them across the Straits Settlements. Although this met with success, it did not mean the end of the societies: some became social organisations, while others kept their criminal activities going underground. The remnants of the secret societies were still going in the last days of empire, with crackdowns such as Operation Dagger, Operation *Pereksa*, and Operation *Sapu* in the late 1950s.

Life as a coolie in Singapore may have been preferable to a miserable existence as a peasant in China, but it was still quite horrible. Home was usually a sleeping shift on a mattress on a bunk in a tiny and unventilated back room, with a small cubby hole for personal effects. In 1924 a rickshaw-puller earned around 20 to 24 Straits dollars a month, and was able to send up to $10 of that back to his family in China.

Many coolies sought escape from their hard lives through opium. It offered oblivion. One traveller wrote of the arms and legs of one smoker hanging down "as if they did not belong to him; and he leered on us with meaningless, but very good-natured smiles. The effect of excess of opium is more like idiocy, than normal intoxication. It steals away the brain like drink."[3]

Singapore's first coroner, Robert Little, documented the preparation of opium in the mid-nineteenth century. He described a process that brings to mind modern-day backyard manufacture of crystal meth. There was boiling and straining through paper and cloth, and mixtures with the consistency of black treacle. As well as the main product, a residue called *tye* was sold off cheaply. Those unable to afford even that could buy the waste *samshing* ashes left behind after *tye* had been smoked.

In 1848 there were forty-five licensed outlets in town, and six in rural areas (plus other illicit outlets). Shops selling opium were required to have a red board hanging outside, printed with the license number. The opium itself was sold in little triangular packets made of bamboo leaves and paper, stamped with "Monopoly Opium" in red letters. The most popular type was *three hoon*, containing 17.5 grains—enough for six smokes. It cost 40 cents, which to a coolie might be half a day's wages.

There was an inevitability about opium's place in Singaporean society. Trade in the narcotic contributed to the foundation of Singapore, thanks to the realities of British trade policies, and its strategic position between China and India. Between 1814 and 1818, opium accounted for between 30 and 50 per cent of Bengal's exports to China and the East Indies. It was even used as a form of currency during Singapore's early years. As mentioned earlier, William Farquhar helped fund the island's administration by auctioning off monopoly concessions. Domestic use was encouraged, especially among coolies: it brought in money while damping down the febrile, strained atmosphere of a hard-working, hard-living port city full of desperate, mostly male immigrants.

Pressure for a clampdown on the pervasive trade in opium was growing by the turn of the twentieth century. At that time there were well over 500 licensed opium shops in the colony. Measures were introduced gradually. In 1907 the Singapore Anti-Opium Society was founded, and in 1909 the Chandu Revenue Ordinance ended the revenue farming system. In 1928 opium smokers had to register, and in 1933 they were required to show a permit (including a photograph), with limits on how much they could buy each day. That year a rehabilitation clinic was set up by the Anti-Opium Society's president, Chen Su Lan. In 1934 the register was closed, other than for medicinal uses. One study by the Anti-Opium Society in 1935 suggested that 10 per cent of the adult Chinese population in Malaya, rich and poor, was addicted. In 1943, during the Japanese occupation, opium was outlawed.[4]

Despite prohibition in the post-war years, opium-smoking continued into the 1980s. But by then it ran up against the will of the PAP, which was busy transforming Singapore into something far more wholesome. The age of opium was over, and the flipside of the economic miracle was a cleansing of Singaporean society, with drug abuse being one of the law and justice system's main targets. Woe betide anybody who is caught with drugs at Changi airport.[5] The narcotic crutch of so many coolies and labourers passed into the smoky depths of the island's history.

At the other end of the socioeconomic scale from the opium-addled misery of the coolies was a class of Chinese moguls, who made fortunes, built influence, and mixed with the cream of colonial society. One was a man named after a place called Huangpo, in Canton, who arrived in Singapore at the age of fifteen in 1830, not long after it was established. The father of young Whampoa owned a shop that sold beef and bread, at the junction of Boat Quay and Bonham Street. When his father died, he expanded into new areas, such as ice-making. Through his shrewd business brain and ambition, allied to the booming port, Whampoa became one of Singapore's wealthiest private individuals, with a string of honours and achievements. He was the first Chinese to be a member of the colony's Legislative Council, was the Singapore Consul for Russia, China, and Japan, and set up Raffles Girls' School. In the George MacDonald novel *Flashman's Lady*, he appears with a perpetually full glass of sherry in his hand.

18

HONG LIM PARK

A VERY QUIET SPEAKERS' CORNER

Hong Lim Park is an unexceptional oasis of (near-)rectangular calm in the centre of Singapore's Downtown Core. As a location it only stands out for two reasons. Firstly, it is edged on one side by the stunning Parkroyal Hotel, which looks rather like a giant 3D-printed wedding cake that has been crashed into a garden centre by joy-riding aliens. Secondly, the park contains an area called, without a hint of irony, Speakers' Corner.

The original Speakers' Corner is over in colonial HQ, in a leafy angle of London's Hyde Park. There, cranks, malcontents, and visionaries roll up, climb onto their soapboxes, and let rip with their searing insights into politics, the nature of being, or simply the benefits of mass vegetarianism. It has been a crucible of white hot debate since the late nineteenth century, peppered with nutty conspiracy theories and revealed truth. As I passed by Hong Lim Park during the lunching hour on that March day, however, the Singaporean version was conspicuously empty. One man was asleep on a park bench, his plastic sandals neatly arranged below, next to a tied plastic bag containing his hawker centre lunch. The thick-bladed, ever-resilient tropical grass was disturbed by nothing more troublesome than a pair of quizzical mynah birds. Otherwise, nothing.

This was hardly a surprise: Singapore is never going to be a soapbox free-for-all. Anybody wishing to galvanise the world with their insights, or gather to protest some iniquity or other, first has a raft of regulations to negotiate. It seems there are over a dozen pages of terms and conditions, and a further set of laws and constitutional clauses. Some topics will always be out of bounds. If you use your soapbox for anything that might cause undue friction between Singapore's different ethnic or religious groups, for example, you can expect to see the inside of a police station rather quickly.

The rulebook, and the willingness of the state to enforce it, can be intimidating. A *Reuters* report in 2017, about a protest against a 30 per cent rise in water bills, contained the allegation that many others would have turned up had they not been afraid to join the protest. The police issued a stern counter-complaint, saying the *Reuters* report gave a "false and misleading" picture of how Speakers' Corner worked.[1]

Other public displays of a political nature could also fall foul of the law. In July 2017, a migrant worker called Prabagaran Srivijayan was executed for drug smuggling. He had never admitted his guilt, and human rights groups had called on the government to reconsider his case. When seventeen people held a vigil the night before his execution, they were told they were not allowed to light any candles. The candles were then confiscated, and the participants were informed that they faced charges of being in an unauthorised public gathering under Section 16(2)(a) of the Public Order Act, Chapter 257A.[2]

The godfather of this uncompromising line on public dissent was Lee Kuan Yew. He recognised the dangers that destabilising forces, including communism, might wreak upon his newly independent nation. This went back to the days of the *Konfrontasi* with Indonesia, and the split within the PAP between Lee's own moderates and the radical hotheads of Lim Chin Seong. He drew lessons from the industrial unrest he saw in post-war Singapore, seeing how strikes and high wages made foreigners nervous about investing their money there. "I had to fight left-wingers, Communists, pro-Communist groups who had killer squads," he told the *New York Times*, as he approached his ninetieth year. "If I didn't have the guts and gumption to take them on, there wouldn't be a Singapore."[3]

Lee Kuan Yew's guts and gumption could be applied quite ruthlessly. When the implacable opposition politician J.B. Jeyaretnam died at the age of eighty-two, *The Economist* described him as "a courteous, dignified figure, vaguely reminiscent, in his muttonchop whiskers, of a Victorian statesman."[4] However, to the Singaporean state, Mr Jeyaretnam had been a mortal enemy. In 1981 he had been elected to parliament, winning a by-election after campaigning on local issues. Three years later, he increased his majority. In 1986, however, he was found guilty of perjury, jailed, and banned from parliament and legal practice for five years. This was overturned by the Privy Council in London, who ruled that Mr Jeyaretnam had been the victim of what it called a "grievous injustice." He returned to parliament in 1997 for a few more years, but in the meantime, he was slowly ground down in the courts. In total, he ended up paying around S$1.6 million in damages and costs. The fact that Mr Jeyaretnam had maintained his opposition to the way the PAP was running Singapore was testament to his character. That the PAP continued to wield a big stick against his sustained opposition was testament to their determination not to let anybody undermine what they were working hard to achieve.

The message from this was clear to all: if you opposed the government, and in doing so endangered Singapore, you would be dealt with. The miracle was too important, and too fragile, to brook any significant internal resistance. Mr Lee was characteristically blunt when commenting on Mr Jeyaretnam's travails. "If you are a troublemaker," he said in 1997, "it's our job to politically destroy you. As long as J.B. Jeyaretnam stands for what he stands for—a thoroughly destructive force—we will knock him." He went on with matter-of-fact menace, "Everybody knows that in my bag I have a hatchet, and a very sharp one. You take me on, I take my hatchet, we meet in the cul-de-sac."[5]

The cul-de-sac where LKY took on perceived troublemakers was often the courts, where the authorities wielded wallet-draining defamation suits like particularly sharp hatchets. In 2017, *The Economist* published a report that questioned aspects of the government's line on freedom of speech, and its use of the courts to harry opponents. The report noted that criticism often resulted in defamation suits over "accusations that American or European politicians would have shrugged or laughed off." It cited a Supreme Court decision to uphold the conviction of three activists who had protested the management of the Central Provident Fund. They had been found guilty of creating a public nuisance and disrupting an event being held in Hong Lim Park.[6] This report, entitled "Grumble and be damned," elicited a tart response from Singapore's high commissioner in London, Foo Chi Hsia. The protestors "were not charged for criticising the government," admonished High Commissioner Foo, "but for loutishly barging into a performance by a group of special-education-needs children, frightening them and denying them the right to be heard."[7]

Despite the high commissioner's suitably uncompromising letter, Singapore's pugilistic mix of authoritarianism and democracy is not one-dimensional. A key lesson of the 2011 general election, for instance, when the ruling party suffered significant electoral losses, is that the PAP cannot afford to let other parties appeal to the day-to-day trials and tribulations of people's lives while they busy themselves sorting out headline issues like Singapore's economy. This is particularly dangerous in a social media age, when dissenters need not apply for a permit to let off steam at Speakers' Corner.

A key element of the PAP's solution has been to ramp up its community-based ground war. In my own old corner of Singapore, a leafy area stuffed with expats and home-grown millionaires, the local MP was near-omnipresent. Every two months, the glossy "We Love Bukit Timah" would be popped through the letterbox. The "bi-monthly newsletter of the Bukit Timah Division Citizens' Consultative Committee" was full of vivid colours, Facebook contact details, QR codes, and a large photo of the MP ("@SimAnn.SG") having a selfie taken with a grinning school-girl. Out of twenty-six photos in the first issue of the newsletter, in 2017, the indefatigable Sim Ann appeared in seventeen.

There were posters and billboards in every park and public space, advertising community get-togethers: a visit to the Singapore Biennale, and numerous opportunities to watch *Star Wars* films with neighbours. The Bukit Timah Lunar New Year Celebration Dinner featured "Special Guest: Grassroots Advisor Ms Sim Ann—Senior Minister of State, Ministry of Culture, Community and Youth, Ministry of Trade and Industry." The meagre S$2 entrance fee for "Dads for science @ the park" included an "Appreciation Ceremony for National Servicemen" marking fifty years of Singapore's National Service, an opportunity to "win prizes by doing fun science activities together!", and a world of burgers, ice-cream and lucky draws. MP Sim Ann was of course the guest of honour there, too.

This reinvigorated ground war is not just aimed at reminding Singaporeans how hard Sim Ann and her colleagues are working to make their lives better. It also has the objective of keeping the government plugged in to local community issues. Various committees and local representatives are in place to engage with people on a block-by-block, estate-by-estate basis. They can identify and sympathise with the annoyances and challenges that people face in their real lives, and either find local solutions, or pass the issue up the chain. The PAP government has always gained legitimacy through its sheer effectiveness, so its campaigning on the ground is really a case of keeping some of the focus on the level of the HDB block.

When I discussed this with Nominated Member of Parliament Kuik Shiao-Yin, she said that the ground war had been an effective response to the PAP's setbacks in 2011. She put that result down to a mixture of two types of opposition voter: there were some deeply disgruntled Singaporeans, fired up by online conversations with other malcontents; and there was a stable of voters who were simply angry, who wanted to send a message to the government. The response from the government, to listen and act on the day-to-day issues, was then enough to appease the latter group and persuade them that they were being listened to. "That is what people want," she said. "They allowed people to express anger, and then did something about it. Anger is healthy; contempt is the dysfunctional version."

The problem for the government, however, is that legitimacy in the social media age is no longer just about performance, but also about process. Beyond the economy and the stratospheric international rankings, those moaning about the way the government runs its business can now take their grumbles and gripes online. With Singaporeans having easy access to platforms that allow frank and safe discussions about fiery issues, the government can no longer be sure that the way it controls a situation will not become a contested issue itself—a state of affairs that can lead to healthy anger becoming dysfunctional contempt.

An example of this was the "election" of Singapore's eighth president, Halimah Yacob, in 2017. Yacob was, by all accounts, a personable, capable, and well-qualified candidate for the job. She was a former speaker of parliament. As the PAP's candidate, and a good one at that, she probably would have won without any help. After all, the PAP had bounced back from its bruising experience in 2011, winning the support of seven out of ten voters in 2015. But what is the point of entertaining risk when you hold the levers of power, and the country's future is at stake?

Direct presidential elections had been introduced back in 1991, ostensibly to increase voter engagement and state legitimacy. Despite this, in practice it has hardly been an exercise in listening to the popular will: restrictions on who could stand meant that only two out of five votes held subsequently involved a choice of more than one candidate. Then the law changed again, and the restrictions for the 2017 election, in which Yacob ran for president, became even tighter.

In the months before the election, social media platforms buzzed with talk about the requirement that the election candidates that year had to be from the Malay community. This was because of a law supposed to ensure that all three of the main ethnic groups had a pop at the job; if nobody from a certain group had been elected president for five terms, the next election was reserved for that community. This time, therefore, the president had to be Malay. But was this social engineering, a fig leaf for the country's Malay community, or fair representation in a multi-ethnic society? Given that surveys consistently showed that nine out of ten Singaporeans would prefer prime ministers and presidents to be of their own race, perhaps this was necessary.[8] Thanks to this electoral requirement, however, many Singaporeans found themselves discussing race in public for the first time, often in uncomfortably frank terms. Just why were many Malays poorer and less well-qualified than, say, Singapore's Chinese? Were their children happier and less stressed? Were the Malays ever going to be as loyal to Singapore as the Chinese?

Were the Chinese too dominant? Why had all three of the country's prime ministers (who had much more power than the president) been Chinese? It felt strange to my ears and eyes, but I heard and read things being discussed in the context of this election that I thought were taboo in Singapore. This was not just taxi uncle talk.

Some people also pointed out that there was a happy side-effect for the PAP of the Malay-only restriction: the man who had failed to beat the PAP candidate by only 7,383 votes in 2011, Tan Cheng Bock, would not be permitted to run. But even without Tan, it looked like there would be a field of three.

There was, however, a further tightening of the rules. As things stood, candidates had to have held a very senior government job, or have run a profitable private company with S$100 million in shareholder equity. That bar was then raised, to S$500 million. When a committee examined the candidacies, they found that only Halimah Yacob was eligible to stand, and so she was deemed to have been elected unopposed. Job done.

This was no way to increase either legitimacy or engagement. One seasoned journalist, P.N. Balji, argued that the whole affair demonstrated that Prime Minister Lee Hsien Loong failed to understand how politics was changing. He said that the Malay community had come out of the whole sorry business feeling wounded, with a sense of simmering injustice thanks to their apparent reliance on positive discrimination.[9] The hard-won legitimacy that Lee Kuan Yew had secured, through the sheer effectiveness of his government, was not as easy to come by in an age of MRT malfunctions and online griping about faltering meritocracy and cars that cost too much. That meant that the electorate was more sensitive to the kind of sharp political practices that would have garnered a simple shrug under LKY. There were already grumblings about how the next prime minister would be appointed, when Lee Hsien Loong reached the age of seventy. Would that be an opaque inside job, or would public opinion count for anything?[10]

The 2017 presidential elections also demonstrated that, whatever its control of the nuts and bolts of the political process, the government was no longer always in control of discourse. There had been anger, and much of that anger had been sublimated into bubbles of online contempt over the government's cack-handed managing of the presidential contest. P.N. Balji concluded that the main result of the election was the resounding but simple message, "Don't take Singaporeans for granted."[11]

Such apparent missteps, however, are arguably the product of trying too hard not to take Singaporeans for granted: the very opposite of complacency. The government is engaged in a difficult balancing act, made harder by the online world, and in this case it had leaned too far to one side. This is a natural risk for a capable government that is used to feeling the levers of state firmly in its hands. As the economist Tyler Cowen has observed, there is a debate over the brain drain into the Singaporean government, rather than out of it.[12] As a result, sometimes the government can be too clever, and imagine itself too able to affect how the island nation functions; paradoxically it can be too complacent about its lack of complacency.

I met up with one of those brains who had been drained into government at Relish, an upstairs lunch spot in the colonial-era Cluny Court. In its own way, Relish is as representative of modern Singapore as a hawker centre. It combines a studiously chichi atmosphere with a location near both the French Embassy and the Botanic Gardens. By 10.00 a.m. every morning it is clogged up with chic French wives in lycra, yoga mats tossed airily over one shoulder. It is the type of place that serves pink fizzy drinks adorned with sprigs of garden herbs, in the kinds of glass jars that grandmothers employed to dispose of a glut of strawberries. Elsewhere in the building you can stock up on turmeric lattes, multicoloured meringue blobs that are designed to be snapped by manicured nails, and any manner of trinkets from boutiques with names like "Groovy Gifts." Thankfully, Relish also serves up an excellent burger and chips for wilfully non-chichi customers like me.

Governance in Singapore is taken very seriously, said my lunch partner. In the US it is the opposite, and as a result there is under-investment and low expectations. "Here the government is given resources and expected to deliver." I was talking to someone who was one of those very resources, with a CV that in most other countries would have taken them straight into a blue-chip private-sector job with a gold-plated bank account. They also had an engaging openness when it came to the big issues that confronted Singapore, from migration and the labour market, to challenges such as MRT breakdowns and the HDB system.

When I asked about the pressures of education and the Primary School Leaving Exam, the conversation took a surprising turn. "Singapore," my lunchmate suggested, "has a problem with failure." Indeed, the size of the country means that failure carries massive costs. We talked about the HDB system, which sets lifetime trajectories that are dominated by saving and conventional employment, rather than the risk-taking and entrepreneurship that is part of a modern knowledge economy. The PSLE did something similar for children, crowding out any room for self-discovery or creativity, in the name of a high-pressure exam that could set a course for life.

My lunch partner also spoke about the strange case of Amos Yee, a shaggy-haired young nuisance whose impact on Singaporean public life has been way out of proportion to his provocations. "It's the Streisand Effect, times a thousand." The reference was to Barbara Streisand's attempt to suppress photos of her Malibu home, back in 2003, thereby drawing much more attention to it. Similarly, attempts by the Singaporean authorities to shut down an adolescent troublemaker, simply for being a teenager and a troublemaker, only drew more attention to him.

Amos Yee is a former child actor and ex-Catholic, with a track record for uploading controversial videos mocking everything from Chinese New Year celebrations to the ban on homosexuality. When independent Singapore's guiding light died, Yee was just sixteen. He responded in true sixteen-year-old style: "Lee Kuan Yew is dead, finally," he said on a video uploaded to YouTube. "Why hasn't anyone said, 'fuck yeah, the guy is dead'?" On his personal website he posted a drawing of LKY having sex with Margaret Thatcher, and claimed that under the late prime minister's watch, Singapore had become one of the world's most depressed countries, as well as one of the world's richest.

Instead of simply rolling their collective eyes and turning their backs, the authorities promptly arrested the teenager. He was eventually sentenced to four weeks in jail. After his release he used his augmented public profile to cause even more trouble, merrily calling for the Singaporean people to rise up against oppression. In December 2016, Yee fled to the United States and asked for political asylum. He was promptly interred in the McHenry County Adult Correctional Facility in Woodstock, Illinois. Singaporeans allowed themselves a smile at his continued incarceration. On Facebook he posted the defiant message that this was "simply a non-traumatic mild inconvenience, and not some absolutely life-ruining experience."

Yee's application for asylum in the US was agreed in early 2017. A judge in Chicago ruled that his treatment in Singapore constituted "persecution on account of Yee's political opinions." The Singaporean Ministry of Home Affairs responded the day after this ruling, noting that he had been charged with publishing an obscene image and with hate speech against Christians and Muslims. Yee's online ramblings had included wisdom such as a suggestion that Muslims "follow a sky wizard and a pedophile prophet," and the laconic "Fuck you, Christian shits."[13] Singapore's high commissioner in London, Foo Chi Hsia, wrote another letter to *The Economist*, reiterating that Amos Yee had used bigoted rather than simply crass language, noting that "Singapore does not countenance hate speech, because we have learned from bitter experience how fragile our racial and religious harmony is."[14] At the time of writing Amos Yee remains in the US, with his online rants now attracting little more than amused and scornful disapproval back in Singapore.

The trouble with the way Yee's case was handled, suggested my lunch partner, was that he was really just a teenager being a teenager. His juvenile and obnoxious online postings would simply have been dismissed in most countries as attention-seeking, childish drivel. Instead, in Singapore, they were considered destabilising enough to warrant a stamp down, with the full force of the law. Even the appointment of the second solicitor general as his prosecutor (presumably at an astronomical hourly rate, backed by vast state resources) was designed to reaffirm the Lee Kuan Yew-era message that Singapore comes down on cases of disobedience like a tonne of bricks. In reality, Singaporean intolerance of disobedience can seem to blur into intolerance of non-conformity and failure. This serves a purpose of sorts, while unfortunately also underlining that Singapore is not a place for mavericks or risk-takers.

In geopolitics there is a concept called "strategic depth." It means having the space to absorb a reversal, before once again seeking an advantage. In 1941, the USSR had absorbed the advances of the Nazi Wehrmacht into its territory, and the loss of millions of its own soldiers, before gathering its strength and marching to Berlin. It had strategic depth in spades.

Singapore does not have this capacity to absorb reversals. It is simply too small, and that leads the government to try to control every situation, calibrating its actions and attempting to get the balance exactly right. "At its most draconian, Singaporean prag-matism can refer to an austerity of action and thought where every single interaction is pregnant with cold calculation, where every calorie, it seems, must be expended only towards some higher economic purpose," notes the writer Sudhir Vadaketh.[15] Indeed, it is often very good at this, led and staffed as it is by extremely capable people.

This, argued the historian P.J. Thum, is a danger in itself. The longer the PAP state continues, the less flexible it becomes. Yes, it finds solutions to the problems it comes across, such as the S\$8 billion Pioneer Generation Package, which was announced after the 2011 election signalled that many older Singaporeans were feeling materially left-behind. But, he said, such schemes fail to respond quickly enough to fix such problems as were starting to develop. Economic crises are set to evolve into politi-cal ones. "Do we have a government that can respond to these changes?" he asked me. The answer in his eyes was no: the political class was too embedded in the system, and that system was too rooted in a stifling form of "economic performance legitimacy." "Today, Lee Kuan Yew would not have a chance of getting into government," he argued, for LKY was an inveterate outsider, unafraid to break things.

* * *

On the other hand, in an age of Trump, Brexit, fake news and Erdoğan, Singapore's government seems to be managing things rather well. Multi-ethnic Singapore has its internal disagreements, but it is neither rocking nor reeling, let alone tearing itself apart. What might make a critical difference to this is identity politics, of the sort that has fired up angry zero-sum voters across the globe. That has not gained a real foothold on the island, yet.

One reason for this is that the value of performance legitimacy has been inculcated in the Singaporean people. Its citizens are far

more interested in having a stable and effective (PAP) government than one that appeals to a single burning facet of their
identity. They also appreciate that stern PAP strictures against
appeals to race or religion are rooted in a very real need for solidarity. There is a folk memory of race riots, reinforced by the
Little India riots of 2013. Singaporeans are also quite a conformist and innately conservative bunch.

Take, for instance, issues connected to sexuality and gender,
which have energised so many young people across the West. In
Singapore, gay sex between men is still illegal. Lee Kuan Yew
himself said that Singapore would eventually come to recognise
homosexuality as acceptable, but—thanks to the more conservative social stance of the country's Muslims, and of its older citizens—this would have to happen slowly to maintain social cohesion. There is simply a very pragmatic, rather than ideological,
deference being paid to prevailing conservative attitudes.

The laws do not mean that the LGBT community in
Singapore is underground. I had numerous gay and lesbian
friends, and it didn't seem to me that they had to hide their
sexuality under a bushel (granted, an observation from the perspective of a white, straight male). After a hospital visit accom-
panying his husband, one friend said their married status led to
half the nurses offering their whole-hearted congratulations, and
to the other half visibly disapproving. Those nurses who offered
their best wishes would no doubt also feel comfortable with the
annual and very visible "Pink Dot SG" event, held in Hong Lim
Park, in support of the country's LGBT community.

I had wandered along to the Pink Dot back in 2015, after my
wife arranged to meet up with some friends at the event. The
atmosphere had been welcoming, but somehow peculiar: there
was general gaiety, all dressed up in baby shades of pink; but
there was also an air of wariness, as though pride in asserting an
identity was being hedged by awareness of unseen disapproval.

There were certainly none of the exuberant displays of oiled-up sexuality that you might find in Sydney or San Fran.

This sense that there was an accommodation between the LGBT community and the state, rather than something less measured, was reinforced at the 2017 event. My wandering along would not have been welcome that year, as the government had introduced rules that prevented foreigners from attending in any meaningful way. "These are political, social or moral choices for Singaporeans to decide for ourselves," explained the Ministry of Home Affairs. "LGBT issues are one such example."[16] Although the 2016 Pink Dot celebration had been sponsored by the likes of Google and Goldman Sachs, the new rules also prohibited foreign companies from getting involved.

On the face of it, this was another case of the government going through its familiar playbook, forcing an emerging topic into parameters that make it feel comfortable. It is a technocratic and methodical approach, letting their awfully bright people work their way through an issue, before plotting an optimum course ahead. This works better in times of complexity, uncertainty, and triangulation. It might be an unnatural fit with identity issues, where people may feel that something fundamental to their existence is being constrained or curtailed by a government.

This is the danger that Singapore may run with identity politics, of whatever flavour. Powered by social-media-fuelled outrage or intense feeling, it can bring greater demands for more definite, heartfelt and obvious decision-making. I know, from my Relish lunch partner and from countless initiatives around town, that the clever chaps in government are aware of these new dynamics, but that does not mean that they feel in control. Perhaps that is one contributory factor behind the lack of bravery detected by some, such as Professor Kishore Mahbubani. In this, the government is certainly not complacent—other than about their own lack of complacency—but maybe that will not be enough.

19

CBD

"WE ARE PRAGMATISTS"

After Hong Lim Park, my route brushed past some of the towering edifices of Singapore's Central Business District (CBD). These monuments in glass and steel and concrete neatly complemented the chimneys and pipelines of Jurong: modern Singapore's economy is built on financial services and multinationals, as much as shipping containers and zillions of gallons of refined petrochemicals.

My route took me past two sky-scraping bank headquarters, the OCBC Centre and the UOB Plaza, each chock-full of men and women in suits, manipulating columns on Excel charts and putting together insightful Powerpoint decks. There is something slightly incoherent about Singapore's CBD. As with the rest of Singapore it is peppered with building sites, which lend it an air of impermanence. Collyer and Raffles Quays are now firmly inland, untroubled by the lap of tepid seawater. Office workers mill around under occasional expanses of roof, safe from whatever combination of soaking or baking Singapore's weather gods have in store. A few blocks away from where I walked was one of Singapore's most atmospheric hawker centres: Telok Ayer Market, also known as Lau Pa Sat, with its rust-coloured octagonal steel roofing and the smells of 1,001 dishes mingling among its plastic seats.

Development within the CBD has been episodic, leading to an often-fascinating hodge-podge of building styles.[1] Take, for instance, the slightly faded, green-coloured Tunas building, which was one of the first skyscrapers to be built in Singapore. A plaque in the lobby dates it to 1973, when an Indonesian businessman erected it as a very public display of his success. The man still owns the entire top two floors, which now house part of his art collection (apparently six warehouses are needed for everything that he could not squeeze in). They resemble half-forgotten storerooms, full of endless antiques, canvasses, curios, and bad taxidermy. One room is stacked with suitcases. There is a confused-looking buck-toothed bear, a table crammed with blue and white ceramic teapots, and a bird of paradise that looks like it lost a fight with a tumble-drier. A black packet of Gudang Garam cigarettes sits on another table, looking as 1970s as the building itself.

The glories of the Tunas building continue on its circular roof terrace, accessible from the twenty-seventh floor. I counted twenty-seven porcelain horses, seven camels, an ox, and a mermaid. There are spectacular views of the Lego-esque container port, of Sentosa, and of the green pimples of Indonesia's Riau archipelago. The juddering giant fan blades of a skyscraper-sized air conditioning unit mix with the drilling and clanking of a much higher new tower that rises steadily into the air next door. This is a CBD with space for the Tunas building alongside much swankier neighbours, and it feels all the better for it.

Some pockets of first-generation HDBs remain in the CBD, hidden in amongst the various shining temples to commerce and finance. Rents of S$18 per square foot on one side of the road can contrast with S$1.80 on the other, in the lower floors of an HDB complex alongside Uncle Teo's One Stop Shop and the Perfect Exchange money changer. As leases expire they will be replaced by new generations of glassy towers. Plot ratios for empty land dictate to developers how much floor space each new building must have. Those giving space to not-for-profits are able to bend the rules and get more commercial floor space elsewhere. It is a very elegant and very Singaporean system, crafted by clever people and ever so efficient.

The CBD is one of the three or four touchstones of Singaporean expat life. For many, the world revolves around their condo, their office, and Changi airport, with the odd Sunday hotel brunch or Sentosa staycation thrown in, if only to keep up a vague semblance of family life.

The attractions of Singapore as an expat base are easy to see. The tax rates are almost as low as the crime rates, and the family gets a poolside base for easy excursions to Bali, Thailand and Hong Kong.[2] Sure, the trailing wives (and, like me, husbands) might sometimes be bored out of their minds, prevented from meaningful work by the shifting quicksands of working visas. But the kids are happy in the pool, the international schools are first class, and the nail bars are everywhere. There is childcare on tap, English is spoken almost everywhere, and the very bored can log on to online banking and watch their accounts grow ever larger. It may be an expensive place to relocate, but a few years padding out a bank account with a multinational in a pool-side condo remains a very enticing draw for expats. Despite growing restrictions, there were around 110,000 expats in Singapore in 2015, working for more than 7,000 multinationals.[3]

This is largely what Lee Kuan Yew was aiming for. He knew that attracting international capital and international labour went hand-in-hand. Modern Singapore was designed to be a perfect location for multinationals eager to boost their growth rates by advancing into Southeast Asia, or even the whole of the APAC region, with minimal dissent from employees' sybaritic spouses or their kids. Expats would not pay much income tax, but they would spend big on wines, cars, and condos. Thousands of excellent and aspirational office jobs would be created, and Singapore would become one of the world's business hubs. New industries, such as an international schooling sector, would follow. "Much of Singapore's success is thanks to good luck and good timing," points out David Skilling of Landfall Strategy. "It's being at the right place at the right time, and as you know you have to make the most of your luck."

Now, however, there are two looming threats. First, the government is making it harder to bring in expat talent, without first scouring the Singaporean labour market for suitable candidates. Second, Singapore is becoming a very expensive place to post an expat worker, just as the liveability gap with the rest of the region closes fast.

The rise in the viability of neighbours is important. Rather than set up an entire regional HQ in Singapore, companies are starting to spread functions across other suitable parts of Asia— say, having an IT department in Ho Chi Minh City, or procurement over in Jakarta. Only the top management needs the carrot of Singaporean civilisation, while massive amounts of money can be saved by setting up shop in cheaper locales. Airline networks are far more robust, and do not just rely upon Singapore Airlines or Cathay Pacific flights. Even Garuda, from the age-old airline basket-case that was Indonesia, has transformed itself into an excellent option, winning a coveted five-star Skytrax rating.[4] Other cities have developed their own swanky condos, with infinity pools and gyms. They have adequate shopping, WiFi, 4G signals, and international-brand schooling for children. Some boast pro-business politicians and respect for the rule of law. Even Chinese cities can be pretty decent places to live in, at least on the days when there is something other than toxic soup to breathe. They are also right at the scene of the economic action, rather than in a city state small enough to walk across in a day.

There is yet another paradox here: the rise of Asia helped to fuel the Singapore miracle, but now freshly risen Asia is stealing part of Singapore's lunch. It is eating away at some of the unique selling points of Singapore, while also introducing other dynamics that may undermine the city state's economic health.

To understand just how important the rise of Asia has been for Singapore, look at it from the perspective of that half-century miracle. First Japan took off, spearheaded by world-beating firms like Toyota and Sony. Then it was the turn of South Korea, with a zone of burgeoning economic vitality that extended south through Taiwan and Hong Kong, and into markets such as Malaysia. Then, of course, there was China.

Singapore benefitted grandly from all this, leveraging clean and effective government and a blessed geographic position. It linked rising Asia with the oil of the Middle East while developing a comprehensive petrochemical sector. Its port was modern and efficient, gorging on global trade from the far southeastern tip of the Eurasian land mass. It became a reliable financial centre, and multinationals found that it made an excellent choice as their regional base. Singapore's miracle was achieved on the back of rising Asia, as well as the domestic achievements of Lee Kuan Yew and his acolytes.

Around 4 billion people live in Asia, producing 40 per cent or so of the world's goods. China has become so important that it is the first or second most important trading partner for seventy-eight different nations. With growth ever harder to find in the more developed economies of the West, Asia is the place that shareholders and directors have been hunting for action. China, in particular, has proved itself able to get multinational executives very excited indeed.

However, Japan, back in the 1980s, was considered something special too. There were assumptions and extrapolations, and the lines on growth charts continued to point ever upwards. Then, as the 1990s were ushered in, Japan began to confound expectations. Could China, with its easy growth behind it, also stutter and stall?

The nature of both governance and growth in China gives some pause for thought. Its early decades of Communist Party rule were a particularly low point in the history of governance. Under Chairman Mao, its grand heritage of wise mandarins and perspicacious officials was crushed under the idiocy of backyard steel-making and Red Guard brutality. The odd million or two died here, and the odd million or two died there, all in the service of a crooked and pitiless ideology. Then Deng Xiaoping engineered the great take-off by helping farms to become more productive, thereby freeing up plenty of potential workers who could be shipped off to factories. Yes, there was slightly more to it than that, but the core dynamic of the Chinese miracle is deceptively simple.

In retrospect, pulling China out of its self-destructive Maoist nose-dive was always going to have a very large upside, for the country itself, and for economies clever enough to connect with it. With a rather more sensible generation of leaders in charge, the Chinese Communist Party has proven itself to be an extremely effective governing force, able to design and implement extraordinary projects and programmes. The inconvenient trifles that might have concerned Western governments, such as human rights or environmental standards, have not raised eyebrows in Beijing. Its leaders had also watched the Soviet system destroy itself, and were not about to let any Mikhail Gorbachev do something quite so silly off in the East. Meanwhile, millions sweated, and millions had cause to be grateful for Deng Xiaoping's common-sense revolution.

The outsized impact that this has had on the world can also be sketched in simple terms. China is enormous and started out from a very bad place. In 1962, its gross national income (GNI) per capita was US$70. By 1990 it was US$330; it then more than trebled by 2001. In 2016 the figure stood at US$8,250.[5] At the same time, China's population was galloping up to, and then past, the billion-person mark. Thanks to its late development, proven technologies were already out there, along with a stable and open trading system. Its factories might have been quite miserable places to labour hour after hour, but the world loved the fact that it could knock products out on a large scale, and at a "China price" that nobody else could match.

The seismic reawakening of China moved the world economy, and has been particularly good for Singapore. But will these trends continue in the same skyward direction? In his book *The End of the Asian Century*, Michael R. Auslin lays out a risk map for China and the rest of the continent. There are five areas of risk: the economic miracle might grind to a halt, partly through a failure to reform; Asia's demographics are unstable, and either include far too many old people, or far too many too young ones; there are numerous unfinished political revolutions; the regional community is full of antipathy and antagonism (not something that China's recent geopolitical forays have done much to improve); and, as the US struggles to come to terms with its commitments in the region, there is real risk of conflict.

The seasoned China-watcher Jonathan Fenby draws a similar picture in his book, *Will China Dominate the 21st Century?* He details the country's triumphs, but also writes about demography, the environment, water and energy, corruption, Beijing's challenge to the international order, and the "middle income trap." His final chapter heading is simply "Why China will not dominate the century." There is, of course, a large and fertile gap between not dominating and continuing to blossom, but the overriding point made by both Fenby and Auslin is that we should not expect those graphs to continue to point ever upwards. Singapore has benefitted greatly from China's rise, but geographical realities change.

This adds an extra driver to the urgency about reinventing Singapore's economy. If the country can no longer rely so heavily upon multinationals, and if the Asian economic outlook is no longer quite so vigorously sunny, what else can the country do to stay pre-eminent among the pack? Fintech (financial technology) is likely to be a crucial element of this, as Singapore's important financial sector is squeezed by Hong Kong and the increasingly sophisticated sector developing in China. It is also able to reap the benefits of its two sovereign wealth funds, which, according to a senior economist at the Macquarie Group, are estimated to administer just shy of a trillion US dollars.[6] This should continue to allow strategic investments in new industries and infrastructure, and cushion any shocks.

Singapore will also have to maintain some of the qualities that have always differentiated it from the rest of the region. First and foremost, that means the rule of law and an uncompromising attitude towards corruption. This reputation has been crucial for Singapore's positioning. While Hong Kong (with which the island's inhabitants habitually compare their country) has been struggling to come to terms with being drawn ever more firmly into Beijing's orbit, Singapore has remained the safe haven for international capital and Western companies. This is just as Lee Kuan Yew intended. The rule of law, allied to effective government, and a safe and transparent business environment, has been a killer combination for a business centre close to the Asian action.

However, questions have been raised over Singapore's sterling reputation in these areas. Although Transparency International ranked the country seventh (that is, as trustworthy) in its Corruption Perceptions Index 2016, there have also been disquieting revelations about the government-linked Keppel corporation being caught up in the massive Petrobras corruption scandal.[7] Singapore has also had to act fast to ensure that its financial centre is not tainted by any links to the Malaysian 1MDB scandal, with the Monetary Authority of Singapore closing down the local branch of the Swiss BSI bank, over what it called "serious breaches of money laundering requirements."[8] The optics of that unsightly squabble over Lee Kuan Yew's bungalow have not helped.

The towers I wandered past on the edge of the CBD were high, mighty, and formidable. The women and men in their business suits, sipping coffees and chatting to each other, are the indomitable foot soldiers of a world-class financial and multinational sector that has performed a key role in forging the Singapore miracle. The government saw the opportunities that rising Asia was opening up before it, and seized them. The towers were testimony to the government's tactical brilliance. But the work is far from over, and there will be a sizeable amount of running needed just for Singapore to stand still. That reputational advantage is something to burnish and treasure, while a multitude of new challenges are faced down without the same tailwinds as before. As David Skilling notes, Singapore's economic model faces diminishing marginal returns, and keeping it productive will be harder, more time-consuming and complex. As with the notion of Singapore as a "smart" city, the country can no longer rely purely on attracting foreign companies; it has to start developing domestic champions, which is hardly easy when the local market is so small. Those foot soldiers in business suits cannot afford to be complacent.

20

BOAT QUAY

STEPPING OUT IN SINGAPORE

I stepped out onto the front of the Singapore River through an alley next to the Penny Black pub. Shop houses with riverfront terracing stretched away to my left, decorated with fish tanks full of sullen lobsters, and open menus that never seemed to reflect the true plated cost of the seafood on offer. Other than on the odd wander with my toddler, I had only ever visited Boat Quay three times. Once I sat down there for a quick meal with my wife—an occasion only memorable for the size of the subsequent bill. On two other times I had joined the odd assembly of locals and displaced oil-and-gas workers that were, loosely, the Singaporean branch of Middlesbrough FC supporters' club. It was a curious mixture: gruff, pink-faced Teessiders, feeling momentary nostalgia for the buffeting of North Sea winds and a Jurong-esque skyline; and a gaggle of Singaporeans whose strange affection for an underwhelming club a world away marked them out from the glory-hunting masses of Southeast Asia. On one occasion we lost a play-off final, and on the other we won promotion. Both times, the beer cost S$15 a throw.

SINGAPORE, SINGAPURA

Boat Quay, like Clarke Quay just up river, is the spiritual centre of Singapore's nightlife. Backpackers wander around, their daily budgets running through their heads and then their fingers. Heavily made-up women call at any stray, foreign man, promising him company over a drink or two. Lobsters scramble over each other in those restaurant fish tanks, next to groupers suspended in the greenish water, burping out streams of tiny bubbles. On the opposite bank from the Penny Black is the Asian Civilisations Museum, and an altogether more dignified stretch of riverfront, leading up to the country's parliament.

I had never associated Singapore with nightlife. When *Time Out* surveyed thirty-two of the world's major cities in 2018 to find the most exciting, Singapore came in a miserable thirty-first.[1] It is certainly no Bangkok, but rather a place where they ban chewing gum and use the cane on miscreants. Famously, its puritanical streak led to a prohibition on men having hair longer than 2 inches above the collar. In 2005 I had used it as the jumping-off point for a tour of Vietnam, Laos, Thailand, and Cambodia, visiting an old university friend who introduced me to *dim sum* and air conditioning. It sat in sanitised, concreted contrast to the ruins and *tuk-tuks* and tumult of the rest of Southeast Asia. When I moved here, it was the day after my son turned one, and I had lost the will to drink beer with strangers and stay up till sunrise. Luca gave me all the reasons I needed for red eyes and feeling knackered. I was happy to be in boring old Singapore.

One book changed my perceptions of night-time Singapore. *Sarong Party Girls* was an unlikely hit: the story of an apparently immature and shallow young woman, called Jazeline Lim Boon Huay, and her search for an *ang moh* to marry.* Jazeline was

---

* *Ang moh* means "white person" in the Hokkien dialect of Chinese. Jazeline specifies that she wants one that is not too hairy, red-faced or pig-nosed.

trying to break out of the *longkang* HDB housing estates, full of *Ah Bengs* digging in their ears with their finger nails.† She resented the Eurasians, who acted fancy because of a drop of white blood from a long time ago. Ironically, she dreamed of having a half-*ang moh* child herself—the "Chanel of babies"—while handing out acidic observations, including that ugly children have "backside faces." She also grumbled about an old acquaintance who boasted about her new life in London's grungy Hackney (a "bumfuck place"); she would have much preferred to live somewhere with a name familiar from English football—Manchester, Liverpool, "or Aston Villa." Cool things were *Atas* and *Shiok*, while bad things were "Very Hardship." An attractive woman was "tall tall skinny skinny one," and an idiot was a *Goondu*. I will not translate what it means to call another woman a *Chee Bye*, but when Jazeline once said she wanted to *hantam* someone, it carried the threat of physical violence. Jazeline Lim Boon Huay was an ordinary girl, keenly aware of status and hopes for a new, better life that seemed stubbornly just out of reach. *Wah!*

The solution was to try harder to snare her own *ang moh*, which was to say that she was a dedicated "Sarong Party Girl" or SPG.[2] She went to fancy bars, drinking bottles of spirits costing eye-watering amounts, thanks to the bulky wallets of the men she hung out with (at one point she remembered drinking three bottles that cost a staggering S$2,888 each). Jazeline visited KTV lounges, where karaoke sessions with business contacts degenerated into orgies with prostitutes. She felt the heat of intense competition from mainland Chinese girls, who would do any-

---

† *Longkang* is a Malay word meaning "ditch, sewer or dump." *Ah Beng* describes loutish Singaporean men, and is derived from the Hokkien word *beng*, which is common in many Chinese male names. The *Ah Beng*'s female counterparts are *Ah Liens* and *Ah Huays*.

thing to escape having to go back there. (China was so *longkang* that her own ancestors risked their lives to leave for Singapore.) *Kani nah!***

The whole book was full of sharp observations. Jazeline unpicked the meaning behind one *ang moh* owning a Mini, rather than something fancier like a BMW or Mercedes: she decided that, because a Mini was not something a company would buy, it indicated that the owner was wealthy enough to pay for the COE himself. She was disappointed to find that one potential love interest worked in the industrial areas of Jurong, rather than in the CBD, indicating that he was in oil and gas rather than banking. The nagging self-doubt of citizens of such a small country was captured in her observation that one bar was "confirm happening" as the *New Times* had written a story that a Perth-based newspaper had mentioned it. The job of the government, in her opinion, was to keep coming up with apparently cool neighbourhoods for Singaporeans, to make up for life on a tiny island. *Die lah.*††

The book's author, Cheryl Tan, told an interviewer from Today Online that the idea for the book came to her after a visit to a bar with local friends. One real-life Sarong Party Girl spoke about a "Chanel baby," and Ms Tan realised that this was a sub-culture that said a lot about Singaporean attitudes to race, money, culture, and history. Jazeline's own desire to be an SPG stemmed "from a desire to fashion a better life for herself—one that is outside of the traditional patriarchal set-up that she sees around her and abhors." Her boundless materialism was a reaction to the dull and colourless HDB life that her parents worked long hours for. The book was also a celebration of the Singlish

---

** A very dirty Hokkien expletive, translating to something like "Fucking hell!"

†† "How embarrassing."

dialect: in Ms Tan's words, "direct, a little bossy, funny, sarcastic, witty and cheekily vulgar."[3/4]

Sarong Party Girls is a serious book about the way Singaporeans see the world, masquerading as an airport page-turner, and Jazeline was in danger of being an Elizabeth Bennet for modern times. Although the glimpse into Singapore's sleazy underbelly was fascinating, I was also struck by how close to the bone some of the insights were. Jazeline's rampant materialism resonated with my own experience of Singaporean values. After all, Lee Kuan Yew's miracle was legitimised by putting money in the pockets of the country's citizens. He saw materialism rather than idealism as the best bulwark against the very real threat of communism, and the most effective way of tying citizens to his project. S. Rajaratnam, one of the PAP's co-founders, himself noted that "money is about the only thing that rouses powerful emotions in the average Singaporean." While warning about the neglect of values that involved care for elderly family members, he also spoke of "the religion of moneytheism that prosperity breeds in all societies."[5] Once, when my son was invited to the fourth birthday party of a friend, we were asked to contribute to the friend's educational trust fund. What was wrong with getting them *The Cat in the Hat*?

Now, thanks to the creeping feeling that there was a glass ceiling on their aspirations, that value system was becoming a liability for Singapore. It also led people to value security and material wealth in their professional lives, rather than take risks and hope for other measures of fulfilment. Propagating a start-up culture on the island would take more than seed money and clever names for the buildings of One North.

Another uncomfortable truth lay at the heart of the book: however you cut it, race is something that matters in the minds of many Singaporeans. Just as Indian food is supposed to make the homes of South Asians smell, and Malays are considered lazy, *ang mohs* are the best route to a comfortable life of high-end shopping, business class travel, and Chanel babies. The SPG phenomenon is real, and debated enthusiastically online by the wives of bankers. One good friend, after a fancy event involving her husband and his fellow finance workers, was both angry and scathing about the SPGs that she had seen gathering around them, every time their wives' backs were turned.

The book also casts a critical eye over the male-dominated and hierarchical culture of the Singaporean workplace. Women are often little more than decoration, and things generally happen only when and if the boss says so. God forbid anybody disagrees, fails to recognise the status of those higher up in the pecking order, or leaves before the boss does.

The most intriguing insight from the book, however, related to the generational shift in outlook between Jazeline and her mother. Jazeline rejected outright the humble certainties, of HDB flat and stable job, that her mother's generation had fought for. She craved the tantalising lifestyle advertised by social media, glossy magazines, and the glitzy boutiques of Orchard Road. Such a dissonance between generations is not exactly unique to Singapore, but it ought to be of particular cause for concern there. The Jazeline generation had replaced hard work and a sense of vulnerability for extreme complacency and the search for an easy way out. The miracle had built a good life for the people of Singapore, but rather than appreciate that, they wanted trinkets. *Kani nah!*

* * *

The changing face of Singapore sleaze can be charted by its portrayal on the big screen. Back in 1947 it was being styled as the "city without a conscience" in the tagline of *Singapore*, a film starring Ava Gardner and Fred MacMurray. In 1978, the movie *Saint Jack* depicted a pimp and ship's chandler called Jack

Flowers, flitting between the grubby local world around the port and the expatriate world. Despite being shot on the island, the film was banned in Singapore for thirty years for its negative portrayal of the country. By the late 1970s, the city was changing, and cleaning up that equatorial sleaze was a key part of the LKY plan. HDBs and skyscrapers were far less photogenic than opium dens, wharves, and desperate sailors lurking in shop houses. When it did reappear on the silver screen, in 1999, Singapore was the setting for a bloodless tale of high finance and banking, with *Rogue Trader* tackling the story of Nick Leeson and Barings Bank.[6]

The crime rate in this sanitised city is still remarkably—for most Westerners, staggeringly—low. Bicycles are left outside supermarkets, unlocked and unmolested (although this may be because it is too hot for a vigorous cycle-borne getaway). Occasional street signs notify passers-by that a crime—often very minor—was committed nearby.[7] Singapore's police say there were 135 days in 2016 with no reported crime.[8] In a densely packed city of several million people, ranging from playboys to toilet attendants, that is genuinely astonishing.

The trifling crime rates did not come about by happy accident. They were a deliberate plank of LKY's drive to attract global talent to Singapore. In crime terms, Singapore was normal well into the 1990s. Every so often the crime rate spiked: it went up by a quarter in 1979, and by another 18 per cent a year later. The highest number of reported crimes was in 1988, with 46,753 cases.[9] There was lots of house breaking and thievery, and historical issues such as opium use, prostitution, and gambling were still causing problems. The police were feared almost as much as the criminals.

One of the more lurid cases involved ritual murders committed by a man called Adrian Lim, his wife, Tan Mui Choo, and his mistress, Hoe Kah Hong. In 1983 they were convicted of luring two young girls to his Toa Payoh flat, where they were killed. The court heard of blood-drinking, black magic, sex, trances, and 'treatments' involving electric shocks. The seventh-floor apartment had an altar, crucifixes, Hindu and Chinese idols, and lots of joss sticks. All three perpetrators were hanged in 1988, after a final bath and some cake.[10]

Gangland violence persisted for some time. One case involved an enforcer and hitman known as "One Eyed Dragon" (his real name was Tan Chor Jin). He was part of the 369 or *Salakau* (the number 369 in Hokkien) secret society, which made its money through drugs and prostitution. His life of crime came to an end thanks to a very Singaporean liking for chicken rice. His last crime was the killing of a nightclub owner, Lim Hock Soon. Tan forced his way into the man's apartment, made him tie up his wife, thirteen-year-old daughter, and maid, and then shot him six times. Although he escaped, the One Eyed Dragon was tracked down to a room in the semi-swanky Grand Plaza Parkroyal Hotel in Kuala Lumpur. An undercover policeman was able to plant a bug while delivering a midnight order of Hainanese chicken rice to Tan's room. As soon as they heard snoring, police officers burst in. Tan was hanged in 2009.

A serious clampdown on criminality was underway from the early 1980s. The then-minister for home affairs, Chua Sian Chin, said a new social ethos had to be created in Singapore, "wherein those who violate accepted codes of conduct are frowned upon and wrong-doers are made to feel a deep sense of shame for their misdeeds." He also harked back to the old *kampongs* (villages), and decried the loss of the "warmth, concern and cohesiveness of the old traditional communities," falling respect for the elderly, and the "get rich quick" syndrome.[11]

Part of the answer to Singapore's criminality was community policing, based on the Japanese *kōban* system of locally visible units. Chua Sian Chin's successor as minister for home affairs,

Professor S. Jayakumar, visited Japan to see the system in action. "If parents bring a little kid saying their pet has gone missing, and the child is crying because of the missing pet," he said, "the police officer has to drop whatever he's doing and try his utmost to find the cat. Because if he succeeds, he has won over that family, and the child and parents would consider policemen as friends."

The first of the new Neighbourhood Police Posts was established in 1983, in Toa Payoh. A large sign saying "At your service" hung above the door, and the officers inside were visible through the slotted glass windows. By 1993 there were ninety-one of these NPPs, and Sin City's fightback against crime had begun. A muscular crime-fighting mascot, Captain V, toured the island in cut-out form, on top of an anti-crime battle bus. Private donors funded the National Crime Prevention Council.

The whole approach was very Singaporean, in that it was measured, effective, and thorough to an almost absurd degree. Take the simple idea that after a few drinks and a good night out, some people may want to dance on top of a bar. Regulations were in place to stop this, in the form of laws that confined such activities to specified dance floors. However, in 2002 there was a rethink that reached the top level of government. The prime minister, Goh Chok Tong, noted in his National Day speech that "perhaps we should allow dancing on bar-tops." Part of the reasoning was that it was worth rebranding Singapore as a place to party, the "London of Asia," in the wake of the SARS epidemic.[12] There was a consultation, and a study group travelled to Shanghai, Beijing, and Hong Kong, presumably taking notes while watching people dancing on bar-tops. The result was a relaxation of the dance-floor rules, and the equipment of suitable bar-tops with poles (as a safety measure).[13] It was an example of public policy-making that would have delighted Jazeline Lim Boon Huay.

The other, more infamous, answer to Singapore's crime problem was an unflinching attitude to punishment. On the one hand, there is the rattan cane. This came to international attention in 1994, after a sixteen-year-old from Hong Kong was arrested for driving his father's car without a license. The boy's interview in custody put investigators on the trail of several other boys from the Singapore American School, including a nineteen-year-old American, called Michael P. Fay. Unfortunately for him, not only did they find stolen road signs at his house, but the media had also been covering a series of incidents across Singapore where cars were being vandalised, and their tyres slashed. Following a confession to these offences, Mr Fay was sentenced to six strokes of the cane, and four months in jail. This led to something of an international outcry, with President Bill Clinton even weighing in by saying that the strokes were extreme and mistaken. The Singaporean government stood by the punishment, but eventually reduced the sentence to four strokes. After returning to the US, Mr Fay described the caning. He said the prison officials had told him that he had shouted out, "I'm dying!" after the first stroke. The bleeding had been halfway between gushing and a few drops, "like a bloody nose," and he was left with brown scars across both buttocks.[14] Whatever the damage to Mr Fay's rear end, it was a convenient and internationally noticed signal that Singapore was taking a hard line on even minor criminality. Caning remains an accepted punishment in Singapore's schools, although—just like National Service—it can only be afflicted upon the male population.

On the other side of the Singaporean justice system, there is the hangman's noose.

It is not easy to be an effective executioner, according to Darshan Singh. If the hangman is inexperienced, he said, the condemned would "struggle like chickens, like fish out of the water." He, in contrast, knew what he was doing, having executed 850 people in the forty-six years up to 2005. He made sure they were calm, and told them to be brave. He weighed the condemned person a week before, and again on the day of the hanging, and carefully consulted a 1913 copy of the British Home Office's "Official Table of Drops." This allowed him to calculate exactly how long the rope had to be to break the neck. In his early days he used a new noose for every hanging, but as they cost several hundred dollars, they started to be reused. His Friday shift as a hangman began at 5.30 a.m., and ended in time to allow some lunch, then hockey or cricket at the Singapore Recreation Club. (His prowess with the cricket bat was apparently useful when he was called on to use the rattan cane, for a fee of 50 cents a stroke.)

Singh took the whole business in his stride. He had joined the colonial service in the mid-1950s, but at the age of twenty-seven, volunteered to take over as hangman from a Mr Seymour, because of the extra money that came with the rope. He found that he had an affinity for it. At one point he worked his way through eighteen men in a day, in batches of three, following a murderous riot on the penal island of Pulau Senang. On another occasion, he hanged seven men in just ninety minutes. In 2001, Singh's friends helped him celebrate his 500th hanging with a couple of bottles of Chivas Regal.[15] Despite this bloody tally, the only one of his executions that bothered him was that of a troublesome prisoner called Mimi Wong. She was a dance hostess who had murdered the wife of her Japanese lover. In jail, Wong used to strip naked and throw urine at prison guards. After hanging her in 1973, Singh was off sick for a month, and never spoke to his wife about Mimi Wong's final moments.[16]

Singh's usual breezy approach to breaking the necks of the condemned gained him overnight notoriety in the early years of the millennium. An Australian man named Nguyen Van Tuong had been arrested in Changi airport, on a stopover from Cambodia to Melbourne, in 2002. He was found to have 396.2 grams of heroin on his person, in packages strapped to his body and stuffed into his bags. In Singapore, the import or export of more than 15 grams of heroin carries a mandatory death sentence, and in 2004 Nguyen was sentenced to hang. This caused an outcry in Australia, which became more shrill after Singh gave a press interview suggesting that he hoped to carry out the execution himself, describing why in rather too much detail. When the Singaporean government awarded the job to somebody else, Singh suggested that he was missing out on the S$470 executioner's fee because of the adverse publicity in the Australian newspapers.[17] In contrast, Singaporean papers ran features that portrayed him as a loyal civil servant who had been duped into saying unwise things by crafty reporters.

Although they doubtless welcome the publicity that it brings to their tough line on crime, the Singaporean authorities have been less keen on allegations that there is anything unfair about their use of capital punishment. One British reporter, Alan Shadrake, ended up being jailed for writing a book that made just those claims. He had developed an interest in the subject thanks to two particular cases. One involved the drug-smuggling Nguyen, and the second, a British businessman called Michael McCrea. McCrea had killed both his girlfriend and his driver (a close friend of his), abandoning them in a silver Daewoo on the seventh floor of Orchard Towers car park, before fleeing the country. He had successfully fought extradition back to Singapore from Australia, because of the threat of execution if he returned (he was later convicted of manslaughter in Australia, and sentenced to twenty-four years in jail).[18] Following up his new-found interest in Singapore's death penalty, Shadrake ended up tracking down Darshan Singh. They hit it off, he remembered: "We're old codgers together. I used to talk to him about Manchester United. He loved it."[19]

As well as plenty of juicy and gory details gleaned from Singh, Shadrake's subsequent book, *Once a Jolly Hangman*, carried some alarming allegations. He argued that Singapore knowingly used its death penalty disproportionately against the young and the poor, rather than against those of higher socioeconomic status.[20] Although Singapore has no issue with being made to look tough on crime, it has a real problem with being accused of such unfairness. When his book was published, Shadrake made the mistake of turning up to a launch event in Singapore itself, despite the British High Commission advising against it. Around 150 people attended, and the seventy-six-year-old went to bed, job done. At 6.30 a.m., however, he was woken up by policemen, carted off to the cells, and interrogated. He was eventually sentenced to six weeks inside, and a hefty fine.[21]

Despite the canings and the hangings, the real internationally recognised flag-bearer of Singapore's stance on crime is the ban on chewing gum. This was first raised as an issue in 1983, by the minister for foreign affairs and culture, S Dhanabalan. Adverts for gum were stopped, and school tuck shops were no longer allowed to sell it. The issue became more acute in the early 1990s, following a spate of vandalism, including incidents where MRT train doors malfunctioned thanks to globs of gum stuck over their sensors. The Housing Development Board alone reportedly spent S$150,000 each year cleaning up the mess made by pre-masticated splodges. In 1992 the Regulation of Imports and Exports (Chewing Gum) Regulations [sic] became law, banning the import, manufacturing and selling of all kinds of gum. The law has now been relaxed to allow therapeutic products such as nicotine gum to go on sale, thanks to the implications of a free-trade agreement with the US.[22] Even with this nod to globalised commerce, the issue has become emblematic for Singapore, and its determination to become near crime-free remains a key part of its appeal to multinationals and their cosseted workforce. "If you can't think because you can't chew," Lee Kuan Yew commented in an interview with the BBC, "try a banana."[23]

21

MARINA BAY

INSTAGRAM CITY

The Cavenagh Bridge is the point at which the Singapore River stops even pretending that it is a river at all. From then on, it lets itself go like a relieved forty-five-year-old with big bones and a penchant for doner kebabs, into a basin that is the epicentre of Instagram Singapore.

My mid-walk stomach burbling with an ill-considered Big Mac and a rather welcome large Coca Cola, I judged that my fast-disintegrating feet would not thank me for taking the short detour to that ersatz symbol of Singapore, the Merlion.* I turned past the grandly columned façade of the Fullerton Hotel, and traipsed across to the north bank. A statue of Raffles himself stood just a few dozen metres to my left, where he alighted to make history, but those feet of mine were in no mood for diversions.

* The Merlion is half lion, half mermaid. Some love it, but I hate it. Although it has its roots in the original designation of Singapura as the Lion City, the creature seemed to emphasise the synthetic nature of the place rather than link it to its fascinating heritage. Somewhat inevitably, it was dreamt up as a logo for the local tourism board.

207

Off to the left was the Padang sports field, where for the best part of two centuries the cream of Singapore had met to trade wickets, hurl balls, and strike deals. On the nearside was a modest memorial to the Indian National Army of Subhas Chandra Bose, hinting at complicated wartime accommodations.[1] On the other side of Esplanade Drive there was a marked increase in the density of pouting selfie-takers, adjusting, snapping, then readjusting. This meant one thing: Marina Bay Sands.

Move over, Raffles Hotel: MBS is the new hot hotel in town. Even if you are not staying there, it is the iconic image of twenty-first-century Singapore. It looks like half a split banana, raised 200 metres high on three tower blocks. The infinity pool—goodness knows how many iPhones have been lost in its waters—was built for social media. The main exercise going on in the pool is holding one in the air and gurning out a smile. Precisely 500 jacks regulate the 1000 tonnes of water (especially on a windy day), preventing the whole damn thing from collapsing and breaking Instagram. In his quest to have one large pool, rather than splitting it up into something more technically sensible, architect Moshe Safdie had to develop a complex expansion joint that would not leak.

Marina Bay Sands was opened in 2010 as part of a seemingly promising drive to triple tourist income over the following decade. It cost a whopping S$8 billion to build. A full 70 per cent of revenues come from the casinos, with MBS suites given out for free to high rollers/losers. There are fifty butlers at the guests' disposal, serving the more exclusive among the 2,500 rooms. The cavernous lobby feels like the bowels of an elongated ziggurat. Its theatres hold a combined 4,000 seats. 160,000 computer-chipped uniforms whirr around on automated racks and conveyors; each time one of the 9,000 staff logs in, their particular uniform magically appears at a little window in front of them. The kitchens cook half a tonne of rice each day, and 5 tonnes of flour are used for the daily bread bake. More than a thousand pool towels are handed out to swimmers every day.

Yes, I took a sweaty selfie with the building in the background, and stuck it up on Twitter. I am scathing, but not proud.

The extraordinary revenues from the casinos of MBS and Sentosa are something of an eye-opener, given Singapore's firm line against gambling. In truth, gambling has been a confirmed part of life on the island since its early days under the British. It was an early source of tension between Raffles and William Farquhar, who, as we saw, used "vice revenue" to fund public works. In 1823 the more puritanical Raffles cracked down on such activities, stating that "whoever games for money or goods shall receive eighty blows with a cudgel on the breech, and all money or property staked shall be forfeited to Government." Despite the warnings about being cudgelled on the breeches, the gambling continued, bringing in 71,283 Straits dollars in 1827. In 1829 all gambling was outlawed across the Straits Settlements.[2]

This suppression, however, failed to account for demand from the rapidly growing Chinese population. Many had gambled with their lives when fleeing misery on the mainland for new beginnings at the very tip of Eurasia, and were temperamentally attracted to games that could change their lives at a stroke, whatever the potential downside.

The game most associated with Singapore's Chinese immigrants was *Chap ji kee*, which means "Twelve cards" in Hokkien. A card is drawn out of a bag and placed in a box. Gamers lay bets on six red playing pieces (field marshal, prime minister, minister, chariot, horse, and cannon), and six black (general, scholar, elephant, chariot, horse, and cannon). Once the card is revealed, anybody who chose correspondingly wins ten times their stake—giving an unmistakable mathematical edge to the banker. The game sat comfortably within the Chinese underworld of secret societies and—in the view of the authorities—organised crime, and it was systematically supressed.

Chap ji kee, however, was too lucrative to abandon, and so it evolved to stay ahead of the law. To avoid suspicious crowds, bets were collected door-to-door. The collectors themselves developed clever cryptic notation systems and accounting methods. Credit lines were extended to those who needed temporary liquidity. Lookouts were posted at the draw to facilitate quick exits, and organisers could fiddle the outcome by making sure the least-backed card was the one that just happened to be drawn from the box. As the game was driven further underground it gained in organisational complexity, with layers of collectors, promoters, and sub-promoters. China Street became known as *Kiau keng cheng* ("Front of the gambling houses" in Hokkien) and *Po tsz chheung kai* ("Gambling hall street" in Cantonese).

Although the game spread into the poorest communities, with minimum bets as low as 10 cents and characters replaced by simple numbers to help illiterates, the vice came to be associated with middle-class women. One *nonya* (lady, auntie) managed to run up a debt of S$50,000, and was forced to pawn her jewels (replacing them with fakes). A raid in 1909 led to the arrest of eleven *nonyas* in a house on Tank Road. The magistrate advised the husbands to have their wives chastened by a fortnight behind bars, rather than escape with a fine.

During the Japanese occupation *Chap ji kee* was encouraged, and it positively flourished in the post-war years. Two syndicates dominated: *Lau Tiun*, which was based in Tiong Bahru and Upper Serangoon Road; and *Shanghai Tai Tong*. When the latter's leaders were arrested and deported in 1948, two other gangs swiftly took over its territory and its gaming interests. By the 1970s the *Lau Tiun*, *Sio Poh*, and *Tua Poh* had a combined annual income of S$100 million. A survey in the *New Nation* in 1973 found that 95 per cent knew that the game was open to scams, but most played anyway. Women continued to place small, inconspicuous bets, through an intricate network of collectors who were also the local fishmongers and market stall-holders.

The pervasive spread of what came to be known as "The house-wives' opium" and its underworld links are what informed the official Singaporean hard line against gambling. The *Chap ji kee* ecosystem represented a mortal threat to the kind of society and country that the PAP was trying to build. The net gradually tightened during the 1960s and 1970s, and the Singapore Pools, a state-owned lottery company, was introduced as an acceptable gambling pressure valve in 1968. The Singapore government was busy redesigning society with a firm guiding hand, and its approach to gambling has been a reminder of its technocratic and paternalistic approach to its citizens' lives.[3] Singapore still gambles heavily, however, with annual gambling losses per resident adult adding up to over US$600, way ahead of most other countries.[4]

Meanwhile, the same technocratic and paternalistic government has also placed gambling at the centre of its development policy, through the mega-casinos of Marina Bay Sands and Sentosa. "I don't like casinos but the world has changed," Lee Kuan Yew told the *International Herald Tribune* in 2007. "If we don't have an integrated resort like the ones in Las Vegas [...] we'll lose. So, let's go. Let's try and still keep it safe and mafia-free and prostitution-free and money-laundering free."[5] As a result of this clear-headed pragmatism, the casinos are controlled and profitable, and Singaporean citizens are even welcome to join in the fun: although unlike foreigners, who can enter for free, locals have to pay S$100 a day (or S$2,000 a year) for the privilege. The PAP first tamed *Chap ji kee* in the name of creating a modern country, and then signalled a change of course for the economy and country with the building of the sky-high banana split of Marina Bay Sands. It is designed to turn Singapore into a destination rather than a stopover, while tapping into the lucrative East Asian megabucks gambling market.

The entire Marina Bay complex encapsulates Destination Singapore. There is the ArtScience Museum, shaped like a robot's half-open palm, and the twin durian fruits of the

Esplanade concert halls. When I hiked past, the Float—a 10,000-square-metre stage, bobbing a few metres offshore—was playing host to a toddlerscape of inflatable white shapes (and a sperm whale), all with cutesy eyes and smiles. The Float has a serious purpose beyond the art installations and selfies: Singapore is actively researching floating structures, including solar farms, shipping fuel containers, and even homes, as a solution to its land-scarcity problem.

I ducked through a gap in the grandstand that faced the Float, onto Temasek Avenue, and through a coach parking lot. Then it was up a few flights of concrete steps, and onto the edge of the Benjamin Sheares Flyover, where traffic zipped past and my vertigo kicked in. The view was spectacular. Off to my left was Kallang, which was still by reputation the centre of Singapore's red-light district. The Kallang River had once gone by the name of *Sei Kai Hor*, or Dead Chicken River, as it was always full of the carcases of dead farm animals. Gardens By The Bay East was just across the water ahead of me, with the genuinely lovely main chunk of Gardens By The Bay stretching off across the water to my right. In sight—if I'd been able to look at anything other than my shoes, methodically counting off the steps of vertiginous terror—were the Flower Dome, and the Cloud Forest Dome, with its internal waterfall. There were the bizarre filigree arboreal structures of Supertree Grove, then Dragonfly Lake and the water park where my over-excited son skipped in and out of sprays and jets on many a Sunday morning. This was prime Destination Singapore, but all I wanted to do was leave, to get going and descend the steps on the other end of the Flyover, back to the safety of ground level. Once there, all would be fine. I would be at the beginning of the end of my walk, with leafy East Coast Park stretching ahead of me. I would have the chance to sip some water, breathe a little, and try to work out why my socks felt like they were filling with liquid.

22

EAST COAST PARK

THE STATE OF FUN

At the foot of the steps, I delayed checking my feet for as long as I could. I drank some water, and scanned the trees and shrubs for a suitable place to pee. I checked my map, and compared my scribbles to the real world. I rubbed my thumb along the irritated muscles in my thighs and calves. And then I loosened my shoelaces.

My socks were bright red, which, given that they had started off as white, was a bad sign. I peeled one off to expose the heel. A flap of watery skin hung off the inside, stretching from just below my ankle into the thick leather on my sole. There was blood and some other damp and angry secretion. I lifted the flap back into place and tried to tape all the damp matter back together. I worked my sock back on, tied my shoe with all the firmness that my nervous system would allow, and turned to the other foot. The situation there was exactly the same, as was my rudimentary treatment.

My main problem was that I was still well over 15 kilometres from my finish, and my flayed feet were only a marginally bigger concern than my spasming muscles. I had actually allowed myself a dab of deluded optimism about reaching East Coast Park: the final strait, surrounded by the greenery of one of Singapore's many manicured leisure spaces. I would track along with the beach to my right, hundreds of assorted ships moored just off-shore, and, ahead of me, that steady stream of A380s and 747s touching down and taking off from Changi getting steadily closer with every stride. Now, alas, each stride would be a hobble and every meander of the path an unnecessary added metre of agony. It might not be a walk to challenge Apsley Cherry-Garrard's *Worst Journey in the World*, but it might come quite close. Minus the frostbite, penguin eggs, and constant brush with icy death.

As it happens, my hobbling was quite successful at first. Being surrounded by trees and greenery—the thundering traffic on the East Coast Parkway (ECP) excepted—was every bit of the sensory relief that I had expected. Just beyond the ECP was a line of top-flight high-rise condos with ocean views: The Palms; The Waterside; The Seafront on Meyer; Hawaii Tower; Casa Meyfort; The Sovereign. There were cyclists and in-line skaters and joggers, and I knew I would be able to refuel with a sugary drink within a kilometre of two. I might even be able to buy some paracetamol.

I was back on reclaimed land. The old coastline used to follow that line of high-rise condos with their enticing names. The streets of bungalows beyond—Margate and Ramsgate and Bournemouth Roads—used to enjoy something of a colonial-era sea breeze. Reclamation came, and the new coastline became a buffer for the land, grabbing enough real estate for the condos, the ECP, and the long green sward of the East Coast Park.

This was an important part of the grand PAP plan. Once Singapore's economy was in gear, circuses were slated to follow the bread. In the recent past it was the large entertainment complexes such as Great World City that provided the kicks and the relief from a working day. Even further back, of course, it was prostitution, opium, and gin, or whichever combination suited best. Now it is the parks, recreation areas, and—most of all—Sentosa.

Where the Botanic Gardens are Singapore's verdant showpiece, the central forests and reservoirs its green heart, and the various parks its civic amenities, Sentosa is the country's purpose-built, government-sanctioned theme park. The island is appended to the southern tip of Singapore much as Singapore itself dangles from the far end of the Malay peninsula. Hop on the jostling monorail or take a taxi across the causeway, and you arrive in a place that has been officially designated as the "State of Fun." It is half expected that the batteries of CCTV cameras are programmed to zoom in on any wayward scowl.

Resorts World Sentosa offers a choice of activities, from a branch of Universal Studios to high-stakes gambling. There is Siloso Beach, Palawan Beach, and Tanjong Beach, each with a range of refreshment options, imported sand, and enticing islands just offshore, reachable by rickety bridges or a flying fox. You can take a cable car, learn to skydive or surf, visit Madame Tussauds, or lose the children in KidZania. There is, of course, a Merlion, should you need another photo-opportunity. There is a choice of two golf courses, and—beyond that—the yacht club and a selection of the most exclusive properties in Singapore. Scanning through property websites I found an ultimately forgettable, rather angular, glass-clad landed house on Ocean Drive for S$87.6 million (or, as I write this, not far under £48 million). It is, of course, only on a ninety-nine-year leasehold, but has a smashing view, taking in multicoloured steel containers and the shipping lanes across to Seringat Island. Thankfully, the advert acknowledges that the price is negotiable.[1]

Sentosa was not always this much fun. The roads along the spine of the island tell of a different heritage: Artillery Avenue and Allanbrooke Road (I presume after Field Marshal Alan [sic]

Brooke, the chief of the Imperial General Staff during the Second World War). Rather than a strategic component of modern Singapore's commitment to social harmony and having fun, it was a strategic component of British Singapore's maritime prosperity. The containers that you can see from the S$87.6 million house are part of Keppel Harbour, and the island was recognised from very early on as affording the entire port area very effective protection.

The island was also known to have a particularly inclement climate, and was the epicentre of British research into malaria. It became a fortress, and there is a good if under-visited museum at the western tip, based around Fort Siloso and its battery of guns. This battery was partly responsible for the wrong-headed popular notion that Singapore fell to the Japanese (approaching from the north) because its guns "were facing the wrong way."

The precise original name of the island is difficult to pin down. In the early days of British Singapore, it was Pulau Panjang, which means Long Island. It then became known as Pulau Blakang Mati, or "Island of Death from Behind." Although this would have been a superb name for an island that was then designated as "Asia's favourite playground," in 1972 a contest held by the Singapore Tourist Promotion Board came up with "Sentosa," meaning something like "peace and tranquillity" in Malay.

That new name lit the touch paper on a new role for the island. But even as it was being transformed into the State of Fun, it had a less savoury side. A political prisoner, Chia Thye Poh, was the island's only permanent resident while under house arrest there. He had been politically active back in the 1960s, representing Jurong Constituency for the Barisan Sosialis, a left-wing party formed by splitters from the PAP. He was also something of an activist, warning of strikes and street demonstrations. Arrested in 1966, he refused to sign a promise to renounce violence and sever any ties with the Communist Party of Malaya (he said that that this would have implied that he had at some point advocated violence or been a member of a communist party). Although he was neither charged nor tried, Chia was then imprisoned for twenty-three years under the Internal Security Act. After his release from prison, he was placed under house arrest in a small, meticulously tidy cell in the guardhouse of Fort Siloso. He was obliged to remain on the State of Fun from nine o'clock every evening until six in the morning, with further restrictions placed on what he could do during daylight hours. In 1998, all remaining restrictions were removed, and he was allowed to leave the State of Fun.

* * *

For those who imagine that Sentosa is all a bit ersatz, there are other, more authentic ways to find out how Singaporeans enjoy themselves. They could, for instance, go prawning. The Hai Bin prawning pool, which I visited with my wife and son, is tucked behind a light rail stop and a garden centre, and just along from a floodlit driving range. There was a metal roof that thundered when the rain came down, and a confusion of throbbing jungle was visible just across a waterway. This was a way to enjoy free time that the Pioneer Generation would recognise.

My hour of prawning fun did little more than cement my son's confirmed view that I was largely useless at catching creatures with a rod and line. For my S$18 I was given a slim, bendy rod, a net to hook on the side of the pool, and a small plastic dish containing slivers of chicken heart. "First time, ah?" said the man who took my money, before thinking to offer a smile halfway between condolence and hope.

I speared some chicken heart onto my hook, and showed Luca how to dunk the line into the Coke-coloured water. Behind us sat an entire extended family, camped out for the day, the mother and granny on their tablet computers while a young girl waged calculator-based war against her maths homework. An excited burble signalled a woman snaring some sort of armoured monster next to us, its multi-segmented blue arms dangling feebly as it was hoisted out of the water. "Auntie, what do we do with this thing, ah?" asked a friend of hers, ready with a pair of pliers for wrestling out the hook. The victorious angler spotted my son and insisted that he have his photo taken with the beast. This he did, while glancing at me with understandable fear.

Opposite us, a frustrated trio of men with their own rods hanging uselessly in the water looked away in denial. Another man walked up to our pool, peered into the murk as though in possession of a prawning-specific sixth sense, and pulled an impressively professional extendable rod out of a padded carry-pouch. The man who had taken my S$18 appeared, shaking his head ruefully at my sadly predictable lack of success, and tipped a tub of wriggling, glistening prawns in, right next to my rod. He set up a second baited rod for us, immediately felt a tug, and handed it over to me. I tried to replicate the same mixture of delicacy and Hemingway-esque strength that I had seen in the other prawners, but somewhere my touch let me down, and my hook came up empty. My hour was looking prawnless.

Maybe our approach was simply too amateur. I read about one forty-four-year-old business consultant who was hooked after his first visit. He became obsessive, buying live prawns so that he could study their feeding habits at home. He travelled to Taiwan to learn techniques from a prawning master, in scenes that are presumably reminiscent of Luke Skywalker's meeting with Yoda. The man is now a master himself. He spends S$800 a month in places like Hai Bin (his third favourite venue, apparently), trails an entourage of fawning fanboys wherever he goes, and catches so many prawns that he has to give his surplus to local pensioners. He was the prawning equivalent of a card-counter that gets banned from casino after casino in Monte Carlo and Atlantic City.

Others around Hai Bin nurtured a similar sense of purpose. My wife pointed out the potent-looking red paste that the successful auntie next to us was fashioning around her hook. A cabinet next to the cash register was filled with a mesmerising array of Shrimp Assassin lures and concoctions. One prawning master, his bait-of-choice ready-rolled into perfectly regular little balls, held the end of his rod with all the tactile delicacy of a chopstick. Another couple sported a purpose-built plastic case, full of compartments and cubby-holes, each containing a specific lure or potion to guarantee prawn after prawn after prawn. One of the frustrated trio of men unhooked an impressively clawed specimen from his tackle, as all three affected to be unimpressed. Everyone other than us was Chinese.

We did have one catch that day, even if it was second-hand. A smiling gentleman, equal parts pity and curiosity, called us over just as a frenetically struggling prawn broke the water. He plucked off the claws, showed my son where the hook was embedded in the poor creature's frothing mouth, and offered it to us.

This Singapore was a million miles from the glitzy boutiques of Orchard Road or the state-sanctioned fun of Sentosa. The aroma of smouldering charcoal rose up from the barbeque pits and mingled with Robbie Williams' "Angels." Cages of song birds and budgies hung from the ceiling among old Carlsberg adverts. The prawning at Hai Bin would go on for twenty-four hours straight, followed by another twenty-four, and then another. Some would come to spend time with other aunties, as couples, as prawn masters. It was a place for a post-clubbing cigarette with a mate, or an escape from an HDB flat full of kids doing maths homework and wives watching soap operas. Odd Anglo-Italian families might wander in and be greeted with politeness, consideration, and pity. It was there, open all day and all night, because that is what Singaporeans wanted to do with their time, whatever the government's planners and zoners decided for them.

I was just packing up our own—obviously unlucky—rod when the auntie next to us snagged another whopper. She would eat well at the barbeque pit, even if most of the ones she was catching were 60 per cent claw. Opposite her, the trio of over-serious and under-lucked men noted her catch, then looked back to their own floats, bobbing away in that Coke-coloured water.

* * *

I swallowed a couple of paracetamols with a chaser of sugar-rich sports drink, and continued to hobble my painful way along East Coast Park. In one way or another the greenery stretched the best part of 10 kilometres along the southeast coast of Singapore, hemmed in on one side by the thundering East Coast Parkway, and on the other by the open sea. The shimmering artificial beach was held in place by numerous jetties and stony fortifications. Beyond that was an armada of ships at anchor: freighters and tankers, cargo carriers and car transporters, all patiently facing into the current and riding out the day under the hot sun.

The ECP, more than the carefully-managed Sentosa, was a true representation of Singapore at play. On such a thin sliver of land everything was planned. The stalls selling the life-giving sports drinks were evenly spaced, with clusters of seafood restaurants and fast-food joints filling the gaps. There were occasional encampments of concrete bungalows, and camping areas full of flimsy S$30 tents, where—so I have been told—many Singaporeans have their first unchaperoned adventures with the opposite sex. I started making my way around the seaward edge of a lagoon used for cable-led water skiing, only to be confounded by building works. I swore, retraced my steps, and took the clockwise path. Every unnecessary step hurt twice as much.

The footpath kept pace with a well-used cycle path. Men in full lycra racing kit trundled past uneasily on their carbon-fibre bikes, unable or unwilling to pick up speed above that of an asthmatic Labrador. Pairs of young women, holding hands in ill-advised attempts at stability, tottered by on roller blades. Flocks of schoolkids shuffled on and off the cycle path like sheep, looking anxiously for cues from their teachers telling them where it was safe to walk and where it was not. Every concrete bench that I passed was occupied by a resting South Asian labourer, taking a lunchtime breather with a quick nap or mobile phone check. Others sat in groups on the concrete floors of open-walled shelters, scooping up curry from paper wrappings, with the occasional word to each other.

I thought I would be enjoying this green, breezy stretch of my walk. I would pause and taste the salt in the air, walk barefoot through the sand and lapping surf, and cast my eyes from the steel hulks offshore to the aluminium monsters slowly descending towards Changi, just a little way off in the distance. The satisfaction of having walked across the entire country in a single day would be within reach. Each step would be spring-loaded.

But each step was not. I made out the vividly marked tail of a Tiger Air A320 as it lost height on its final approach, winced, cursed, and continued.

23

CHANGI AIRPORT

GEOGRAPHY CHANGES

That Tiger Air Airbus continued its descent, hidden from my sight by the trees of East Coast Park. Its passengers left behind the awesome sight of those dozens of enormous ships at anchor, passed over a ribbon of sand, then the East Coast Parkway, the Laguna National and Tanah Merah Country Club Tampines golf courses, and touched down on Changi's Runway 1. They would taxi to their stand, taking in the gargantuan double-decked Singapore Airlines and Emirates A380s, the round-hulled Cebu Pacific A330 on its way back to Manila, and construction projects in every direction. They would disembark, cocooned by the climate-defying air conditioning, and race to immigration. After a few business-like moments they would arrive to pick up their hold luggage, which would invariably be there waiting for them. The whole experience would be frictionless, and a marvel of modern travel. I once landed at Changi in a Garuda 737 on a flight from Jakarta, disembarked at the most remote corner of the airport, and was home—20 kilometres away as the crow flies—a barely believable forty-five minutes after stepping off the plane.

If anything in Singapore exemplifies the miracle of its first half-century, it is Changi. It is consistently ranked as the best airport in the world, with magazine articles gushing about its efficiency, comfort, and the fact there is a swimming pool for use by transit passengers. There may be some awful taxi drivers in Singapore (one almost killed us after a late-night arrival at Changi), but there are also Ubers and Grabs available, and nobody is going to try to cheat you out of an extra dollar or two. It goes without saying that the whole place is the product of land reclamation. It takes a remarkable, focused and determined government to bring something like this into being.

Changi's reputation is only enhanced by the airline that calls it home. Singapore Airlines, or SIA, is also consistently ranked as one of the world's best. It built its reputation as a high-quality connector airline, particularly on the "kangaroo route" from Europe to Australia. There was no domestic market, but it took full advantage of the capabilities of the new Boeing 747 "Jumbo Jets," positioning itself as a high-quality linkage between somewhere over there and somewhere else. SIA was, in effect, Singapore's strategy with wings: it leveraged geography and technology, and was globally competitive on price and quality. Even in the late 1970s, my grandmother used to swear by SIA when she visited us in New Zealand.

But, as in other areas where the Singapore miracle has transformed the island's fortunes, what worked in those first fifty years may not be quite so robust in the future. In terms of quality SIA is no longer head and shoulders above the rest. Rivals from the Gulf, such as Qatar Airlines, have waded into the that game and come out on top. Price, which was never SIA's strongest suit, is becoming a real problem in a world where new planes and low cost carriers (LCCs) are setting the rules. SIA fares are often comfortably among the most expensive, although demand is cushioned by the unstinting loyalty of the Singaporeans themselves. On longer routes they face added competition from the likes of Emirates and the Chinese airlines, while LCCs are starting to make serious inroads on medium-length regional routes, helped by the advent of highly efficient longer-range small jets.

Finally, Singapore's geography may no longer be quite as advantageous for SIA as it once was. In the past, using the 747, Southeast Asia was the natural stopover between Europe and Australasia. The Gulf has stolen a large chunk of this pie, thanks to a geographical inheritance—between Europe and booming East Asia—that has usurped that of Singapore. The home bases of Qatar, Emirates and Etihad sit within an eight-hour flight of two-thirds of the world's population, and within a four-hour flight of a third.[1] The Gulf has also marketed itself as a glitzy winter-sun destination in its own right: even with Marina Bay Sands and Brand Raffles, Singapore is struggling to stay in the tail wind of the Instagram king, Dubai. Staggering sums have also been invested on the quality of the Gulf connector airliners, marketing budgets, and the airports that service them. Meanwhile, Chinese airlines are getting better, are cheaper, and are well-positioned to muscle in on the Kangaroo route. And that is before the new breed of ultra-low-cost carriers is taken into account.[2] SIA, like Cathay Pacific up in Hong Kong, clearly has it all to do if it is to stay competitive.

The challenge of changing geography is affecting Singapore in other ways, too. Its core proposition as a port was always its critical position on the sea route from East Asia to India, the Gulf, and Europe. After independence in 1965 it benefitted hugely from the rise of Japan, followed by South Korea, Taiwan, and then China itself. Investments in fuel refining, bunkering, and port infrastructure, especially after containerisation, have been very well-rewarded. But will this geographical bounty continue?

It is easy to argue that it will not. As China shifts higher up the value chain, developing more domestic consumption, that will surely result in fewer exports to be shipped via Singapore. Other trends might also play a part, including the development of an ice-free globally-warmed polar route between Asia and Europe, or the continued rise of local supply chains, perhaps fuelled by 3D printing. If the world shifts towards a post-carbon economy, Singapore's petrochemical industries, and its position linking the Middle East to East Asia, might also become far less relevant.

One other geography-bending possibility that has intrigued dreamers for a century or two, and probably given Singaporean authorities the occasional cold sweat, can be found just over 1,000 kilometres up the Malay peninsula. The idea is simply that a canal can be cut through one of the narrower parts of the peninsula, obviating the need to scoot down towards Singapore at all. This proposition dates back to at least 1677, when it was put forward by a French engineer. By the nineteenth century the British considered a "Kra canal" to be a genuine potential threat to their interests. That view was revised after the Indian Mutiny of 1857, when it was recognised that a canal would help the swift transfer of reinforcements between India and East Asia.

Several expeditions took a close look at the slightest section of the Malay peninsula, the Kra Isthmus in Thailand and Myanmar, and most concluded that a canal would be a rather daunting proposition: the land is hilly, and the underlying rock is granite. One British survey of 1863 suggested building a railway, rather than a canal. In 1883 Alfred J. Loftus published an account of his own expedition. In amongst his thoughts about dinners of braised monkey, accompanied by brandy and cigars, and the problems of leeches, he noted that "in my opinion the Isthmus of Krá as a means of transit from one sea to the other would be utterly useless, either by canal or railway."[3] In 1897 a treaty was signed with Siam (now Thailand), agreeing that the Siamese were the only ones who could build this unlikely canal without British consent.

The idea, however, has not entirely disappeared. It gained a new lease of life in the 1970s, although the canal scheme was spiked: Thailand simply did not have the infrastructure to support such an expensive project, and there were concerns that it would lead to a *de facto* partition, severing the bulk of the country from the restive southern (Muslim) provinces. In 2017, an organisation called the Thai Canal Association for Study and Development, which was formed by retired Thai generals (with some Chinese involvement), did yet another feasibility study into the canal. The suggestion was that it could be tied into the Chinese "Belt and Road" initiative, and that it would cost US$28 billion.[4]

While in truth the Kra canal still seems as far away as it did for Alfred J. Loftus, as he munched on a few slices of braised monkey, this should not obscure the wider issue. The geography that first attracted Raffles, and allowed Lee Kuan Yew to build a miracle, may not remain on Singapore's side for very much longer. Geography is not static.

The challenge that Singapore now faces is that its size means that it has little wiggle-room to fall back on as geography evolves. So much of its miracle leveraged its location, from Indian opium to Chinese electronics, and from Middle Eastern oil to a stable safe haven for multinationals in Southeast Asia. There is an echo here of other economies that have been marginalised by changing geographic realities, including Genoa, as trade moved from the Mediterranean and Black Seas to the Atlantic; and Buffalo, NY, as New York's link to Lake Erie became less important. Again, complacency is something that Singapore can ill afford, no matter how marvellous Changi airport is, or how loyal SIA's local fan-base proves.

* * *

Singapore's geography may have fuelled its rise, but it has also been a source of insecurity. Small size always brings risks, and that nutcracker positioning, between Malaysia and Indonesia, has helped fuel the feeling of vulnerability that drove the Singapore miracle. It may now be far better friends with its immediate neighbours, but new security problems have arisen.

The one that I heard about, time and time again, from government employees as much as taxi uncles, was the risk of terrorist attacks. The understandable working presumption is that any such incident would most probably be perpetrated by Islamist extremists. In addition to its sizeable Muslim minority in its Malay community (and very many Muslim migrant workers from Bangladesh), both of Singapore's neighbours are overwhelmingly Muslim.

With such large—and, it must be emphasised, largely very friendly—Muslim populations in the immediate region, there is a real concern that fallout from conflicts such as that in Syria may wash up on Singapore's shores sooner or later. The number of Singaporeans who have fought under the black flag of ISIS (the Islamic State of Iraq and Syria) is thought to be well into double figures.[5] Many more radicalised Indonesians and Malaysians are known to have been involved, and many of them have returned to Southeast Asia. They have been joined by others, with intelligence sources worried that many extremists end up being "dumped" in Malaysia.

For these pockets of radicalised extremists, nearby Singapore may present a tempting target. Writing in *The Diplomat*, Bilveer Singh argued that Singapore can be viewed by extremists as an illegal creation within the Muslim Malayosphere, occupied by infidels (mainly the Chinese) operating anti-Muslim policies both regionally and internationally (including the hosting of a US military base).[6] Singapore's materialistic and Western ethos would certainly represent fair game.

The impact and profile of any successful attack can easily be imagined, beyond the casualties. In August 2016, six people were arrested after the discovery of an apparently ISIS-inspired plot to fire rockets from the neighbouring Indonesian island of Batam towards the Marina Bay Sands area. Singapore's Terrorism Threat Assessment for 2017, from the Ministry of Home Affairs, names ISIS as the nation's most serious threat.[7] Speaking as a former broadcast journalist, I have no doubt that images as iconic and visually striking as an under-attack MBS would be difficult to shift from rolling TV news bulletins across the world. Indeed, on such a well-connected and international island, any attack would be global news for days, accompanied by copious professional and amateur video footage.

Anything of this order would be utterly catastrophic for Singapore. It could devastate an economy that relies upon the presence of multinationals, its open links to the region and the wider world, and a totally safe environment for tourists and expats alike. The country's recent arms-length relationship with expats has compounded the feeling that their presence—on both sides—is not much more than a mutually beneficial economic relationship. They are mobile, and would disappear in an instant.—along with richer Singaporeans—on the first flights to Perth, Dubai, and London. Terrorism could be a mortal threat to the Singapore miracle, and the authorities are anything but complacent about it.

"Singapore views terrorism as the primary threat for national security," said Dr Collin Koh of the Maritime Security Programme at the Nanyang Technological University. "Especially if you look at the threat of Islamic State coming to Southeast Asia." I had called Dr Koh to ask about piracy in the Malacca Straits, but the conversation soon veered towards the topic of terrorism. His view was that the congested sea lanes around Singapore heightened the risk of an attack, perhaps on the industrial installations that I had seen on my Southern Islands fishing trip. "We're an important petrochemical hub," he noted.

"Many of our installations are on the waterfront, in close proximity to very busy shipping lanes." In such a congested, busy
environment it was hard to get early warning of an attack. There
had also been scenario planning for an assault on harbour or
passenger terminal facilities from a ferry that could be hijacked
near an Indonesian island. The possibilities are endless, mind-
boggling, and very scary.

You can get a flavour of official concern about all this by stepping into some MRT carriages. As well as standard warnings
against the dangers of dengue fever and sneezing one's germs all
over other people, one MRT train that I travelled in was plas-
tered in public safety adverts aimed at raising awareness of possible terrorist attacks. I dutifully downloaded the SGSecure
smartphone app, as advised. Among its features was one allowing
people to send photos of anything suspicious to the authorities.
"Be alert to tell-tale indicators of suspicious or malicious intent,"
it said, along with graphics explaining which clothes or behaviours were particular cause for alarm.

The anniversary of the British surrender at the Ford Motor
Factory is now known as Total Defence Day. The five pillars of
the country's "total defence" system are military, civil (wider society, including families and friends), economic, social, and psychological ("being a resilient people").[8] For somewhere as out-
wardly stable, safe, and secure as Singapore, these public
messages are a chilling reminder of the worst that could happen.
However, they do not cover all possible threats on the security
front, to the island nation and its economy.

Piracy is one threat. This is not exactly new in this corner of
Southeast Asia, with the region's myriad small islands and overgrown creeks providing fantastic cover for pirate boats. Back in
Singapore's early years, many of the raiders came from pirate bases
as far away as Mindanao and Borneo. One of the great imperial
characters of the time, an Englishman called James Brooke, made
his name in bringing pirates from the latter to heel.

Brooke was born in India, ran away from school in England, and fought in the British East India Company's Bengal Army. He was seriously wounded in 1825 at the Battle of Rungpore, in the First Anglo-Burmese War, after leading two charges by Indian volunteers. In the second of these he was shot, thrown from his horse and left for dead. When the battlefield was being cleared they found that he was still breathing. He was evacuated to England, where he recovered, with all of his sense of bravado intact.[9]

After coming into an inheritance of £30,000, Brooke bought a schooner called *The Royalist* and headed towards Southeast Asia. In 1838 he arrived in Borneo, where he helped to crush an uprising against the sultan of Brunei. In gratitude, the sultan made Brooke the governor of Sarawak. Brooke successfully suppressed the pirates that had made the coast of north Borneo their home, and, after restoring the sultan to the throne following another uprising against his rule, he became the famed "White Rajah of Sarawak." At one point, Brooke joined forces with Sir Henry Keppel in Singapore, before hunting down the base of the fearsome Dyak war prahus.[10] These were giant estuarine craft with outriggers powered by up to 200 oarsmen, carrying warriors armed with swords and blowpipes on their roof.

Modern piracy in the Malacca Straits may not be quite as colourful, but it is a serious and persistent problem. Attacks spiked in the early 2000s, at one point making the region the probable successor to the Horn of Africa as the world's pirate hotspot. Many attacks took place in the congested Straits, in waters that lay outside the immediate jurisdictions of the three littoral states. One area of particular concern was a section of relatively open sea, just beyond Raffles Lighthouse in the southwestern edge of Singaporean territory, close to several Indonesian islands and the unkempt Sumatran shoreline.

The targets of these modern pirates are very different to those that were attacked in the Indian Ocean off Somalia. They tend to be carriers of commodities such as palm oil or logs. Their ships are boarded, often at night, and taken to a remote creek or island. Their cargo is then simply pumped or unloaded onto another vessel. In effect, the pirates are running sophisticated operations that involve infiltrating complex and sometimes highly regulated supply chains, rather than simple demands for ransoms. They require forgers, along with experts in technology and finance. In some cases, the ships themselves are recommissioned with new papers. This is not just simple theft; through these methods pirates are able to circumvent regulations in industries such as fishing and palm oil, with implications for sustainability, and are tied in to wider crime networks.[11]

Singapore's government, as we know, is far from complacent, and strong measures have been taken to combat this new form of resurgent piracy, in concert with the country's neighbours. It seems to have worked, although other parts of Southeast Asia remain hotspots (the Sulu Sea, off the northeast coast of Borneo, is apparently the latest danger area). However, there is a wider geopolitical risk, which Dr Koh also pointed out to me.

"The biggest issue in the South China Sea is how the rule of law is being looked at and implemented," said Dr Koh. It sounded a lot less lively than pirates. "A very small country like Singapore is very sensitive towards how bigger coastal stats regard the rule of law at sea. The South China Sea is a threat to Singapore now because of normative issues."

This was an oblique reference to China, and its ambitions in the expanse of sea that opens up to Singapore's northeast, with Borneo and the Philippines archipelago to the east, and Malaysia, Thailand and Vietnam to the west. China's rise has been destabilising. It may not (yet) have led to outright war, but it has certainly tipped the status quo in a direction where war between major powers—whether through miscalculation or mistake—is not inconceivable.[12] In 2012 East Asian military budgets outstripped those of Europe's NATO members for the first time, rising 7.8 per cent from the year before.[13] There had been friction between China and Vietnam for years, but the former's interest in the aptly named Mischief Reef, on the eastern side of the South China Sea, threatened a host of other nations: Philippines, Malaysia, Brunei, and Indonesia. Lee Kuan Yew told the BBC that the interest was akin to "a big dog going up to a tree and raising its leg and marking its presence, so that smaller dogs in the region will know that a big dog has been past and will come back."[14]

That big dog has become ever more aggressive, referring to the South China Sea as "blue national soil," and scrabbling around for evidence that the contested "Nine-Dash Line" (which in effect lassoes much of the sea as Chinese territory) has some sort of historical basis.[15] If you happen to have an ancient map that marks that sea as definitively Chinese, dig it out of your attic and offer it to the Chinese: they will happily shower you with gold in return. In the absence of durable evidence, Beijing is using tactics such as browbeating and bribing neighbouring states, while literally building up tidal lumps of rock with a permanent Chinese presence.

Strategically, Beijing's game is clear: it is establishing itself incontrovertibly within the chain of islands and archipelagos that separate the coastal waters of Eurasia from the blue waters of the Pacific Ocean itself. This chain stretches from the Yellow and East China Seas, past the Japanese island of Okinawa, through the Straits of Taiwan, and down into the South China Sea. As the resurgent power in the region, re-establishing itself in the waters lying just off its coast, this may seem reasonable. However, what is incontrovertible is that this has raised the political temperature in the region.

Chinese ventures in these waters are also a direct threat to the security of several states, or encroachments into what they long thought of as their own territorial waters. Japan is now re-examining its post-war pacifist constitution. Taiwan's own notions of independence from the mainland are being squeezed, along with any confidence that it could defend itself against an amphibious attack. Fishermen from the Philippines and Vietnam feel their livelihoods under threat. As noted earlier, military spending, including on technologies such as submarines, is being ramped up. These ventures are a direct threat to the United States, which has treaty obligations to protect Taiwan, along with a commitment to both international law and the freedom of navigation for crucial shipping routes. There has been a series of stand-offs and near-misses, as each side probes and tests the other.

Given that its fifty-year miracle was earned on the back of a benign trading environment, with international law upheld and booming economies from Japan and South Korea to China and Taiwan, this ramping up of tension is a real worry for Singapore. An incident in the South China Sea, or an outbreak of something serious in relations between China and either Japan or Taiwan, could lead to a dramatic collapse in shipping. "The problem to sea lines of communication in the South China Sea is on the minds of every prudent defence planner," commented Dr Koh. "You assume that there is a chance the South China Sea will enter into a conflict that would endanger shipping lanes or force ships to reroute."

Even without such a conflict, Singapore's diplomatic balancing act is becoming far more difficult. It has trodden a precarious line between Chinese and American interests, acting as a friend to Beijing while making sure the Changi Naval Base has been built to fit the exact dimensions of US Navy vessels. Singapore's armed forces train in Taiwan and Australia, under Israeli guidance. For Singapore, says the American political thinker Robert D. Kaplan, the balance of power is not cynicism so much as the preservation of order. He also describes the island's foreign policy and security elite as the most cold-blooded in the world, when calculating the balance of advantage.[16] It is no surprise that Singapore remains wedded to National Service (for men) and a military that boasts fighter jets and AWACS observation planes, as well as frigates and submarines.

The balance may become even more difficult to maintain given that, as *The Economist* warned, "weaker allies such as Vietnam, the Philippines, Malaysia and Indonesia may conclude that bowing to Chinese military and economic power is a safer bet than hoping for a declining America to fight their corner."[17] The plight of another small state—Qatar—which in 2017 found itself isolated and under pressure from surrounding countries, was another warning.[18] Like Qatar, Singapore does not just rely upon the wider region for water and food security, but for the airspace needed for its viability as a transport hub.

The difficulties of maintaining the status quo and continuing to balance between the big powers, in the era of resurgent Chinese military power, was amply demonstrated in 2016 and 2017 by the Terrex saga. This incident began when an international court in the Netherlands ruled in favour of the Philippines in a territorial dispute in the South China Sea with Beijing, in a case called the South China Sea Arbitration. Prime Minister Lee Hsien Loong responded with some comments about the need to uphold the rule of international law, which some saw as an unwise slight against a prickly China. Not long after that, Singapore found that nine of its Terrex armoured personnel carriers were being impounded in Hong Kong, ostensibly because of a paperwork irregularity.[19] (The fact that they had just been involved in a training exercise in Taiwan is also unlikely to have pleased Beijing.) Although the vehicles eventually made their way back to Singapore, the saga was interpreted as a deliberate shot across the bows by Beijing. Plainly, any pretence to neutrality while trying to maintain friendly relationships with both the US and China will be extremely difficult from now on.

24

TANAH MERAH FERRY TERMINAL

LITTLE RED DOT

You know an insult has failed to hit the mark when its target adopts it as their own. The Indonesian president, B.J. Habibie, intended "Little Red Dot" to be a breezily dismissive slur on the miniscule island that had somehow become a nation. When, fifty years of remarkably successful survival under its belt, Singapore marked its miraculous half-century, its celebratory SG50 logo was drawn in the shape of a little red dot. It symbolised not just survival against the odds, but a collective pride at the country overcoming its physical limitations and becoming far more than the sum of its parts. Meanwhile, Indonesia sprawled across Singapore's southern horizon: gigantic, chaotic, and full of half-realised potential.

The spur of land that marked Tanah Merah ferry port was visible from underneath the Changi flight path. A year or so earlier I had taken a ferry from there to a resort in Bintan, one of Indonesia's Riau Islands, with my family. It had weaved past dozens of ships at anchor before picking up speed and discharging us at a harbour in the north of Bintan, where minibus transfers lined up, waiting to whisk passengers off to their resorts. There was a visiting elephant, charming service, and something of a sea breeze. Some go to play golf, or rack up drinks bills that are a fraction of Singapore prices. I chose to go for a dip in the limpid waters off the white sand beach, bobbing about pleasurably while I watched distant tankers steaming up into the South China Sea. When I climbed out of the water I found the hair on my legs had been tangled up in blobs of oil with the consistency of chewing gum. A pot of what seemed to be white spirit sat on a stool next to the beach, ready to help ill-advised bathers like me scrape their skin clean. I walked back up the beach and into the resort gardens smelling like a painter's rag.

The oily surprises hidden in those clear waters were a reminder that Bintan was still very much on the Straits, and just a stone's throw from Singapore itself. Indeed, the resorts on the north coast of Bintan are really just a physical extension of the city state itself, but under a different flag and jurisdiction. Similarly, neighbouring Batam can be seen as a convenient low-wage industrial estate for Singapore, while cities like Tanjung Pinang and Johor Bahru are reservoirs of labour. Geographers and planners refer to this extended geography as the Indonesia–Singapore–Malaysia or SIJORI growth triangle.* Despite early hostile relations with its neighbours, this interconnection is a mutually beneficial response to Singapore's economic miracle. It provides the island nation with *de facto* extensions of its territory, and provides the neighbours with welcome economic growth.

By the time I was within eyesight of Tanah Merah ferry terminal, I was very well acquainted with Singapore's geography. My socks were bloody, and the tendons and muscles of my legs were wretched after almost as many concreted kilometres as

---

* SIJORI comes from SIngapore, JOhor (in Malaysia) and RIau (in Indonesia).

independent Singapore had years. I was, however, nearing my twin goals. It was, provided I struggled to the ferry port, a country that you really can walk across in a day. I had also seen the Singapore story laid out before me, as I tramped past industrial zones, heritage sites, HDB communities, leisure parks, and the sky-scraping edifices of global finance. This was an explanation of a miracle that began with Raffles and was finished off by Lee Kuan Yew, all on a teeny, tiny island just north of the equator.

The walk also explained the path that might lead to the Singapore miracle continuing. The industrial muscles of Jurong remained formidable, even as Singapore began to chart a path to the modern knowledge economy, with the NUS campus and One North as their statements of intent. The government, with its strategy groups, top-line talent, and PAP community outreach, was obviously up for the fight for both innovation and legitimacy. And an air of confidence wafted around the CBD like the smoke from the charcoal grills of Telok Ayer market. It was no surprise that some of the guiding intellectual lights behind the UK's conscious uncoupling from the European Union looked east, and declared their intention to build a free-trading Singapore-on-Thames.[1]

I had also had plenty of time to reflect on the headwinds that the country now faced. What if its geography was no longer such an asset, or the international climate not quite so benign as during the previous half-century? What if the government ran out of clever ideas, or the legitimacy to implement them? What if a terrorist attack destroyed the country's reputation for safety, or friction in the South China Sea rolled back the steady stream of ships through the Straits? What if Singaporeans simply became complacent about their achievements, and lost the hunger, sense of vulnerability, and appetite for hard work, that had underpinned their economic miracle? As the then-head of the civil service, Peter Ho, put it, "What persuaded their parents and grandparents will not wash with the third generation."[2]

It was the last of these—the sense of growing complacency, among Singaporean citizens if not their government—that concerned me the most. Like a dinghy facing a storm on the high seas, this small country had to feed off a sense of vulnerability to survive. That was easy enough when the roof was made of attap palms and you had every reason to mistrust the neighbours. But now, cossetted by air conditioning and rain-proof walkways, with a Filipino helper to attend to every physical need, and those previously-hostile neighbours now hoping that economic crumbs from your table land in Johor and Batam, it is harder to retain that hunger and vulnerability. In 2010, a reflective Lee Kuan Yew told the *New York Times* that "I've got to tell the next generation, please do not take for granted what's been built. [...] If you believe that it's permanent, it will come tumbling down and you will never get a second chance."[3]

Complacency could also pose a threat to the vaunted—and undoubtedly highly effective—Singaporean style of government. How could LKY have performed his slightly authoritarian miracles if the internet had allowed citizens an easy outlet for any disquiet? The 2011 election was a sign that PAP legitimacy was not guaranteed. Further achievements would need to be trumpeted to the masses, and that nagging sense of inequality assuaged. But what if that meant taking counter-productive measures, such as rolling up the red carpet that had been laid down for multinationals and their expat workforce? The government had a difficult balancing act on its hands.

The PAP would also need to continue its far-sighted stewardship of the economy, whatever storm brewed up around it. One indicator of how exposed the country's economy was to more general downturns in the global economy came with the financial crisis of 2008 and its aftermath. In 2007 the economy grew by a vigorous 7.7 per cent, before a combination of the crisis in finance and a regional export slump led to a dramatic slowdown to just 1.2 per cent the following year. In the first quarter of 2009 Singapore's GDP had declined an alarming 19.7 per cent from the previous quarter (and 11.5 per cent year-on-year). In that same three-month period, manufacturing (in particular, electronics, precision-engineered goods, and pharmaceuticals) contracted by 29 per cent, year-on-year.[4]

The crucial fact about Singapore is that it is small enough to walk across in a single day, and that means that it simply does not have the strategic depth to absorb complacency and catastrophes, setbacks and stumbles. If Singaporeans have lost their sense of vulnerability, then they need to check a map, read the newspapers, and rediscover it quickly. Even when in early 2018 the government announced that adult Singaporeans would each receive a one-off bonus of up to S$300, thanks to a hefty budget surplus, this was laced with stern injunctions about possible tough times ahead.[5]

Helpfully for Singaporeans, a reminder about that vulnerability appears almost annually in the later months of the year. Between August and November in 2015, my family would often wake up with the smell of burnt peat in our nostrils. We would look out of the windows to check how far up the street we could see. Sometimes my son's nursery school would be closed. Pedestrians would pass our gates with masks over their faces. If it was bad, their eyes would be red, agitated, and watery. It became second nature to monitor online maps for concentrations of deadly PM2.5 particles that would sear into the rubbery pink tissue of our lungs.

When it is bad, "the Haze" is enough to make an impact on economic activity. Anything that relies upon people being outdoors, from bars to sports clubs, shuts down. My wife switched her commute from buses to the underground MRT, and tried to work from home as much as possible. We invested in enormous electric air filters, and became experts in the different particles that each of them sucked out of the air. Expats, and anybody else with money, flexibility and time, booked themselves or their families onto flights to Australia, Japan, or Europe.

Few events or issues remind Singapore about its place in the world as much as the Haze, a gigantic seasonal cloud of smoke that tends to envelop parts of Southeast Asia at the height of the local dry season. Its origin tends to be the gigantic islands of Sumatra and Borneo, where marshy land is being cleared for cultivation, often for palm oil. The marshy land is drained, and the peaty soil dries out. Fires, lit deliberately to destroy the thick undergrowth, continue to smoulder underground. In dry weather, they burst out and sweep over vast areas, the clouds rising up, large enough to cover entire countries. Conditions at the centre of this hellish phenomenon are deadly—researchers estimated that 100,000 people were killed in the Haze of July to October 2015. Several thousand of those fatalities had been in Malaysia and Singapore.[6]

The appearance of this ungodly cloud of coughing and death was something of an affront to Singapore. After all, despite this being a piddly little island in an unpromising neighbourhood, with air as hot and heavy as a bowl of inhaled soup, it had achieved the miracle. But the 2015 Haze showed that there was only so much escaping that the island could do. Many Singaporeans, moved both by the local impact and the horrors that it was causing the communities that were surrounded by the flames, mobilised to help. But that sense of Singaporean technocratic control, that all it took to deal with a problem was brains and willpower, failed in the boundless, smoky bogs of Kalimantan and Sumatra. Fixing things on a small island was possible; the world, alas, was more complicated; Indonesia, it turned out, was even more complicated than that.

An enticing option for Singapore is to find a way to bend geography to its will. It is already familiar with the idea of steadily accreting territory because of its land reclamation projects. It has also extended its *de facto* territory through the SIJORI triangle, and its clever use of high- and low-end immigration in the service of its labour market. It is home to multinationals and a potent regional finance centre.

This, of course, is not an alien notion in a hyper-globalised world. Despite the boutique farms of Kranji, Singapore's decision to get rid of the stinking pig farms of the north in the 1970s entailed a firm commitment to outsourcing the island's food. Those pig farms are now to be found in Singapore's "near abroad," in places like Batam. Singapore currently has US$380 million invested in Australian agricultural projects, and is involved in a US$18 billion project to build a mega-farm in northeastern China. The clever people who make the government run so smoothly treat such issues as management problems.

The time might come when braver and more radical solutions need to be found. One of the more inventive geography-bending ideas for Singapore's future came from an Australian academic. Benjamen Gussen mooted setting up a Singaporean "charter city" on one of the various chunks of Western Australian territory that is suffocatingly hot and largely populated by things that kill humans.[7] At heart this was to resolve a supply and demand problem: he said there was worldwide demand for another global city in the Singapore mould, and a copious supply of those baking, orangey chunks of Western Australian bush.

The idea was to establish a green-field charter city in some suitable spot of around a thousand square kilometres. Dr Gussen suggested calling it "Dilga," after the Aboriginal Karadjeri goddess of fertility and growth. Four partners would each hold a quarter of the equity in the venture: Western Australia would provide the land; Singapore would provide the infrastructure; an Australian military base would be next door; the rest would come from the private sector. Between them, they would draft a basic law that would be deposited with the United Nations.

Migrants would be attracted by a ten-year income tax holiday, easy citizenship, and low unemployment. Tourists would come for theme parks, casinos, and resorts. It would help Australia deal with its refugee quota, while also showcasing green tech (in particular, solar energy and water desalination).

The plan went beyond the idea of building one city; it proposed the perfection of a template that could be used, cookie-cutter style, to build a series of mini Singapores around the world. In effect, it would take the miracle and franchise it. Who would not want to live in a clean, economically virile, safe, and efficient copy of the Lion City? They could even design their own version of the Merlion.

As Dr Gussen acknowledges, the bare bones of this are not original. Carthage began as a charter city called Qart Hadasht, back in 760 BC. In their own way, Hong Kong, Macau, and Visakhapatnam Special Economic Zone are all variations on comparable ideas. In 2016, a *Straits Times* opinion editor, Chua Mui Hoong, wrote about Australia's potential as a hinterland for Singapore, based on the two countries' strategic ties. The year before, the managing director of the Monetary Authority of Singapore envisaged setting up retirement communities down in Perth. Perhaps there is a space for Singapore to become a branded country—or a city-scale management consultancy, applying its own solutions for big bucks to others who want some of that miracle for themselves.

This is outlandish, but not a daft idea. Geographers and policy-makers now tend to think in terms of functional regions that cross borders, or lie within them, rather than traditional national units. In Britain there are economically integrated regions such as the M4 Corridor, the Northern Powerhouse, and Silicon Glenn. The Blue Banana is a suitably bending conglomeration of densely populated Europe that cuts across Wales and England, crosses the channel, then turns south towards Italy's old industrial triangle of Genoa, Milan, and Turin. Visiting businessmen tremble at the thought of what the Pearl River Delta could mean for their profit margins. Singapore itself is at the heart of SIJORI. Perhaps, as conventional wisdom turns its back on the nation as the building block of order, a super-functional consultancy, carrying Singapore-miracle branding, might be a natural market leader.

The impact of global warming might hasten the importance of geography-bending ideas for Singapore's future. Back in 2007, Lee Kuan Yew told the *New York Times* that the country was already having conversations with Dutch water experts about dykes. This, he said, would be okay if the water level rose by a metre (although the fallout from a similar rise for Indonesia would cause other significant regional problems). But, he said, laughing, "If the water goes up by three, four, five meters [...] what will happen to us? Half of Singapore will disappear! The valuable half—the seafronts!"[8]

When I discussed the impact of Singapore's tight geographical confines with the sage-like Kishore Mahbubani, he told me that people had to use their imagination more. They might spend their working days in HDBs, he said, but they were rich, and the city state was well connected by air, ferries, and causeways. "They can have second homes in Batam, Thailand, Cambodia, Malaysia, no problem," he said, adding that retirement within this wider and cheaper regional orbit was also a potential answer to any shortfalls in pensions.

Professor Mahbubani's exhortations for Singaporeans—citizens and senior politicians alike—to use their imagination was a constant theme of my interview with him. "Success creates its own problems," he said. "Singapore's fundamental challenge is the Kodak challenge.[†] Despite decades of success, complacency

---

[†] Kodak famously invented the digital camera, but ignored it as their core business was physical rolls of film. In retrospect, this was not a wise decision.

proved fatal for the famous manufacturer of camera film. "While you're still doing very well, to change course dramatically is very difficult. But this is a time for Singapore to change course dramatically." In short, Singapore was becoming too complacent to make the brave and bold decisions that would keep it afloat on the high seas.

Professor Mahbubani, who witnessed the full flourishing of the Singapore miracle during his own lifetime, was fulsome in his praise for Lee Kuan Yew and the senior PAP figures who had steered the new country so effectively. In contrast, he condemned the current leadership with faint praise: he called the government "thoughtful" and noted their awareness of the need to make dramatic changes, but drew attention to their reluctance to follow through. But why this reluctance? I asked him. "Don't forget, change is risky," he replied. "And we have created an incentive system. Our public servants are the highest-paid in the world. You have a system that rewards you if you're competent and do well. But if you take a risk, you might lose your comfortable income. Success creates risk aversion."

The professor turned the question around to me: "When was the last time the government ever did anything really radical and different?" I paused, then mumbled, the cogs in my mind whirring to little effect. It felt like being in a tutorial back at university, with an internationally feted expert putting me on an uncomfortable spot, ready to pounce on any sloppy or half-baked ideas. What about the rethinking of migration after the wake-up call of the 2011 elections? I knew it was a weak example. "But these are not fundamental," he retorted. "There's nothing you can point to that is revolutionary in the last ten years, that is very bold." Governments rarely do anything revolutionary unless faced with a crisis, I noted. "But that's the problem! You define the problem precisely. You're saying to me that only a crisis will move the Singapore government, and that's the problem: they have to move before the crisis."

This, with a certain amount of expert prompting from Professor Mahbubani, placed the charge of complacency on the shoulders of the government, rather than just the people. The citizens could be forgiven for their complacency, just as they could be forgiven for feeling aggrieved about immigration, for their relentless zero-sum approach to coaching their children through exams, or for favouring a predictable career as an accountant rather than gambling everything on a start-up. The government, however, had a different job. It had the responsibility to make the difficult decisions before they were necessary, rather than simply manage pressures.

Take, for instance, the response to the 2011 election. Was the fuss over the selection of a female Malay president, while restrictions were tightened on the Pink Dot event, a fumbling attempt at micromanagement? What about the tougher rules on employing expats? Was not the Singaporean economy built upon drawing in highly skilled foreign capital and labour? Was the continuing reliance on Filipino domestic helpers and Bangladeshi labourers really a sop to the households and companies that relied upon their cheap work, whatever the cost to productivity or to developing real twenty-first-century sectors, such as elderly care or building? I would never have argued that Singapore's government did not know the challenges it faced, or that it did not have superb thinkers and administrators. But, perhaps, it was no longer truly brave, and there were a host of complex "VUCA" challenges on the horizon that required brave answers rather than technocratically competent ones. They were on a small dinghy in a savage ocean, and to flourish rather than simply survive would take the spirit of 1965. The good professor was not convinced that this would happen.

"There won't be a major implosion," said Professor Mahbubani. "There'll be a gentle, comfortable slide downwards. Gradually we'll find that our neighbours become more competitive. They'll do bolder, more imaginative things. There are lots of reasons why people will continue to use us. If you want to set up a law firm to service the region, obviously you do it in Singapore. Everything works here." But even that would not be enough in the long run. "We'll just gently slide downwards."

Before I left Professor Mahbubani's office, with its view across the trees of the LKY School of Public Policy campus, our conversation briefly turned to the book that I had written about Genoa. There were similarities, I said, as the Genoese had been dealt an unpromising hand and were forced to come out fighting. The city state had levered hard work, invention, and geography, and had risen from nothing to become a vital cog in the nascent semi-globalised medieval economy. But Genoa then lost its vitality, and scrabbled around for a purpose, crowded out by France and Spain, as the world shifted away. Then followed 600 years of slow and steady decline. "Six hundred years of decline is not too bad!" he said, and shook my hand as I headed out of the door.

* * *

The last stretch of my walk hurt. I crossed the sea outlet of a canal, limped past the ropes and aerial walkways of an outdoor adventure centre, and joined the Coastal Park Connector footpath through some sparse jungle. I joined Tanah Merah Coast Road and turned right, passing an intricate arrangement of traffic cones that reminded me of England. I took the turn off to the ferry terminal, touched the terminal building with my fingers, and sent my wife a message. I found a seat, called up an Uber, and went inside. I slurped down another sugary sports drink, and noticed that my hands were shaking. An app on my phone told me that I had walked 53 kilometres.

When the driver appeared in her Honda Vezel, she asked me if I had just come from Indonesia. No, Tuas, I replied. Oh, said the driver, as she pulled out on to the main road. A wide-body jet was descending into Changi ahead of us. I asked how bad the traffic would be. Not bad, she answered, as it was still well before the rush hour. My phone told me that the journey home would take something like twenty-five minutes, on Singapore's smoothly functioning highways, lined by rows of immaculately pruned rain trees and vivid bougainvillea bushes. It was a small island, and I would be home soon.

NOTES

1. THE SOUTHERN ISLANDS

1. Rose George, *Deep Sea and Foreign Going: Inside Shipping, the Invisible Industry That Brings You 90% of Everything*, London: Portobello Books, 2013.
2. Pound-for-pound, of course.
3. He announced his retirement from the post of Dean at the Lee Kuan Yew School of Public Policy at the University of Singapore in 2017, as I was writing this book.

2. TUAS CHECKPOINT

1. Another early name for the island was Temasek, which is now used in the name of Temasek Holdings, a Singaporean national wealth fund.
2. Philippe Regnier, *Singapore: City-State in South-East Asia*, London: Hurst, 1987.
3. "Transcript of a press conference given by the Prime Minister of Singapore, Mr. Lee Kuan Yew, at Broadcasting House, Singapore, at 1200 hours on Monday 9th August, 1965," National Archives of Singapore, 9 August 1965, http://www.nas.gov.sg/archivesonline/data/pdfdoc/lky19650809b.pdf
4. John Curtis Perry, *Singapore: Unlikely Power*, New York: Oxford University Press, 2017.
5. This signature technique of taxi uncles seemed to be based on an ill-advised theory about saving fuel. It also meant that my son vomited in 90 per cent of taxis during his second and third years.
6. "Malaysia a 'dumping ground' for deported ISIS fighters," *The Straits Times*, 17 May 2017, http://www.straitstimes.com/asia/se-asia/malaysia-a-dumping-ground-for-deported-isis-fighters

7. In May 2018 Najib Razak was sensationally voted out of office. Many Singaporeans reacted with surprise, some relief, and a mental note that election upsets do happen.

8. Zhang Jiayi, "Debunking the myth of the lazy Malays," *Yayasan Mendaki* (Council for the Development of Singapore Malay/Muslim Community) (2014), http://www.mendaki.org.sg/qws/slot/u50178/2.%20Publication%20&%20 Resources/2.5%20Others/2.5.4%20YM%20Occasional%20Papers/ MENDAKI%20Occasional%20Paper%20Series_Zhang%20Jiayi.pdf

9. Perry, *Singapore: Unlikely Power*, 2017.

10. The electoral defeat of Najib Razak led some newspapers to speculate openly that a reunion was viable, if not likely.

3. THE AYE TOLL ROAD

1. "Raffles Country Club to make way for KL-Singapore High-Speed Rail," Channel NewsAsia, 4 January 2017, http://www.channelnewsasia.com/news/ singapore/raffles-country-club-to-make-way-for-kl-singapore-high-speed- rai-7537076

2. Rudyard Kipling noted that "the food is as excellent as the rooms are bad" in the famous Raffles Hotel. Evidently not all the food was good: "The turtle steaks of Raffles' at Singapur still live in my regretful memory," he wrote.

3. The treaty, in effect, set the border between what is now Indonesia and what are now Malaysia and Singapore. Some in Britain had even advocated abandoning Singapore, for fear of weakening the tottering Dutch empire, as they were more concerned with balancing French power.

4. John Curtis Perry, *Singapore: Unlikely Power*, New York: Oxford University Press, 2017.

5. Joseph Conrad, *The End of the Tether*, first published in *Youth: A Narrative and Two Other Stories*, Edinburgh/London: William Blackwood and Sons, 1902, http://www.gutenberg.org/files/527/527-h/527-h.htm

6. The "junk season" stretched between November and March, when the northeast monsoon helped junks and other boats on their way down from China. The "Bugis season" took boats up towards Indochina and China.

7. Rudyard Kipling, *From Sea to Sea and Other Sketches: Letters of Travel*, London: Macmillan and Co., 1900, https://archive.org/details/fromseatosealet02kiplgoog

8. For more on gambling, see Chapter 21.

9. Raffles' interest in the natural world extended to keeping a tiger cub as a pet, and an orangutan dressed in human clothes. He was a co-founder of the

Zoological Society of London and London Zoo, and the world's largest flower, the *Rafflesia* (which smells of rotting flesh) is named after him.

10. "Henry Keppel Surveys New Harbour, 29th May 1848," History SG, March 2015, http://eresources.nlb.gov.sg/history/events/6f5184c7-d976-4f15-8da3-a77dab180981

11. Algernon West, *Memoir of Sir Henry Keppel, G.C.B., Admiral of the Fleet*, London: Smith, Elder & Co., 1905, p. 161, https://archive.org/stream/memoirsirhenryk00westgoog#page/n182/mode/2up

12. *The Straits Times*, 15 July 1845, p. 1, http://eresources.nlb.gov.sg/newspapers/Digitised/Article/straitstimes18450715–1.2.2.4

13. *The Straits Times*, 20 July 1920, p. 10, http://eresources.nlb.gov.sg/newspapers/Digitised/Article/straitstimes19200720–1.2.70

14. "The Armenians of Singapore: An Historical Perspective," *Armenian Weekly*, 6 January 2015, https://armenianweekly.com/2015/01/06/armenians-of-singapore/

4. JURONG

1. Samanth Subramanian, "How Singapore Is Creating More Land for Itself," *New York Times*, 20 April 2017, https://www.nytimes.com/2017/04/20/magazine/how-singapore-is-creating-more-land-for-itself.html

2. See Chapter 22.

3. https://data.gov.sg/dataset/total-land-area-of-singapore

4. "A High Quality Living Environment for All Singaporeans: Land Use Plan to Support Singapore's Future Population," Ministry of National Development (Singapore), January 2013, https://www.mnd.gov.sg/landuseplan/e-book/files/assets/common/downloads/Land%20Use%20Plan%20to%20Support%20Singapore.pdf

5. David Owen, "The World is Running out of Sand," *The New Yorker*, 29 May 2017, http://www.newyorker.com/magazine/2017/05/29/the-world-is-running-out-of-sand

6. "Sand, rarer than one thinks," UNEP Global Environment Alert Service, March 2014, https://na.unep.net/geas/archive/pdfs/GEAS_Mar2014_Sand_Mining.pdf

7. Vietnam's Ministry of Construction does allow some sand from sea and river dredging projects to be sold in this way, although the investigation suggested that this was unlikely to have led to such large quantities.

8. "Tracing Vietnamese 'sand drain' to Singapore—P1: Where do the ships go?", *Tuoi Tre News*, 2 March 2017, http://tuoitrenews.vn/features/39825/tracing-the-vietnamese-sand-drain-to-singapore-p1-where-do-the-ships-go

9. Zhangxin Zheng, "Sand exported unethically from Vietnam ends up in Singapore," Mothership.sg, 10 April 2017, http://mothership.sg/2017/04/sand-exported-unethically-from-vietnam-end-up-in-singapore/

10. It was more officially known as "A proposed industrialization programme for the state of Singapore," United Nations Industrial Survey Mission 1963.

11. Philippe Regnier, *Singapore: City-State in South-East Asia*, London: Hurst, 1987.

5. PANDAN

1. Carolyn Khew, "Singapore's water success has H2O expert worried," *The Straits Times*, 21 March 2016, http://www.straitstimes.com/singapore/environment/singapores-water-success-has-h2o-expert-worried

2. For more on Singapore's Speakers' Corner, see Chapter 18.

6. WEST COAST ROAD

1. http://www.hdb.gov.sg/cs/infoweb/residential/buying-a-flat/new/hdb-flat

2. Singapore was good at this type of thing. Young fans of Lee Kuan Yew could complete an entire comic book series about their hero: *A Boy Named Harry*; *Harry Grows Up*; and *Harry Builds a Nation*.

3. See Chapter 9.

4. "Why 80% of Singaporeans live in government-built flats," *The Economist*, 6 July 2017, https://www.economist.com/news/asia/21724856-subsidies-are-irresist-iblebut-come-social-controls-why-80-singaporeans-live

5. "Creating 'vertical villages' in Singapore," BBC News, 27 November 2017, http://www.bbc.co.uk/news/av/business-42115818/creating-vertical-villages-in-singapore

6. Tyler Cowen, "A safety net we all can stand behind," Marginal Revolution, 15 May 2017, http://marginalrevolution.com/marginalrevolution/2017/05/safety-net-can-stand-behind.html

7. Suruchi Mazumdar, "The racist reality of house-hunting in Singapore: 'Sorry, your wife is Indian,'" Quartz India, 29 August 2016, https://qz.com/768706/the-racist-reality-of-house-hunting-in-singapore-sorry-your-wife-is-indian/

8. Helier Cheung, "'No Indians No PRCS': Singapore's rental discrimination problem," BBC News, 2014, http://www.bbc.com/news/world-asia-26832115

7. NATIONAL UNIVERSITY OF SINGAPORE

1. Depending on the international ranking you read, NUS was either the best

university in both Singapore and Asia, and twenty-second in the entire world (according to the *Times Higher Education* in 2018), or the fifteenth in the world but only the second in Singapore (in the QS World University Rankings, which placed Nanyang Technological University ahead of NUS).

2. "Programme for International Student Assessment 2015," Organisation for Economic Co-operation and Development, 2015, https://www.oecd.org/pisa/pisa-2015-results-in-focus.pdf

3. Gonzalo Viña, "Half of UK primary schools adopt 'Asian' style maths," *Financial Times*, 12 July 2016, https://www.ft.com/content/693e5d6a-4829-11e6-8d68-72e9211e86ab

4. Jeevan Vasagar, "Why Singapore's kids are so good at maths," *Financial Times*, 22 July 2016, https://www.ft.com/content/2e4c61f2-4ec8-11e6-8172-e39ecd-3b86fc

5. "Many Pathways, One Mission," Ministry of Education (Singapore), 2007, https://www.moe.gov.sg/microsites/many-pathways/

6. This should not diminish some of the strong foundations bequeathed by earlier British rule. This includes places of learning such as NUS, Raffles Institution and the Anglo-Chinese School (established in 1905, 1823, and 1886, respectively).

7. Philippe Regnier, *Singapore: City-State in South-East Asia*, London: Hurst, 1987.

8. "Many Pathways, One Mission," Ministry of Education (Singapore), 2007, https://www.moe.gov.sg/microsites/many-pathways/

9. "Singapore tops Asia in preparing students for the future: EIU study," Channel NewsAsia, 20 September 2017, https://www.channelnewsasia.com/news/asia/singapore-tops-asia-in-preparing-students-for-the-future-eiu-9232606

10. "Fearing exams more than parents' death," News24, 21 November 2001, https://www.news24.com/xArchive/Archive/Fearing-exams-more-than-parents-death-20001121

11. Sandra Davie, "Singapore students suffer from high levels of anxiety: Study," *The Straits Times*, 20 August 2017, http://www.straitstimes.com/singapore/education/spore-students-suffer-from-high-levels-of-anxiety-study

12. "Student, 10, jumps to death over school workload," Singapore Window, 22 August 2001, http://www.singapore-window.org/sw01/010822af.htm

13. Calvin Yang, "Super tutors who earn at least $1m a year," *The Straits Times*, 23 May 2016, http://www.straitstimes.com/singapore/super-tutors-who-earn-at-least-1m-a-year

14. Ibid.

15. Jeevan Vasagar, "Why Singapore's kids are so good at maths," *Financial Times*, 22 July 2016, https://www.ft.com/content/2e4c61f2-4ec8-11e6-8172-e39ecd-3b86fc

16. Singapore has tried to tackle the life-long learning challenge by setting up voucher-based "individual learning accounts" that can be spent on a range of courses.

17. Bobby Jayaraman, "Let's kill the drill approach in schools," *The Straits Times*, 17 February 2017, http://www.straitstimes.com/opinion/lets-kill-the-drill-approach-in-schools

18. Amanda Erickson, "People in Singapore don't read much literature. Can these tiny books change that?", *The Washington Post*, 11 February 2017, https://www.washingtonpost.com/news/worldviews/wp/2017/02/11/people-in-singapore-dont-read-can-these-tiny-books-change-that/

19. Maggie Hiufu Wong, "McDonald's offers to lock up your smartphone for more family time," CNN, 17 October 2017, http://edition.cnn.com/travel/article/singapore-mcdonalds-mobile-phone-locker/index.html

20. Stavros N. Yiannouka, "Is education the secret of Singapore's success?" World Economic Forum, 10 April 2015, www.weforum.org/agenda/2015/04/is-education-the-secret-to-singapores-success

21. "Worldwide Educating for the Future Index," The Economist Intelligence Unit, 2017, http://educatingforthefuture.economist.com/

22. "Singapore and the World: Looking Back and Looking Ahead," The Online Citizen, 4 June 2017, https://www.theonlinecitizen.com/2017/06/04/singapore-and-the-world-looking-back-and-looking-ahead/

23. Adrian W.J. Kuah, "It's about time we learn to take our time," Today Online, 5 June 2017, http://www.todayonline.com/singapore/its-about-time-we-learn-take-our-time

8. NUS SPORTS FACILITIES

1. It was also extraordinarily well-rewarded. Singapore's national reward for winning a gold medal was US$753,000, the highest in the world. Indonesia was next with US$383,000, then Azerbaijan at US$255,000. http://sports.yahoo.comnews/u-s-ranks-ninth-on-list-of-countries-paying-out-bonuses-for-gold-medals-184751327.html

2. Belmont Lay, "Joseph Schooling is S'porean. He won a medal for S'pore. But he did it in the most un-S'porean way," Mothership.sg, 18 August 2016, http://mothership.sg/2016/08/joseph-schooling-is-sporean-he-won-a-medal-for-spore-but-he-did-it-in-the-most-un-sporean-way/

3. "World's Top 20 Highest Paid Political Leaders," Richest Lifestyle, 2015, https://richestlifestyle.com/highest-paid-political-leaders-in-the-world/

4. Michael D. Barr, *The Ruling Elite of Singapore: Networks of Power and Influence*, London: I.B. Tauris, 2014.

5. William Keng Mun Lee, "The economic marginality of ethnic minorities: an analysis of ethnic income inequality in Singapore," *Asian Ethnicity*, vol. 5, no. 1 (2004), https://doi.org/10.1080/1463136032000168880

6. Fann Sim, "Singapore is kiasu, competitive, self-centred: survey," Yahoo! News, 23 August 2012, https://sg.news.yahoo.com/singapore-is-kiasu—competitive—self-centred—survey.html

7. Justin Ong, "Singapore should kill 'kiasu' culture: NMP Kuik Shiao-Yin," Channel NewsAsia, 5 April 2016, https://www.channelnewsasia.com/news/singapore/singapore-should-kill-kiasu-culture-nmp-kuik-shiao-yin-8089162

9. NATIONAL UNIVERSITY HOSPITAL

1. Several well-known figures have made a similar choice. Robert Mugabe has been a frequent visitor, as have wealthier citizens from across Asia.

2. Duncan Sutherland, "Ida Simmons," Singapore Infopedia, National Library Board (Singapore), http://eresources.nlb.gov.sg/infopedia/articles/SIP_2013–05–14_135054.html

3. https://www.cpf.gov.sg/employers/employerguides/employer-guides/paying-cpf-contributions/cpf-contribution-and-allocation-rates

4. Aaron E. Carroll and Austin Frakt, "What Makes Singapore's Health Care So Cheap?", *New York Times*, 2 October 2017, https://www.nytimes.com/2017/10/02/upshot/what-makes-singapores-health-care-so-cheap.html

5. John Micklethwait and Adrian Wooldridge, *The Fourth Revolution: The Global Race to Reinvent the State*, London: Allen Lane, 2014.

6. http://app.psd.gov.sg/data/SpeechatAdminServiceDinner2005final.pdf

7. Tyler Cowen, "A few notes on Singaporean (and other) health care systems," Marginal Revolution, 26 August 2013, http://marginalrevolution.com/marginalrevolution/2013/08/a-few-notes-on-singaporean-and-other-health-care-systems.html

8. Seth Mydans and Wayne Arnold, "Modern Singapore's Creator Is Alert to Perils," *New York Times*, 2 September 2007, http://www.nytimes.com/2007/09/02/world/asia/02singapore.html

9. https://data.worldbank.org/indicator/SP.DYN.TFRT.IN?

10. Julian Ryall, "South Koreans 'will be extinct by 2750,'" *The Telegraph*, 25 August

2014, https://www.telegraph.co.uk/news/worldnews/asia/soutkorea/11054817/South-Koreans-will-be-extinct-by-2750.html

11. Ong Hwee Hwee, "Singapore population report: 10 things to know about citizens, PRs, babies and more," *The Straits Times*, 30 September 2015, http://www.straitstimes.com/singapore/singapore-population-report-10-things-to-know-about-citizens-prs-babies-and-more

12. Seb P. Smith, "Singapore's demographic time-bomb," Medium, 2015, https://medium.com/@sebpsmith/singapore-s-demographic-time-bomb, no longer available.

13. One senior foreign journalist told me that she had been called in for a friendly chat in a ministry, after running a story about an example of poverty in Singapore. The officials explained that the person in question was only suffering hardship because of inadvisable personal choices. It's hard to imagine such an extraordinary official intervention in any other developed country.

10. ONE NORTH

1. Peter Ho, "Governing in the Anthropocene: Risk & Resilience, Imagination & Innovation," Lecture II of the IPS-Nathan Lectures, 19 April 2017, http://lkyspp2.nus.edu.sg/ips/event/201617-ips-nathan-lectures-lecture-ii-governance-in-the-anthropocene-risk-resilience-imagination-innovation

2. "Singapore tries to become a fintech hub," *The Economist*, 12 January 2017, https://www.economist.com/news/finance-and-economics/21714384-city-state-wants-fintech-bolsters-not-disrupts-mainstream

3. Monica Kotwani, "Singapore's security industry, plagued by high turnover, to see robots in its midst," Channel NewsAsia, 6 April 2017, https://www.channelnewsasia.com/news/singapore/singapore-s-security-industry-plagued-by-high-turnover-to-see-ro-8703870

4. Linda Poon, "To Entice Riders, Singapore Buses Get a 'Signature Scent,'" Citylab, 8 March 2017, https://www.citylab.com/transportation/2017/03/singapore-buses-now-have-a-signature-scent-to-entice-more-riders/518940/

5. Driving standards in Singapore are very poor. Perhaps this is because the country's size means that very few—whether the owners of Nissans or Lamborghinis—have ever reached the giddy heights of 50 miles per hour. Drivers also have infuriating *kiasu*-infused zero-sum attitudes to other road users. My son learned some very bad words from me when we used to brave the cars and cycle to school.

6. Saheli Roy Choudhury, "Innovators, Singapore wants you, Smart Nations boss says," CNBC, 17 May 2016, https://sg.news.yahoo.com/innovators-singapore-wants-smart-nations-010944370.html

11. KENT RIDGE PARK

1. John Curtis Perry, *Singapore: Unlikely Power*, New York: Oxford University Press, 2017.
2. Henry Frei, *Guns of February: Ordinary Japanese Soldiers' Views of the Malayan Campaign and the Fall of Singapore, 1941–42*, Singapore: Singapore University Press, 2004.
3. Arthur G. Donahue, *Last Flight from Singapore*, New York: The Macmillan Company, 1943, https://archive.org/stream/LastFlightFromSingapore#page/n9/mode/2up
4. Donahue survived, but was killed in 1942 ditching his Spitfire in the English Channel, after trying to intercept a Junkers 88 bomber.
5. John Baptist Crasta, *Eaten by the Japanese: The Memoir of an Unknown Indian Prisoner of War*, ed. Richard Crasta, New York: The Invisible Man Press, 1999.
6. Thomas Kitching, *Life and Death in Changi: The War and Internment Diary of Thomas Kitching (1942–1944)*, ed. Goh Eck Kheng, Singapore: Landmark Books, 2002.
7. Japanese soldiers had lost an average of 10 kilograms each in the bicycle-assisted advance down the peninsula.
8. Ibid.
9. Frei, *Guns of February*, 2004.
10. Kitching, *Life and Death in Changi*, 2002. Nora Kitching's family only found out about her death three years later in 1945.
11. Crasta, *Eaten by the Japanese*, 1999. I pass 50 metres from the monument to the Indian National Army, next to the Padang sports field, in Chapter 21.
12. "S'pore massacre final pleas," *The Singapore Free Press*, 2 April 1947, p. 1, http://eresources.nlb.gov.sg/newspapers/Digitised/Article/freepress19470402–1.2.2
13. *Sook Ching* is a Chinese term, meaning "purging through cleansing." The Japanese term was *dai kenshō*, meaning "great inspection."
14. Goh Sin Tub, "The Sook Ching," *Biblioasia*, vol. 12, no. 4 (2017), http://www.nlb.gov.sg/biblioasia/2017/01/09/the-sook-ching/#sthash.pDjX6aBk.dpbs
15. Paul H. Kratoska (ed.), *Southeast Asian Minorities in the Wartime Japanese Empire*, ed., Abingdon: RoutledgeCurzon, 2002.
16. "Extermination order 'just' says Jap General," *The Straits Times*, 22 March 1947, p. 7, http://eresources.nlb.gov.sg/newspapers/Digitised/Article/straitstimes19470322–1.2.86
17. This was not unusual. Many Japanese residents were encouraged to take photos and make sketches of Singapore for the authorities back home.

18. Fiona Hodgkins is a teacher and writer who has written extensively about both Bahau and Shinozaki.

19. P.F. de Souza, "Spy and Humanitarian," *The Straits Times*, 19 August 1946, p. 4, http://eresources.nlb.gov.sg/newspapers/Digitised/Article/straitstimes 19460819-1.2.42.4

20. Banana dollars were named after the bananas depicted on the $10 note.

21. T. Fujitani, Geoffrey M. White, Lisa Yoneyama (eds), *Perilous Memories: The Asia-Pacific War(s)*, Durham, NC: Duke University Press, 2001.

22. Tommy Koh, "A world statesman," *The Straits Times*, 27 December 1990, http://leekuanyew.straitstimes.com/ST/chapter3.html

12. HYDERABAD ROAD

1. You can have a go yourself at https://www.sla.gov.sg/SPIO/Property Listing/Residential, if you think you are rich enough. If you are successful, you will need to buy a cupboard full of gin to complete the picture.

2. Joseph Conrad, *The End of the Tether*, first published in *Youth: A Narrative and Two Other Stories*, Edinburgh/London: William Blackwood and Sons, 1902, http://www.gutenberg.org/files/527/527-h/527-h.htm

3. Rudyard Kipling, *From Sea to Sea and Other Sketches: Letters of Travel*, London: Macmillan and Co., 1900, https://archive.org/details/fromseatosealet02kiplgoog

4. In January 1934, the temperature dipped to a chilly 19.4 centigrade. This remains the record.

5. Despite this, prostitution remained enough of a problem for the authorities to call in an expert in 1939, after an epidemic of venereal disease laid the British garrison low. Miss S.E. Nicholl was given a two-year contract at 500 Straits dollars a month, based on her experience surveying prostitution in Rangoon.

6. Farish A. Noor, "Money Making Bodies: Prostitution and Colonialism in 19th Century Singapore," *Biblioasia*, vol. 11, no. 3 (2015).

7. Lim Tin Seng, "Coolies, Triads and Pimps: Chinatown in Former Times," *Biblioasia*, vol. 11, no. 3 (2015).

8. M. Periasamy, "Indian Migration into Malaya and Singapore during the British Period," *Biblioasia*, vol. 3, no. 3 (2007).

9. Bencoolen in Sumatra (now Bengkulu) had been a penal colony for Indians since 1787.

10. Bonny Tan, "Convict Labour in Colonial Singapore," *Biblioasia*, vol. 11, no. 3 (2015).

11. Aw Cheng Wei, "Life in the dumps," *The Straits Times*, 18 July 2015, https://www.straitstimes.com/singapore/life-in-the-dumps

13. SOUTHERN RIDGES FOREST WALK

1. Kurt Ganapathy, "Why Singaporeans must learn to coexist with insects," SG Magazine, 5 May 2016, http://sg.asia-city.com/city-living/news/why-we-should-learn-coexist-singapores-insects
2. Pollen Nation is an NGO that promotes the well-being of Singapore's bees.
3. https://www.lta.gov.sg/apps/news/page.aspx?c=2&id=rj2i4o1u3d7018466v86y82epxjj32mwbvnhu6rpwt8lplkgo6
4. Adrian Lim, "Cross Island Line sparks residents' fears," *The Straits Times*, 2016, http://www.straitstimes.com/singapore/transport/cross-island-line-sparks-residents-fears
5. Sudhir Thomas Vadaketh and Donald Low, *Hard Choices: Challenging the Singapore Consensus*, Singapore: NUS Press, 2014.
6. Our neighbours would eventually be consigned to living high up in a condo block somewhere in the far east of the island. The air of Watten Drive would never again be filled with the pungent, near-deadly smell of Auntie Lily's cooking.
7. "Historian Thum Ping Tjin appears to be involved in coordinated attempt to subvert parliamentary processes: Charles Chong," *The Straits Times*, 2018, https://www.straitstimes.com/politics/historian-thum-ping-tjin-appears-to-be-involved-in-coordinated-attempt-to-subvert
8. Sonny Liew, *The Art of Charlie Chan Hock Chye*, Singapore: Epigram Books, 2015.
9. Sulaiman Daud, "Sonny Liew reveals why NAC revoked the grant for The Art of Charlie Chan Hock Chye," Mothership.sg, 29 September 2017, https://mothership.sg/2017/09/sonny-liew-reveals-why-the-nac-revoked-the-grant-for-the-art-of-charlie-chan-hock-chye/
10. "Lion City march," *The Economist*, 10 March 2016, https://www.economist.com/news/books-and-arts/21694495-touching-thoughtful-meditation-singapores-relentless-progress-lion-city-march

14. MASJID AL-AMIN

1. The other ever-popular choice was "I *heart* SG."
2. Bhavan Jaipragas, "Gyrating Pop Stars, Embezzlement and Faith: Singapore's City Harvest Church Scandal Headed for the Top Court," *South China Morning Post*, 16 April 2017, http://www.scmp.com/week-asia/society/article/2087782/gyrating-pop-stars-embezzlement-and-faith-singapores-city-harvest

15. KAMPONG BAHRU ROAD

1. In my own experience of Wednesday-night football at the Rainforest Sports Hub, most Singaporeans who played football were Malays, with a few Chinese thrown in. More than half wore Manchester United, Barcelona, or Germany shirts. Plucky underdog teams were not very popular.

16. PINNACLE@DUXTON

1. "Free meals for insulted taxi drivers in Singapore," BBC News, 2 May 2017, http://www.bbc.co.uk/news/blogs-news-from-elsewhere-39779406

2. At the time of writing, Uber is retreating from Singapore, with nothing more than a fistful of Grab shares to show for it. Prices are expected to rise as a result.

3. Simon Parry, "Out of a job: Banker who sneered at poor and 'the stench of public transport' sneaks his family out of Singapore ... in economy class," Mail Online, 25 January 2014, http://www.dailymail.co.uk/news/article-2545824/Anton-Casey-British-banker-living-Singapore-provoked-fury-ridiculing-poor-people-parted-ways-company-gone-Australia.html

4. Kevin Rawlinson, "British banker receives death threats for anti-Singapore diatribe," *The Guardian*, 23 January 2014, https://www.theguardian.com/world/2014/jan/23/banker-singapore-insults

5. "Singapore to freeze car numbers," BBC News, 24 October 2017, http://www.bbc.com/news/business-41730778

6. Horacelu, "Anti-Chinese sentiment in Singapore up following Ferrari crash caused by Sichuan man," Shanghaiist, 5 May 2012, http://shanghaiist.com/2012/05/16/ferrari-crash-singapore.php

7. If your car is special in some way, you can apply for a reprieve. Few are given.

8. http://coe.sgcharts.com/

9. "Singapore to freeze car numbers," BBC News.

10. In comparison, 80 per cent of American adults own their own car.

11. IMF.org, https://bit.ly/2DLflHh

12. "Worldwide Cost of Living Report 2017," The Economist Intelligence Unit, 2017, https://www.eiu.com/public/topical_report.aspx?campaignid=WCOL2017

13. Tim McDonald, "Is Singapore really the world's most expensive city?" BBC, 7 April 2017, http://www.bbc.com/capital/story/20170407-is-singapore-really-the-worlds-most-expensive-city

14. "A Study on Social Capital in Singapore," Institute of Policy Studies (National University of Singpaore), 2017, http://lkyspp2.nus.edu.sg/ips/wp-content/uploads/sites/2/2017/11/Study-of-Social-Capital-in-Singapore_281217.pdf

15. Nur Diyanah Binte Anwar, "Negotiating Singapore's Meritocracy: A Subtle Shift?", S. Rajaratnam School of International Studies (Nanyang Technological University), 12 February 2015, https://www.rsis.edu.sg/rsis-publication/cens/co15030-negotiating-singapores-meritocracy-a-subtle-shift/

16. Amelia Teng, "Six in 10 young Singaporeans have considered leaving the country to fulfill their dreams," *The Straits Times*, 15 January 2014, http://www.straitstimes.com/singapore/six-in-10-young-singaporeans-have-considered-leaving-the-country-to-fulfill-their-dreams

17. Lee Wei Ling and Lee Hsien Yang, "What has happened to Lee Kuan Yew's values?", https://www.theonlinecitizen.com/wp-content/uploads/2017/06/What-Has-Happened-To-Lee-Kuan-Yews-Values.pdf

18. "Oxley Road: Full transcript and video of ministerial statement in Parliament by PM Lee Hsien Loong," *The Straits Times*, 3 July 2017, http://www.straitstimes.com/singapore/oxley-road-full-text-of-ministerial-statement-in-parliament-by-pm-lee-hsien-loong

19. http://singfirst.org/manifesto-in-english/

20. https://www.applyprsingapore.com/

21. Faris Mokhtar, "Survey points to social class divide among Singaporeans," Today Online, 28 December 2017, http://www.todayonline.com/singapore/survey-points-social-class-divide-among-singaporeans

22. "Fair Consideration Framework," Ministry of Manpower (Singapore), http://www.mom.gov.sg/employment-practices/fair-consideration-framework

23. "Written Answer by Mr Lim Swee Say, Minister for Manpower to Parliamentary Question on strengthening Singaporean core in 'triple weak' companies," Ministry of Manpower (Singapore), 10 October 2016, http://www.mom.gov.sg/newsroom/parliament-questions-and-replies/2016/1010-written-answer-by-mr-lim-swee-say-pq-on-strengthening-singaporean-core-in-triple-weak-companies

24. Kent E. Calder, *Singapore: Smart City, Smart State*, Washington, DC: Brookings Institution Press, 2016.

25. https://www.population.sg/population-trends/demographics

26. Nasscom is an acronym for the National Association of Software and Services Companies.

27. "More Worries For Indian Techies As Singapore Clamps Down On Work Visas," NDTV, 4 April 2017, http://profit.ndtv.com/news/tech-media-telecom/article-more-worries-for-indian-techies-as-singapore-clamps-down-on-work-visas-1676975

28. "After US, Singapore tightens work visas, advises Indian IT cos to hire more

locals," Moneycontrol.com, 3 April 2017, http://www.moneycontrol.com/news/business/after-us-singapore-tightens-work-visas-advises-indian-it-cos-to-hire-more-locals-2251591.html

29. Linda Lim, "How land and people fit together in Singapore's economy," in Sudhir Thomas Vadaketh and Donald Low, *Hard Choices: Challenging the Singapore Consensus*, Singapore: NUS Press, 2014.

30. For months I passed a building site on Dunearn Road, as I cycled my son to school. The same South Asian man was sitting on the same plastic chair outside the building site every day, six days a week, just keeping an eye on the pavement.

31. Arlina Arshad and Joanna Seow, "Indonesia plans to stop sending new live-in maids abroad," *The Straits Times*, 18 May 2016, http://www.straitstimes.com/asia/se-asia/indonesia-plans-to-stop-sending-new-live-in-maids-abroad

32. Li Xueying, "Singaporean PM: All to enjoy fruits of growth," *The Straits Times*, 9 August 2010, http://www.mysinchew.com/node/43067

33. Yeo Sam Jo, "Pinnacle@Duxton flat goes for $1.12 million," *The Straits Times*, 22 September 2016, http://www.straitstimes.com/singapore/housing/pinnacleduxton-flat-goes-for-112-million In January 2018, there were eighteen properties for sale in the complex for over a million.

34. Lin Zhiqin, "Winning the HDB lottery—The Pinnacle@Duxton," The Edge Property, 27 May 2015, https://www.edgeprop.sg/property-news/winning-hdb-lottery-%E2%80%93-pinnacleduxton

17. CHINATOWN

1. Lim Tin Seng, "Coolies, Triads and Pimps: Chinatown in Former Times," *Biblioasia*, vol. 11, no. 3 (2015).

2. Rudyard Kipling, *From Sea to Sea and Other Sketches: Letters of Travel*, London: Macmillan and Co., 1900, https://archive.org/details/fromseatosealet02kiplgoog.

3. Gracie Lee, "Chasing the Dragon: The Scourge of Opium," *Biblioasia*, vol. 11, no. 3 (2015).

4. Ibid.

5. See Chapter 20.

18. HONG LIM PARK

1. "Singapore says Reuters report on water price protest misleading," Yahoo! News, 12 March 2017, https://sg.news.yahoo.com/singapore-says-reuters-report-water-price-protest-misleading-201625008—business.html

2. "Singaporean cops investigate participants in silent vigil for executed migrant worker," Boing Boing, 12 September 2017, https://boingboing.net/2017/09/12/prabagaran-srivijayan.html#more-545552

3. "Transcript of Minister Mentor Lee Kuan Yew's Interview with Seth Mydans of New York Times & IHT on 1 September 2010," National Archives of Singapore, 1 September 2010, http://www.nas.gov.sg/archivesonline/data/pdfdoc/20100920006/transcript_of_minister_mentor_lee_kuan_yew.pdf

4. "J.B. Jeyaretnam," The Economist, 9 October 2008, http://www.economist.com/node/12376738

5. Han Fook Kwang, Warren Fernandez and Sumiko Tan, Lee Kuan Yew: The Man and His Ideas, Singapore: Marshall Cavendish International, 2015.

6. "The government of Singapore says it welcomes criticism, but its critics still suffer," The Economist, 9 March 2017, http://www.economist.com/news/asia/21718571-three-protesters-get-stiff-penalties-disturbing-public-order-government-singapore-says-it

7. Foo Chi Hsia, "Letters to the editor," The Economist, 16 March 2017, https://www.economist.com/news/letters/21718853-brexit-news-chile-singapore-diamonds-letters-editor

8. Tan Weizhen, "Clear racial preference for Prime Minister, President: Survey," Today Online, 18 August 2016, http://www.todayonline.com/singapore/clear-racial-preference-prime-minister-president-survey

9. P.N. Balji, "Comment: Singapore presidency with an asterisk and a government that was blindsided," Yahoo! News Singapore, 13 September 2017, https://sg.news.yahoo.com/comment-singapore-presidency-asterisk-government-blind-sided-103722232.html

10. Cherian George, "Singapore's mystifying political succession," New Mandala, 7 February 2018, http://www.newmandala.org/singapores-mystifying-political-succession/

11. P.N. Balji, "Comment," Yahoo! News Singapore.

12. Tyler Cowen, "Why Singapore is special," Marginal Revolution, 3 August 2015, http://marginalrevolution.com/marginalrevolution/2015/08/why-singapore-is-special.html

13. "Singapore gov't cautions granting of asylum to Amos Yee will encourage other hate speakers to seek refuge in USA," The Independent (Singapore), 25 March 2017, http://theindependent.sg/singapore-govt-cautions-granting-of-asylum-to-amos-yee-will-encourage-other-hate-speakers-to-seek-refuge-in-usa/

14. Foo Chi Hsia, "Letters to the editor," The Economist, 12 April 2017, https://www.economist.com/news/letters/21720594-yemen-sex-studies-india-wales-singapore-banks-poland-brains-aprils-fool-letters

15. Sudhir Thomas Vadaketh, "The end of identity?" in Sudhir Thomas Vadaketh and Donald Low, *Hard Choices: Challenging the Singapore Consensus*, Singapore: NUS Press, 2014.

16. Sophie Jeong and Spencer Feingold, "Singaporeans rally for gay pride amid ban on foreigners," CNN, 1 July 2017, http://edition.cnn.com/2017/07/01/asia/singapore-gay-pride-rally/index.html

19. CBD

1. That hodge-podge is also impressive. So much so that a swanky housing project in the Gwadar port development in Pakistan uses photos of the Singaporean CBD in its advertising literature.

2. The tax rate varies between zero and 20 per cent for residents, and 15 per cent for non-residents.

3. Kent E. Calder, *Singapore: Smart City, Smart State*, Washington, DC: Brookings Institution Press, 2016.

4. https://skytraxratings.com/airlines/garuda-indonesia-rating

5. https://data.worldbank.org/country/China

6. Samanth Subramanian, "How Singapore Is Creating More Land for Itself," *New York Times*, 20 April 2017, https://www.nytimes.com/2017/04/20/magazine/how-singapore-is-creating-more-land-for-itself.html

7. https://www.transparency.org/news/feature/corruption_perceptions_index_2016#table, https://anticorruptiondigest.com/anti-corruption-news/2018/01/10/keppel-the-story-of-a-bribe/

8. "Swiss criminal probe into BSI bank over 1MDB links," BBC News, 24 May 2016, http://www.bbc.com/news/business-36365928

20. BOAT QUAY

1. James Manning, "The Time Out City Life Index 2018," *Time Out*, 30 January 2018, https://www.timeout.com/london/citylifeindex

2. Cheryl Lu-Lien Tan, *Sarong Party Girls*, New York: HarperCollins, 2016.

3. Joy Fang, "Dissecting the Sarong Party Girl," Today Online, 15 August 2016, http://www.todayonline.com/lifestyle/dissecting-sarong-party-girl

4. A guide to Singlish emojis includes one for my favourite local phrase, "Come I clap for you," which is used as a sarcastic response when somebody is expecting a more positive response.

5. S. Rajaratnam, "Singapore Government Press Release," National Archives of

Singapore, 22 July 1984, http://www.nas.gov.sg/archivesonline/data/pdfdoc/
SR19840722s.pdf

6. Nick Leeson was a Singapore-based British derivatives broker who brought down Barings (Britain's oldest merchant bank), thanks to a series of fraudulent, speculative trades.

7. A common offence listed on these street signs is "outrage of modesty," an archaic term for molestation. This covers a range of crimes from the serious to the bizarre, including an acupuncturist kissing and nibbling a victim's toes.

8. Uptin Saiidi, "Singapore's crime rate is so low that many shops don't even lock up," CNBC, 16 January 2018, https://www.cnbc.com/2018/01/16/singapores-crime-rate-is-so-low-that-many-shops-dont-even-lock-up.html

9. Susan Sim, *Making Singapore Safe: Thirty Years of the National Crime Prevention Council*, Singapore: National Crime Prevention Council, 2011, http://www.ncpc.org.sg/images/media/FinalSoftCopy_NoBleeding.pdf

10. "Guilty As Charged: Adrian Lim and his 2 'holy' wives kidnapped, tortured and killed 2 children," *The Straits Times*, 15 May 2016, http://www.straitstimes.com/singapore/courts-crime/guilty-as-charged-adrian-lim-and-his-2-holy-wives-kidnapped-tortured-and

11. Sim, *Making Singapore Safe*, 2011, pp. 16, 18.

12. SARS stands for Severe Acute Respiratory Syndrome. An outbreak in 2002 and 2003, which began among bats living in caves in southern China, killed almost 800 people in thirty-seven countries.

13. The Government's "Feedback Unit" cited the changes as a successful example of public opinion shaping policy, in Chapter 5 (called "Party On!") of a 2005 report called "Shaping our home: turning ideas into reality."

14. "Teen-Ager Caned in Singapore Tells of the Blood and the Scars," *New York Times*, 27 June 1994, http://www.nytimes.com/1994/06/27/us/teen-ager-caned-in-singapore-tells-of-the-blood-and-the-scars.html

15. "'I am now sending you to a better place than this,'" *Asian Pacific Post*, 20 September 2005, http://www.asianpacificpost.com/article/2104-i-am-now-sending-you-better-place.html

16. Calvin Yang, "Guilty As Charged: Dance hostess Mimi Wong murdered her Japanese lover's wife," *The Straits Times*, 14 May 2016, http://www.straitstimes.com/singapore/courts-crime/guilty-as-charged-dance-hostess-mimi-wong-murdered-her-japanese-lovers-wife

17. Connie Levett and Steve Butcher, "Hangman ignites outrage," The Age, 30 November 2005, http://www.theage.com.au/news/national/hangman-ignites-outrage/2005/11/29/1133026468284.html

18. "Guilty As Charged: Michael McCrea killed a woman and a man he called his brother," *The Straits Times*, 16 May 2016, http://www.straitstimes.com/singapore/courts-crime/guilty-as-charged-michael-mccrea-killed-a-woman-and-a-man-he-called-his

19. Patrick Barkham, "Jailed in Singapore for writing a book they didn't like," *The Guardian*, 27 July 2011, https://www.theguardian.com/world/2011/jul/27/jail-singapore

20. Alan Shadrake, *Once A Jolly Hangman: Singapore Justice In the Dock*, Singapore: Strategic Information and Research Development Centre, 2010.

21. Justin McCurry, "Alan Shadrake faces Singapore jail term for criticising use of death penalty," *The Guardian*, 7 November 2010, https://www.theguardian.com/world/2010/nov/07/alan-shadrake-singapore-death-penalty

22. "Chewing gum is banned," History SG, 2 January 1992, http://eresources.nlb.gov.sg/history/events/57a854df-8684–456b-893a-a303e0041891

23. Peter Day, "Singapore's elder statesman," BBC News, 5 July 2000, http://news.bbc.co.uk/2/hi/programmes/from_our_own_correspondent/820234.stm

21. MARINA BAY

1. See Chapter 11.

2. Janice Loo, "Desperate housewives: the lure of chap ji kee," *The Straits Times*, 29 November 2015, https://www.straitstimes.com/opinion/desperate-housewives-and-the-lure-of-chap-ji-kee

3. The authorities don't always get the balance right. An advert for the National Council on Problem Gambling issued a poster ahead of the 2014 football World Cup. One boy, sitting on a ball with a concerned expression on his face, tells his friend that he hopes Germany wins, as "My dad bet all my savings on them." Unfortunately for the advert's message, Germany went on to win the tournament. A safer example of a reckless bet, of course, would have been to put money on England.

4. "The world's biggest gamblers," *The Economist*, 9 February 2017, https://www.economist.com/blogs/graphicdetail/2017/02/daily-chart-4

5. "Excerpts from an interview with Lee Kuan Yew," *New York Times*, 29 August 2007, http://www.nytimes.com/2007/08/29/world/asia/29iht-lee-excerpts.html

22. EAST COAST PARK

1. Meanwhile, in early 2018, a two-level penthouse at The Berth By The Cove sold

for S$3.25 million, having been bought in 2011 for S$5.64 million. https://www.propertyguru.com.sg/property-management-news/2018/3/169729/sentosa-cove-penthouse-sold-at-24-million-loss

23. CHANGI AIRPORT

1. "UAE will be the hub of the world," *Gulf News*, 2017, http://gulfnews.com/polopoly_fs/1.1933436!/infoDup%5B0%5D/uploadInfo/fileUpload/infoFile/03_Hub%20of%20the%20World.pdf
2. David Fickling, "The Decline and Fall of Asia's Airline Empires," Bloomberg, 19 January 2017, https://www.bloomberg.com/gadfly/articles/2017–01–19/ominous-fading-of-air-power-in-hong-kong-and-singapore
3. A.J. Loftus, *Notes of a Journey Across the Isthmus of Krà*, Singapore: Singapore and Straits Printing Office, 1883, http://reader.library.cornell.edu/docviewer/digital?id=sea:111
4. William Mellor, "Ambitious Thai canal would link Pacific and Indian oceans," *Nikkei Asian Review*, 10 August 2017, https://asia.nikkei.com/magazine/20170810/Politics-Economy/Ambitious-Thai-canal-would-link-Pacific-and-Indian-oceans
5. Zakir Hussain, "How 15 Singaporeans were radicalised by ISIS ideology," *The Straits Times*, 16 July 2017, http://www.straitstimes.com/singapore/radicalised-in-singapore
6. Bilveer Singh, "Why Singapore Is a Terrorist Target," *The Diplomat*, 28 June 2017, https://thediplomat.com/2017/06/why-singapore-is-a-terrorist-target/
7. Ibid.
8. https://www.mindef.gov.sg/imindef/mindef_websites/topics/totaldefence/about_us/5_Pillars.html
9. The wound qualified him for a lifelong pension of £70 a year. Most accounts say Brooke was shot in the lung, although the novelist George MacDonald Fraser, in his book *Flashman's Lady*, suggests that in reality his wound had caused the loss of various crucial parts of his genitals.
10. For more on Henry Keppel, see Chapter 3.
11. Nicholas Walton, "Why piracy should be recognised as a sustainability issue," Futures Centre, 20 October 2015, https://thefuturescentre.org/articles/4674/why-piracy-should-be-recognised-sustainability-issue
12. "The odds on a conflict between the great powers," *The Economist*, 25 January 2018, https://www.economist.com/news/special-report/21735480-great-powers-seem-have-little-appetite-full-scale-war-there-room

13. Bill Hayton, *The South China Sea: The Struggle for Power in Asia*, New Haven, CT: Yale University Press, 2014.

14. East Asia Today, BBC World Service, 6 June 1995, quoted in Hayton, *The South China Sea*, 2014.

15. Robert D. Kaplan, *Asia's Cauldron: The South China Sea and the End of a Stable Pacific*, New York: Random House, 2014.

16. Ibid.

17. "The odds on a conflict between the great powers," *The Economist*.

18. Tyler Cowen, "Economists' View of Qatar Cutoff Is a Little Scary," Bloomberg, 13 June 2017, https://www.bloomberg.com/view/articles/2017–06–13/economists-view-of-qatar-cutoff-is-a-little-scary

19. Ben Bland, "Mystery over seized Singapore army vehicles in Hong Kong," *Financial Times*, 25 November 2016, https://www.ft.com/content/1a0fbcd0-b2e5–11e6–9c37–5787335499a0

24. TANAH MERAH FERRY TERMINAL

1. The irony, however, is that Singapore is no go-it-alone free trader, but one that is intimately bound to international institutions and relationships, and subject to some of the worst vagaries of the international economic climate.

2. Peter Ho, "The Paradox of Singapore and the Dialectic of Governance," Lecture III of the IPS-Nathan Lectures, 3 May 2017, http://lkyspp2.nus.edu.sg/ips/event/201617-ips-nathan-lectures-lecture-iii-the-paradox-of-singapore-and-the-dialectic-of-governance

3. "Transcript of Minister Mentor Lee Kuan Yew's Interview with Seth Mydans of New York Times & IHT on 1 September 2010," National Archives of Singapore, 1 September 2010, http://www.nas.gov.sg/archivesonline/data/pdfdoc/2010 0920006/transcript_of_minister_mentor_lee_kuan_yew.pdf

4. Bettina Wassener, "Singapore Trims Its Economic Forecasts for 2009," *New York Times*, 14 April 2009, http://www.nytimes.com/2009/04/14/business/global/14singapore.html

5. Toh Wen Li, "Singapore Budget 2018: Adult Singaporeans to get SG Bonus of up to $300 after $9.6b budget surplus," *The Straits Times*, 19 February 2018, http://www.straitstimes.com/singapore/adult-sporeans-will-get-sg-bonus-of-up-to-300-after-overall-budget-surplus-in-fy2017

6. Jeevan Vasagar, "Toxic haze in Southeast Asia killed 100,000, study says," *Financial Times*, 18 September 2016, https://www.ft.com/content/925a02d4-7e17–11e6-8e50-8ec15fb462f4

7. Benjamen Gussen, "A proposal for a Singaporean 'charter city' in Australia," *The Straits Times*, 24 January 2017, http://www.straitstimes.com/opinion/a-proposal-for-a-singaporean-charter-city-in-australia

8. "Excerpts from an interview with Lee Kuan Yew," *New York Times*, 29 August 2007, http://www.nytimes.com/2007/08/29/world/asia/29iht-lee-excerpts.html

INDEX

INDEX

INDEX

INDEX

INDEX

INDEX

INDEX

INDEX